Apocalyptic Fiction

21ST CENTURY GENRE FICTION SERIES

The *21st Century Genre Fiction* series provides exciting and accessible introductions to new genres in twenty-first-century fiction from Crunch Lit to Steampunk to Scandinavian Crime Fiction. Exploring the history and uses of each genre to date each title in the series will analyse key examples of innovations and developments in the field since the year 2000. The series will consider the function of genre in both reflecting and shaping sociopolitical and economic developments of the twenty-first century.

Also available in the series:

Crunch Lit by Katy Shaw
Scandinavian Crime Fiction by Jakob Stougaard-Nielsen

Apocalyptic
Fiction

Andrew Tate

Bloomsbury Academic
An imprint of Bloomsbury Publishing Plc

B L O O M S B U R Y

LONDON · OXFORD · NEW YORK · NEW DELHI · SYDNEY

Bloomsbury Academic

An imprint of Bloomsbury Publishing Plc

50 Bedford Square	1385 Broadway
London	New York
WC1B 3DP	NY 10018
UK	USA

www.bloomsbury.com

BLOOMSBURY and the Diana logo are trademarks of Bloomsbury Publishing Plc

First published 2017

British Library Cataloguing-in-Publication Data
A catalogue record for this book is available from the British Library.

ISBN: HB: 978-1-4742-3351-4
PB: 978-1-4742-3350-7
ePDF: 978-1-4742-3353-8
ePub: 978-1-4742-3352-1

Library of Congress Cataloging-in-Publication Data
A catalog record for this book is available from the Library of Congress.

Series: 21st Century Genre Fiction

Cover design: Alice Marwick

Typeset by Newgen Knowledge Works (P) Ltd., Chennai, India
Printed and bound in India

CONTENTS

ACKNOWLEDGEMENTS

Many thanks to Katy Shaw, series editor, for inviting me to contribute to the series and for her encouragement during the whole process. I'm also very grateful to David Avital and Mark Richardson at Bloomsbury for advice and patience. I am indebted to the staff of Gladstone's Library, Hawarden, especially to Peter Francis and Louisa Yates. The library has been a fantastic place to write and equally good as a haven of good conversation and company. Students in the Department of English & Creative Writing at Lancaster University have also been great source of inspiration, in particular those doctoral candidates with whom I worked during the writing of this book: Peter Watt, Lauren Randall, Muhammad Hamdan, Dorcas Wangui and Ahmad Qabaha. A number of my excellent colleagues gave indispensable feedback on draft chapters: many thanks to Brian Baker, Arthur Bradley, Jo Carruthers and Michael Greaney. The failings are, of course, all my own. To other friends whose company and conversation were also vital, thank you: Mum and Dad, Chris, Anne-Marie, Steve Roberts, Peter Redrup, Ian Rowe, Kevin Gritton, James Griffiths, Gareth Johnstone, Simon Bainbridge, Catherine Spooner, Alison Easton, Jenn Ashworth, Mark Knight, Ben Whitehouse, Katherine Venn, Jonathan Roberts, John Schad, Peter Blair, Melissa Fegan, Alex Paknadel, Will Smith, Ashley Chantler, Matthew Bradley, Simon Marsden, David Powers, Nigel Capewell, David Ashbridge, Paul Egglestone and Michael Wheeler. My greatest debt is to Michaela Robinson-Tate to whom this book is dedicated, with love.

1

Introduction: Dreams of the 'ruined' future

'I don't believe in the future. I think we're all doomed', claims one of Douglas Coupland's cheerfully mournful characters in *JPod* (2006).[1] This apocalyptic forecast may be rather glibly predicted, but similarly less than sanguine conjecture is far from rare in contemporary culture. Indeed, the prospect for the years to come, according to a copious body of twenty-first-century fiction, does not look particularly bright. Western civilization, according to such novels, appears to have abandoned its faith in a promised world of progress and continuing prosperity.

An ailing father and his young son walk south, heading towards the distant coast of a ruined, ash-coloured landscape, hoping to survive winter and escape the twin threats of starvation and gangs of cannibals. A pair of brothers journeys eastwards, also on foot, hoping to sail away from the same land, the country that 'used to be America [...] the safest place on earth' but which is now distinguished by deprivation; its people, perhaps a century or more into the future, are illiterate and have no memories of modern technology or the nation's former status as a superpower, the culture of the deep past no more than the half rumour of folktale and song.[2] To the north, 'Snowman', a forlorn former advertising executive with a gift for storytelling (and manipulation), sits in a tree. The world into which he makes reluctant sorties is one of 'dead houses, dead malls, dead labs, dead everything'.[3] This lonely man, continuously on the threshold of delirium, is convinced that he is the last human being; his arboreal dwelling is a makeshift refuge from porcine creatures that lurk on the ground; the 'Pigoons' were once genetically modified as a source of spare organs, but, in a world after human domination, they run free and are more than a little peckish. A little further south and west, a troupe of actors and musicians walk around Lake Michigan performing Shakespeare to the ragtag settlements that represent what is left of humanity twenty years after a pandemic has destroyed most of the world's population. Somewhere in Appalachia, a sixteen-year-old woman is the latest 'tribute' in an annual televised fight-to-the-death contest of the nation's youth; meanwhile, in a city that was once known as Chicago, teenagers are forced to become members of factions determined by dominant character traits and subjected to brutal rites of passage; difference or 'divergence' is not tolerated. These characters and plots are not part of a single, exceptionally depressing literary universe. However, the critical and commercial success of such bleak scenarios, evoked, by turn, in Cormac McCarthy's *The Road* (2006), Jim Crace's *The Pesthouse* (2007), Margaret Atwood's 'MaddAddam' sequence (2003–13), Emily St John Mandel's *Station Eleven* (2014), Suzanne Collins's 'The Hunger Games' trilogy (2008–10) and Veronica Roth's 'Divergent' sequence (2011–13) are evidence that popular contemporary narrative is haunted by dreams of a future that is a place of ruin.

Apocalyptic Fiction explores these narratives alongside a number of other twenty-first-century novels by, among others, J. G. Ballard, Maggie Gee and Tom Perrotta, of what Patrick Parrinder has named the 'ruined' future.[4] The book identifies the dizzying variety of ways in which contemporary authors from Britain, America and Canada envision the decline and fall of civilization, the twilight of Homo sapiens and the possible death of all life on the planet. Whether the world will end with a bang, whimper, sigh of relief or, as for the protagonists of Edgar Wright's comic rites of passage movie, *The World's End* (2013), as a result of a really bad hangover seems to be a matter of perspective. End-of-the-world fiction is emphatically not a recent phenomenon. Indeed, apocalyptic stories are as old as narrative itself. The book treats twenty-first-century 'apocalyptic' fiction as an expansive family of genres with a complex genealogy. It does not attempt to give an exhaustive account of the different categories of 'end-of-the-world' fiction but focuses on some of the recurrent tropes, problems and hopes that preoccupy postmillennial novels of the end. This introductory chapter explores the contours and contexts of contemporary apocalyptic fiction, sets up the parameters of each chapter and gives particular focus to novels not examined elsewhere in the book. It also explores two related questions. Is there a difference, other than scale and the number of deaths, between the phenomena of catastrophe and apocalypse? Why do so many writers in an ostensibly post-Christian era continually return to biblical eschatology to imagine a coming end?

Critical readings frequently emphasize two basic shapes for nightmarish, 'ruined future' fictions: the first, frequently referred to as dystopia, is a world dominated by technology and excessive consumerism that generates endless leisure for a decadent ruling elite and misery for a vast, starving underclass. This kind of society, covertly run by shady bureaucrats who work for corporations rather than for a democratically elected government, is rarely represented as a happy 'end of history', one in which all people (or at least those sensible enough to be rich and to live in the most prosperous nations) achieve material and emotional success; compassionate, enlightened human beings are, apparently, vanishingly rare in such narratives, and those who wish to prosper never ask difficult questions about who pays the price for prosperity. Veronica Hollinger, for example, suggests that the 'technoculture' that best describes twenty-first-century life in affluent, capitalist nations means that many people 'have come to experience the present as a kind of future at which we've inadvertently arrived, one of the many futures imagined by science fiction'. Hollinger explores the writing of William Gibson, godfather of cyberpunk, as a kind of prophetic literature and specifically identifies *Pattern Recognition* (2003) as a novel that represents both realism (its events take place in 2002) and Science Fiction (SF) because it is 'set in the endless endtimes of the future-present. It brilliantly conveys the phenomenology of a present infused with futurity, no longer like itself, no longer like the present.'[5] The catastrophe in such visions is frequently moral rather than literal: personal connection, justice and creativity are sacrificed in order to preserve a passive social order. The alternative vision is of a devastated earth in which this 'technofuture' has failed and life is simply a brutal struggle eked out by the survivors. In a review article for *n+1* published under the bald soubriquet 'The End' (2007), Chad Harbach compares the twin trajectories represented by what he names the 'heighted present' popularized by SF with 'post-catastrophe' narratives. The former, he observes, in 'combining and extrapolating extant technologies (an MP3 player ... in your brain!)' to offer a critique of 'their psychological and political effects'.

> The post-catastrophe novel does the opposite [...] It liberates the violent potential of technology (and its enemy, nature) to create an altered world whose chief characteristic is a bewildering lack of technology. This in turn means a severely winnowed human population, and plenty of hardship and casual brutality. This future doesn't intensify the present moment, it contradicts it: What would happen if we didn't live in an overpopulated, technology-saturated world in which travel by foot is considered eccentric, tacos cost forty-nine cents, and the prerogative to commit violence – despite an amazing profusion of handheld weaponry – lies entirely with the state?[6]

Peter Boxall suggests that for novelists such as Atwood, McCarthy and Sarah Hall, whose twenty-first-century fictions have imagined apocalyptic or dystopian futures, 'the recurrent urge to envisage violent historical change as a kind of universal death has, as its corollary, the image of the dying planet. The contemporary imagination is haunted by the prospect of planetary death, of irreversible environmental disaster.'[7]

The spectre of global catastrophe frequently haunts David Mitchell's fiction: for example, one of the narrators of his debut novel, *Ghostwritten* (1999), is a murderous member of a doomsday cult who has poisoned a Tokyo subway train; two of the six stories in *Cloud Atlas* (2004), 'An Orison of Sonmi-451' and 'Sloosha's Crossin' an' Ev'rythin' After' are set in two different phases of a ruined future that is caused by exploitation of nature. Mitchell's *The Bone Clocks* (2014) concludes in 2043, during a post-oil era popularly known as the 'Endarkenment'. Civil order has not quite collapsed but the world stands on the brink of catastrophe as, for example, resources gradually deplete, radioactive pollution seeps around coastlines and military rule becomes a daily reality. Mitchell's narrator, Holly Sykes, first introduced as a teenager, is now in her mid-seventies; she lives a simple life in rural Ireland and has experienced the loss of family and friends in a long and frequently strange life. Holly is a significant choice to articulate a stark environmental warning. She has witnessed much strangeness, including profound malevolence and acts of self-sacrifice. She is figured as rational, decent and invested in the idea that the world should exist long after her time. Her muted melancholy is not, however, simply bereavement for the people she has lost:

> It's everything: it's grief for the regions we deadlanded, the ice caps we melted, the Gulf Stream we redirected, the rivers we drained, the coasts we flooded, the lakes we choked with crap, the seas we killed, the species we drove to extinction, the pollinators we wiped out, the oil we squandered, the drugs we rendered impotent, the comforting liars we voted into office – all so we didn't have to change our cosy lifestyles. People talk about the Endarkenment like our ancestors talked about the Black Death, as if it's an act of God. But we summoned it, with every tank of oil we burnt our way through. My generation were diners stuffing ourselves senseless at the Restaurant of the Earth's Riches knowing – while denying – that we'd be doing a runner and leaving our grandchildren a tab that can never be paid.[8]

The nightmare of the 'Endarkenment' is envisioned decades in the future but it is clear that Mitchell, like other writers of our ruined future, is equally anxious about the present. We now live in an era of apparent continual catastrophe and the fundamental context for addressing twenty-first-century apocalyptic anxiety is the greatest threat to life on earth: anthropogenic climate change. Despite the occasional broadside from disbelieving voices in the denial camp, often from the political right, there is little serious doubt that a variety of human behaviours – and specifically the perpetual pollution of the planet by wasteful industry – is a root cause of climate change. 'The Earth is now warmer than it has been for over 90 per cent of its 4.6 billion year history', writes geophysicist Bill McGuire, 'and by the end of the twenty-first century our planet may see higher temperatures than at any time for the last 150,000 years'. The consequences of what McGuire calls 'a gigantic planetary trial' that kicked off with the industrial revolution in the late eighteenth century are sobering.[9] Ice caps will melt, flooding coastal cities; ruined agriculture will perpetuate food shortages, starvation and the displacement of vast numbers of people. In *Anthropocene Fictions* (2015), the most meticulous study to date of the literary response to climate change, Adam Trexler notes that there is now a 'considerable archive' of such narratives, though critics have been slow to recognize a genre with a rich (and urgent) recent history. Trexler identifies Ursula K. Le Guin's *The Lathe of Heaven* (1971) as the first novel to engage directly with greenhouse gas emissions, more than a decade before the vast wave of climate change novels was published.[10] More recently, Kim Stanley Robinson's 'Science in the Capital' trilogy – *Forty Signs of Rain* (2004), *Fifty Degrees Below* (2006) and *Sixty Days and Counting* (2007) – engages with hard science far more than the majority of writers discussed in this study. Robinson tests his narrative of Earth on the brink of catastrophe, and specifically of anthropogenic, accelerated climate change, via a scientist protagonist. This man of reason whose role is to enlighten and precipitate radical, perhaps salvific change in humanity's behaviour is a contrast to the more ambiguous protagonists of Ian McEwan's fiction. *Solar* (2010), for example, a tragic–comic climate change novel, follows a decade in the chaotic life of Michael Beard, once a Nobel Prize winner who has all but abandoned any commitment to research. Beard is the scientist as anti-hero; he is a cynical chancer who exploits the goodwill of his many former wives and lovers. Beard's increasing weight and failure to deal with health crises (including an ominous lesion on his wrist) are slightly crude symbols of humanity's failure to attend to the causes of incipient climate disaster. Although my study does not focus on climate fiction – or 'clifi' – since it is such a vast area in its own right, the parlous state of the planet is crucial to every novel discussed. Atwood's 'MaddAddam' trilogy, the focus of Chapter Four, presents two ruined worlds: a post-collapse era in which humanity has been all but wiped out by a man-made pandemic and, in flashback, a near-future dystopian era in which the environment has already been poisoned, the climate altered and all living things treated as little more than a resource for greedy corporations. Cormac McCarthy's *The Road* has been described by George Monbiot, the influential environmental campaigner, as 'the most important environmental book ever written'.[11] This is an extraordinary claim, particularly since the novel does not seek to represent the origins of the parlous, denatured world in which a father and son attempt to survive.

Future fear is not limited to the capacious quantity of novels and short fiction that can be readily described as post-collapse narratives. 'You never know when something disastrous might happen', nervously quips one character in *Station Eleven*, shortly before something disastrous, involving the near extinction of the human race, does indeed 'happen'.[12] Another crucial context for apocalyptic fiction is the attacks on the World Trade Center in New York on 11 September 2001 and the subsequent 'Global War on Terror'. These events have been explored directly in a wide body of novels, including, for example, Jonathan Safran Foer's *Extremely Close and Incredibly Loud* (2005), Ian McEwan's *Saturday* (2005), Jay McInerney's *The Good Life* (2006), Don DeLillo's *Falling Man* (2007) and Mohsin Hamid's *The Reluctant Fundamentalist* (2007), but they also inform, more indirectly, the anxieties of much ostensibly future-orientated fiction. The politics of security and a foreboding sense that life in the West is rather more fragile than had been assumed is a subtext, for example, in Crace's *The Pesthouse* and McCarthy's *The Road*. Similarly, a distinctively post-9/11 focus on violence as spectacle is explored in Collins's 'The Hunger Games' trilogy.[13] A number of interpretations of 'post-apocalyptic' narrative do not emphasize future forebodings but look to the recent past in which versions of the world have been destroyed many times over. In *After the End* (1999), James Berger claims that 'the most dystopic visions of science fiction do no more than replicate the actual historical catastrophes of the twentieth century'.[14] The Holocaust and the dropping of the atom bomb on Hiroshima, for Berger, are the retrospective horizon that shapes the contemporary imagination's expectations of a bankrupt future. One of the problems with understanding speculative fiction primarily as future orientated, 'dystopian' speculations about what might occur somewhere down the line is that it can let us off the hook and evades contemporary political questions. Karl Hand, in his reading of 'The Hunger Games' trilogy, drawing on both Jeremy Rifkin's concepts of 'cultural capitalism' and the Gospel of St Luke's call to action, is not convinced by the view that the nightmare society is a phenomenon that lies somewhere in our future unless we mend our ways: '"dystopia" has already happened', he claims.[15]

Much twenty-first-century fiction is characterized by a certain kind of *pre*-apocalyptic anxiety, narrated by figures who are unlikely to be avid readers of the book of Revelation but who nevertheless believe themselves to be living in the last days; such men and women fear that their societies exist on the brink, for better or worse, of an imminent, radical change. Although they live in worlds that have yet to collapse, their shared terror of approaching disaster resonates with elements of the 'cosy catastrophe' subgenre of apocalyptic fiction as identified by Brian Aldiss in his history of SF, *The Billion Year Spree* (1973). This successful soubriquet, now widely deployed, originally signified narratives of a quiet, very English style of apocalypse in which global disaster is survived by a typically prosperous remnant that adapts, with reasonable aptitude and plenty of common sense, to the new conditions of a post-collapse world. For Aldiss, the 'master of the cosy catastrophe' is John Wyndham, author of SF disaster novels including *The Day of the Triffids* (1951), *The Kraken Wakes* (1953) and *The Chrysalids* (1955). The 'essence' of the genre, in Aldiss's very 1970s' words, 'is that the hero should have a pretty good time (a girl, free suites at the Savoy, automobiles for the taking) while everyone else is dying off'.[16] Other examples might include Ballard's *The Drowned World* (1962) in which London, long submerged beneath floodwaters, has become a tropical lagoon; its protagonist, Kerans, manages to live in old-world style in an upper floor of the Ritz and, when not studying this surreal new Eden and/or fighting the heinous, white-suited Strangman, seduces a woman named Beatrice. The kind of characters who, as Aldiss puts it, 'meet the crisis in the dining room' are even rarer in twenty-first-century post-apocalyptic narratives. Indeed, McCarthy's *The Road* is about as far from 'cosy' catastrophe as it is possible to imagine: in lieu of 'a girl, free suites at the Savoy, automobiles for the taking', the anonymous man has lost his wife to suicide, takes shelter wherever he may avoid cannibals or their prey and, in a post-fuel future, has to make do with his ruined feet and a shopping trolley instead of a looted car.

Twenty-first-century descendants of the typical survivors of 'cosy catastrophe' might be found in contemporary fictions of middle-class life that are charged with an uncanny apocalyptic prescience; these protagonists frequently fear that an incipient disaster will undo their comfortable lives. For example, Nick Hornby's *How to Be Good* (2001) – a tragicomic parable about the mundane realities of love and the difficulties of ethical living – ends with a thunderstorm that has lasted for days ('the kind of rain that you're supposed to get after a nuclear war'); for Katie Carr, Hornby's narrator, these floods seem to portend a dark, diminished future that is the result of human failure: 'We are drowning because we have abused our planet, kicked and starved it until it changed its nature and turned nasty. It feels like the end of the world.'[17] Similarly, David

Nicholls's *Us* (2014) – another ostensibly comic narrative about a disintegrating middle-class marriage – is haunted by apocalyptic dread; speculative pessimism versus a sanguine, Whigish faith in the future is used as an index of the growing estrangement between the novel's sparring couple. Nicholls's narrator, Douglas Petersen, is a fussy, methodical man in denial – he conducts a meticulously planned fight for a twenty-five-year relationship that his wife has already decided is doomed – but he is also full of foreboding. As a teenager of the 1980s, Douglas 'was especially haunted by the prospect of nuclear war' and remembers that those 'public information films intended to educate and reassure the populace' had the reverse impact and induced 'a frenzy of morbid fantasy' in which he would soon 'be hunting for mutant rats in the remains of Ipswich city centre'.[18]

Anxieties of the atomic age – familiar to anybody who grew up with the looming threat of destruction during the Cold War – have not so much evaporated, but have instead been replaced by fears about the state of the world that his own teenage son will inherit. *Us* traces the final summer of a failing relationship but it is also an exploration of another long-standing phenomenon in crisis: Douglas is afraid that the middle classes, in the ascendant since the nineteenth century, are 'doomed' by the accelerated logic of consumer capitalism. Douglas's apocalyptic prospect – a vision of a world in which there is a 'battle for finite resources of food, water, gas and oil [...] where car bomb explosions, typhoons and freak hailstorms are so commonplace as to barely be remarked upon' – is scarcely irrational or particularly out of kilter with widely acknowledged environmental forecasts (*Us*, pp. 331–2). Catastrophe, he suggests, will only be cosy for 'the privileged 1 per cent of businessmen, celebrities and entrepreneurs'. Connie, a nonconformist who yearns for the liberated years of her youth, mocks these millennial presentiments as a '*Mad Max*-like vision of the future' (*Us*, p. 332). To be clear, Douglas is neither a political activist nor a man on the threshold of a religious awakening: he is less concerned with the future of the planet than he is with the continuation of his own comfortable reality – he sees his son's face in a vicious future landscape because he is dimly conscious of his own mortality. Douglas's biography is one of everyday compromise and a product of the subtleties of economic coercion: he gave up his vocation in biological research for a more lucrative life as a manager in commercially driven science. This muted sacrifice of value – exchanging the purity of life itself for short-term material security – may signify Douglas's unconscious guilt in failing to resist the dystopian near-future that he dreads.

We might imagine a particularly awkward meeting between Douglas and Dr Paul O'Rourke, the Boston-born narrator of Joshua Ferris's *To Rise Again at a Decent Hour* (2014). These characters – who coincidentally appeared in novels published in the same year – might meet on one of their tours of Europe. Paul – Red Sox fan, dentist, atheist and insomniac – is less enthused by the aesthetic and religious legacies of the continent than his British contemporary. He recalls a holiday with his erstwhile girlfriend (also, coincidentally, named Connie) who he observes 'took Europe far too seriously' and with whom he visited numerous churches ('simply a place to be bored in').[19] Paul confesses that he perpetually lies awake, anticipating the end of the world, imagining his 'last night on earth, when all options, and not just one night's options, expired'.

> Inside my head, where I lived, wars were breaking out, valleys flooding, forests catching fire, oceans breaching the land, and storms dragging it all to the bottom of the sea, with only a few days or weeks remaining before the entire world and everything sweet and surprising we'd done with it went dark against the vast backdrop of the universe (*TRA*, pp. 42–3).

Are Douglas, Katie and Paul characters who find themselves in the wrong genre? How would they fare in the brutal world of McCarthy's *The Road* or alongside the God's Gardeners in Atwood's 'MaddAddam' trilogy? This trinity are all people who occupy the middle – they are middle class, middle aged – of a mildly privileged world that they all suspect is unstable and unsustainable.

Other twenty-first-century literary protagonists who suffer from such postmillennial forebodings have not always benefited from the same advantages as Douglas and his peers. In Dave Eggers's *Your Fathers, Where Are They? And the Prophets, Do They Live Forever?* (2014), a novel constructed entirely from dialogue, Thomas, a confused and dangerous thirty-something, kidnaps a group of men and women, including an astronaut and a former senator, takes them to an abandoned military base and seeks answers for his disillusioned generation. He confesses to experiencing 'fairly apocalyptic thoughts' and shares a recurring waking dream in which he becomes an avenging angel, an agent of everyday Armageddon:

> I'll be walking down some crowded street and I'll start boiling inside and I picture myself parting all these people like Moses with the Red Sea. You know, the people disappear, the buildings dissolve and when I'm done there's all this empty space, and it's quieter, and there aren't all these people and all their dirty thoughts and idiotic talking and opinions. And that vision actually gives me peace. When I picture the landscape bare, free of all human noise and filth, I can relax.[20]

This is a fantasy of vengeful power by an impotent individual; apocalypse as violent 'cleansing' rather than as revelation; peace achieved by mass destruction. Thomas borrows the Exodus narrative to justify his own sense of marginalization, but misses the context of oppression and the movement towards liberty. He experiences the odd sense of longing for a cause that appears in an era without a common enemy and he is nostalgic for war: 'Everyone I know would have turned out better, if we'd been part of some universal struggle, some cause greater than ourselves'.[21] Thomas's state of mind and conduct are extreme, but his grievance regarding a generational lack of direction echoes aspects of post-youth narratives such as Douglas Coupland's *Generation X: Tales for an Accelerated Culture* (1991).

The quasi-religious register of his destructive anger is also symptomatic of a widespread perception of biblical eschatology as a cinematic montage of cataclysm and retribution. Visions of the end of the world are integral to many world religions: Zoroastrianism, Buddhism and Hinduism, for example, all have distinctive forms of eschatology. The polytheistic religions of the ancient Greeks include stories in which the gods, for a variety of reasons, punish human beings by sending floods or fire. However, in the West, Judeo-Christianity continues to give shape to narratives of catastrophe and particularly those fictions of destruction that seem to portend the end-of-the-world-as-you-know-it.

Apocalypse is widely understood in the shared, popular imagination as a kind of classy synonym for spectacular destruction,

death on a vast scale and the collapse of all that a society might
hold dear (families, cars, the comforts of home). Yet this misses
the *primary* valence of the term – derived from the Greek term
apocalypsis – that signifies revelation, the uncovering of what
was previously hidden. Indeed, the Revelation of St John, the
last book of the Christian scriptures, begins with this Greek term
'suggesting a disclosure or unveiling'.[22] Biblical apocalyptic is
not simply a Christian phenomenon but, as Michael Wheeler,
addressing Victorian forms of eschatology, argues, it is 'a tradition coming down from early Judaism' as well as part of the
gospels, 'in which [...] the end-time and the inauguration of a
new world order, is held in tension with wisdom teaching, which
assumes that the world will continue'. The apocalyptic, because
of its most popular late-twentieth and early twenty-first-century
screen manifestations and Cold War associations with the threat
of nuclear annihilation, 'has come to mean simply the disastrous
end of things'.[23] The theologian Tom Wright, for example, argues
that there is a vast difference between popular understandings of
the world-to-come and Christian eschatology.[24]

The Revelation to John is undoubtedly full of violent imagery but
it is not necessarily a book that glories in gratuitous bloodletting.
In a reading of Christian eschatology compared with contemporary
'climate apocalypse', Michael Northcott argues that in John's vision
there 'is no schadenfreude, no rejoicing in the tribulations that bring
down the powerful from their thrones at the end', but rather 'John's
aim is to encourage the persecuted and powerless Christians whom
Rome threatened to overwhelm under the Emperor Nero, that, provided they remain faithful in loving God and neighbour, the cataclysm will see them vindicated in the end'.[25] This interpretation
emphasizes the advent of 'messianic time' and a new era of justice
and mercy that will replace the corruption and oppression of the
earth and its people. As Judith Kovacs and Christopher Rowland
observe in their indispensable reception history of Revelation, 'the
Apocalypse, no less than the rest of the Bible, hardly offers an unambiguous message' and it is a book that 'has served many agendas,
those of revolutionaries and radicals as well as those of quietists and
supporters of the status quo'.[26] A number of thinkers who are neither Christian nor primarily associated with professional theology
have turned to biblical idioms and ideas. Slavoj Žižek, combative
Marxist–Lacanian, for example, whose work displays a recurrent

fascination with (Saint) Paul has written a book titled *Living in the End Times* (2010). Similarly, Giorgio Agamben takes up the question of messianic time, a concept central to Walter Benjamin's project, in *The Time that Remains: A Commentary on the Letter to the Romans* (2005) in his reading of Paul's letter.

Rival views of the Revelation of St John not only divide theologians and Christian communities but are also interpreted in strikingly different ways by contemporary writers. In an autobiographical introduction to the last book of the Bible, Will Self, iconoclastic novelist and cultural commentator, describes the Revelation of St John as 'a sick text' and the King James Version, in particular, as 'a guignol of tedium, a portentous horror film'.[27] Kathleen Norris, by contrast, believes that the book of Revelation 'has suffered from bad interpretation' and that the narrative itself, far from 'cruel', 'boldly asserts that our cruelties and injustices will not have the last word'.[28]

Even in an era of relative ignorance of the Bible and its specific teachings, a version of the apocalyptic imagination relies on a variety of biblical tropes. The late 1990s witnessed a return to millennial anxiety in both popular culture and philosophy. 'Endism', observed James Annesley in 1996, 'casts a familiar shadow.'[29] The foreboding epithet for what he glossed as the 'cult of the end' is borrowed from a *New York Times Magazine* article on Francis Fukuyama, who famously argued that history itself was heading for its conclusion with the advent of liberal capitalism.[30] Disaster movies were big business for Hollywood in the 1990s, including a popular iteration of the day of judgement story in which a worryingly large asteroid is headed towards humanity in both *Deep Impact* and *Armageddon* (1998); a similar form of absurd cosmic justice, in the shape of a rogue planet, also hurtles towards Earth with unseemly haste in Lars Von Trier's more oblique existentialist drama, *Melancholia* (2011).

Catastrophe on a global scale remains a curiously popular form of screen entertainment. Nations fall, nature is spoiled and the human race might be on the brink of breathing its last after any number of extinction-level events. Such narratives not only seem strange visual companions to popcorn and ice cream, but also are highly marketable. The ways in which we might arrive at this frequently foretold 'ruined future', a future that counterintuitively often resembles our deep past, are disorientating in their diversity. Twenty-first-century screenwriters have become particularly inventive when envisaging the end of the world that we know, but certain forms of catastrophe are particularly popular: pandemics that spread so fast only a tiny remnant of human beings survive; such plagues are, with alarming regularity, accompanied by the return of the dead as zombie hordes; alien invasion, frequently repelled, on screen at least, by Tom Cruise; sentient technology that develops a homicidal antipathy for its human creators; and ecological folly, variously resulting in a new ice age, terminal drought or a global deluge to rival the flood survived by those invited on board Noah's ark. The not-too-subtle subtext of many of these end-of-the-world visions seems to be: we only learn when it's absolutely too late.

Armageddon is also the stuff of television comedy – *The Last Man on Earth* (2015-) and *You, Me and the Apocalypse* (2015) – and Saturday evening family entertainment. In the revived version of the BBC's time travelling drama, *Dr Who* (1963, 2005), the first trip on which the eponymous itinerant Time Lord takes his new companion, Rose Tyler, is to a space station in the year five billion to witness the death of planet Earth, a conclusion hastened by the expanding sun. The Doctor, ostensibly very fond of human beings, appears insouciant about this ending. In the same episode, the mysterious character reveals that he is the last of his species as his own world was destroyed after a long war. He is an exile with a guilty secret, regarded as a hero by many whom he encounters but, he believes, also the person responsible for the annihilation of his people.

This fascination with an anticipated end is not, however, necessarily exclusively a product of either pre- or postmillennial presentiments. Frank Kermode in *The Sense of Ending* (1967), a groundbreaking study of literature's affinities with the apocalyptic tradition and temporality, uses the term 'end-determined fictions'.[31] This might apply to a range of narratives that depend on revelation and resolution, from Virgil and Dante to popular contemporary genres such as detective stories. Paul Fiddes revisits Kermode's theory of temporality in *The Promised End* (2000) and explores the peculiar resistance to closure of postmodern fiction in relation to the eschatological four 'last things' of orthodox Christianity: 'the final advent of the Lord of the cosmos, the last judgement, heaven and hell'.[32] Much late modern thought and art no longer recognizes the transcendental significance of these theological categories. However, contemporary literature displays a continual fascination with the imaginative possibilities of biblical ways of addressing the end. Indeed, for Fiddes 'eschatology [is] the basic mood' not just of theology but also of 'literary creation'.[33]

As Greg Garrard observes, the idiom of eschatology 'escaped the discipline of theology long before the twentieth century'. Garrard cites the 'secular, often politically revolutionary' appropriations of 'apocalyptic rhetoric' by a variety of figures associated with the Romantic movement of the late eighteenth and early nineteenth centuries, including the highly esoteric image-texts of William Blake.[34] This wayward visionary used his wildly reimagined biblical images against the official arbiters of revelation: church authorities and the publicly pious are mocked, their theologies inverted and defamiliarized as part of a prophetic critique of social conformity and the tyranny of wealth.

Nineteenth-century literature and culture frequently explore ethical and aesthetic questions via an eschatological lens. Thomas Carlyle's 'Signs of the Times' (1829), in which the sermonic writer famously characterized his historical moment as 'the Age of Machinery in every outward and inward sense of the word' is a prophetic essay that challenges both materialism and superstition.[35] The title is an allusion to Jesus's warning to the religious authorities that tempted him into giving a sign:

> He answered and said unto them, When it is evening, ye say, It will be fair weather: for the sky is red. And in the morning, It will be foul weather to day: for the sky is red and lowering. O ye hypocrites, ye can discern the face of the sky; but can ye not discern the signs of the times? (Matthew 16. 2–3).

Carlyle was responding, in part, to Millenarian thinkers of his day who anticipated the imminent return of Christ to earth. The essayist's allusion to Jesus's austere advice is likely to have been recognized by believers and sceptics in a culture that prized biblical literacy. The aura of eschatological thinking was also deployed in more explicitly devotional ways: for example, William Holman Hunt's painting of Jesus, *The Light of the World* (1851–3), eventually seen by millions of spectators around the world, interprets Revelation 3. 20 ('Behold, I stand at the door, and knock: if any man hear my voice, and open the door, I will come in to him, and will sup with him, and he with me'); the poet Christina Rossetti, fervent in her commitment to Anglo-Catholicism and, coincidentally one of the models for Hunt's Christ, also wrote a commentary on Revelation, *The Face of the Deep* (1892). The final words of Charlotte Brontë's spiritually ambiguous *Jane Eyre* (1848), spoken by St John Rivers, include the words of messianic expectation from the penultimate verse of the Christian Bible: 'Surely I come quickly [...] Amen. Even so, come, Lord Jesus' (Revelation 22. 20). Perhaps the most successful work of British religious art of the nineteenth century is John Martin's eschatological sequence *The Great Day of His Wrath* (1851–3). During an era in which Evangelical spirituality was extraordinarily influential in popular culture, vast numbers of spectators gathered to see these canvases depicting the four last things. In later years Martin's reputation declined and, as John Wolffe notes, the paintings were sold in the 1930s for 'the derisory sum of seven pounds'.[36] However, the debatable process of secularization coupled with a more questioning, critical approach to scripture did not bring an end to the fascination with biblical versions of the end. Iterations of Christian apocalyptic, for example, inform the 'scientific romances' of H. G. Wells, especially *The Time Machine* (1895) and *The War of the Worlds* (1897–8), both of which are concerned with end-of-the-world scenarios.

The tradition of displaced eschatology, argues Garrard, also animated Modernism, in particular the environmentally inflected writing of D. H. Lawrence.[37] The author was simultaneously fascinated and repelled by the book of Revelation, a text that he knew intimately as part of a rigorous (if resented) training in daily Bible reading during his nonconformist childhood. Lawrence had long abandoned orthodox Christianity, but was not, in the conventional sense, an atheist. He had a fierce sense of spiritual awe for the universe that he, privately at least, was prepared to name 'Almighty God'.[38] There are apocalyptic echoes throughout Lawrence's work: for example, *Dies Irae*, signifying 'day of wrath', was a working title for *Women in Love* (1920), a novel that is charged with a sense of catastrophe, both imminent and immanent. These biblical reworkings coalesce in Lawrence's last completed work, *Apocalypse* (1929–30), a posthumously published, idiosyncratic mediation on the strange influence of the Revelation of St John ('Perhaps the most detestable of all these books of the Bible, taken superficially'). He disliked its allegorical poetry ('distasteful because of its complete unnaturalness') but recognized its appeal for downtrodden people and observes that 'the huge denunciation of kings and Rulers [...] is entirely sympathetic to a Tuesday evening congregation of colliers and colliers' wives'.[39] For Lawrence, the Revelation – a 'rather repulsive work' – is the product of 'a second-rate mind' that 'appeals intensely to second-rate minds in every country and every century'.[40] The essay is marked by contempt for the Christian antipathy for strength and power; Lawrence, like Nietzsche, reads the celebration of love, duty and mutual dependence as envy. He contrasts the alternative visions of Jesus with that of John of Patmos as two radically different forms of Christianity: 'The former would "save" the world – the latter will never be satisfied till it has destroyed the world'.[41] Lawrence's view is, by turns, humanitarian and rational but also deeply elitist and condescending. However, his argument that the book of Revelation – 'strange as it is, unintelligible as it is' – has been an enormous 'source of inspiration to the vast mass of Christian minds' is oddly prophetic of the vast influence of Millennialism in early twenty-first-century culture, a text that may have more popular appeal than Jesus's teaching across the four authorized gospels.[42]

From one perspective there is no great difference between the eschatology that was preached two millennia ago and twenty-first-century popular narratives of the end, despite the apparent move from faith in God to trust in humanity. 'The early Christian belief in an End-Time that would bring about a new type of human life', contends John Gray, 'was transmitted via the medieval millenarians to become secular utopianism and, in another incarnation, the belief in progress'. For Gray, the confidence of some modern secularists that their world view is free from the taint of religion is a delusion. The evidence, he suggests, is witnessed in the results of the 2003 invasion of Iraq, and in the city of Fallujah, 'razed by rival fundamentalists', the 'age of utopias' came to an end.[43]

'Politics has always been a feature of Christian millenarianism, and fundamentalist belief surely feeds nontheological perceptions', claims Lee Quinby, in her 'anti-apocalyptic' critique of Western genealogy.[44] This is particularly the case in the United States, where the influence of certain strands of fundamentalist Christianity has been significant in the last century. In *American Apocalypse* (2014), a history of the Evangelical influence in the modern United

States, Matthew Avery Sutton notes that 'radical evangelicals initially worked to resurrect and refashion early church millennialism, which they applied to the modern world in creative ways.'[45]
The rise of this tradition from its origins on the fringes of mainline
Protestantism to an enormously powerful movement is, he argues,
a result of a constellation of factors including social unrest in the
United States and two world wars: finally, a series of global crises
culminating in the devastation of the atomic bombs dropped by
America on Japanese cities meant that 'fundamentalist doomsayers
no longer seemed so outrageous'.[46] In Avery Sutton's terms, 'a politics of apocalypse' have emerged.[47] These ideas, he indicates, have
been sustained from the Cold War to the twenty-first-century 'War
on Terror' since apocalypticism constructs 'an absolutist, uncom-
promising, good-versus evil faith'.[48] This kind of theology offers the
comfort of a fixed moral compass in a world marked by simultaneously overlapping and competing interests.

Stephen King's *Under the Dome* (2009) is a SF narrative that
both satirizes the excesses of a fundamentalist culture and resonates
with post-9/11 anxieties about security and authoritarian government. At 11.44 a.m. on 21 October in an unnamed year, Chester's
Mill, a small town in the state of Maine, is suddenly and inexpli-
cably separated from the rest of the world by an invisible barrier
that renders it a virtual prison for its few thousand inhabitants.
The narrative is post-apocalyptic in a triple sense: first, it echoes
the popular understanding of apocalypse as a destructive, violent
ending to an era or social order; second, it narrates the impact of a
transformative event and finally, it echoes the primary Christian signification of the apocalyptic as revelation. This last mode, derived
from biblical eschatology, continues to exert a significant influence
on the shape of texts that might otherwise be read as 'secular' or
even atheist in orientation. In King's text, the final, extraterrestrial
explanation of the mystery of the dome's advent is subordinated
to revelations about the corruption of the town's political and religious leaders. Chester's Mill is dominated by a manipulative individual named Big Jim, a wealthy and publicly pious second-hand car
dealer who also secretly runs an industrial-scale narcotics manufacturing business. He uses biblical rhetoric to coerce his God-fearing
fellow citizens into obedience and exploits the panic generated by
events to persecute those who oppose him and to ensure his own
political power. End-of-the-world-as-we-know-it stories are a kind

of cultural leveller, connecting complex neo-modernist writing and pulp fiction. King is a mainstream, commercially popular writer whose fiction taps into zeitgeist anxieties regarding national security, environmental destruction and the decline of democratic institutions. By contrast, Margaret Atwood and Jim Crace, for example, are more likely to be studied on university courses and to receive esteemed literary awards. Yet all three are fascinated by the human capacity for self-destruction on a grand scale. Each of these writers use the trope of a surviving remnant, groups whose social diversity, conflict and fragile cooperation engage with disquiet about the project of liberal capitalism. They also, consciously or otherwise, echo visionary ideas of biblical prophecy regarding the finite nature of human power.

In some instances, contemporary end-of-the-world fiction deploys biblical allusions that are simultaneously precise and oblique. The sparseness and linguistic restraint of McCarthy's *The Road*, a novel discussed in more detail in Chapter Five, reads like a particularly distressing parable of loss. Even the form of the narrative seems to bear witness to semantic deterioration – punctuation evaporates, conversation is stark and repetitious – but the narrative still teems with biblical allusion. In one flashback sequence, the most significant female character – mother to the boy, wife to the man – urges her stoic husband to abandon hope by telling him to 'Curse God and die', a very precise allusion to the Book of Job, the only words spoken by the nameless wife of the righteous man of Uz (Job 2. 9).[49] McCarthy also draws on a distinctively Trinitarian, relational language: the most significant bond is between the father and the son, but the third person of this trinity might be the reason for their continued journey towards the coast – their existence is not simply a matter of survival but because they are 'carrying the fire' – a recurrent promise in the narrative (*TR*, p. 87). The father sometimes makes brutal decisions that might forfeit his ethical integrity, much to the disappointment of his son, but he also 'knew only that the child was his warrant. He said: If he is not the word of God God never spoke' (*TR*, p. 3). Divinity is invoked in a number of ways including the perhaps blasphemous invocation of 'Christ' and 'God' in desperate situations, as near hopeless prayers for deliverance (*TR*, pp. 116–7). They also encounter a roadside mystic, an elderly man who resembles 'a starved and threadbare buddha' who claims, 'There is no God and we are his prophets' (*TR* pp. 179, 181). However, his assumed name, Ely, is a contraction of the biblical prophet Elijah and he is treated as a kind of negative seer who, unlike others, did not 'believe in' the future. The novel has been read from a variety of opposing theological perspectives; some critics read it as a contemporary Christian allegory whilst others suggest that it represents a nihilist critique of belief. Hannah Stark, for example, emphasizes affinities between the novel and the Revelation of St John.[50]

The legacies of Christian apocalyptic thought are vital, in different ways, to the majority of novels explored in this study. Chapters Two and Three, however, focus on the ways in which specific biblical narratives of the end have been interpreted in contemporary fiction. Chapter Two explores rewritings of the first biblical apocalypse, the story of the flood narrated in Genesis 6–9, in which God, angered by the propensity of his creation for sin, brings destruction upon the earth. David Maine and Maggie Gee both published novels under the title *The Flood* in 2004. Their interpretations of the deluge, however, differ in setting: Gee's narrative is set in a kind of looking-glass, semi-submerged contemporary Britain in which manipulative, smarmy politicians vie with fundamentalist preachers; Maine, by contrast, returns to the text of Genesis, drawing on the English translation (1914) of the Douay Bible (1609), and reimagines Noah's story (named Noe, in this version) in a form that gives individual voice to the patriarch's wife, sons and daughters-in-law. The novel is far from deferential to its source material, but it represents both belief and the experience of suffering with rare nuance.

Not all post-apocalyptic landscapes inflected by biblical narrative resemble the scarred, parched, denatured, colour-drained terrain of McCarthy's *The Road* or the 'drowned worlds' of Maggie Gee or David Maine. Occasionally, twenty-first-century catastrophe narratives look uncannily like the world we already know; disturbing events, in some novels, take place on a global scale without the mass destruction of the environment. The apocalypse, in such stories, comes like a 'thief in the night' and simultaneously changes both nothing and everything (1 Thessalonians 5. 2).[51] Tom Perrotta's *The Leftovers* (2011), the focus of Chapter Three, imagines a world that has experienced a 'Rapture-like' event known as 'the Sudden Departure' in which millions of people across the world have, in the blink of an eye, disappeared without trace. The novel is a sceptical treatment of a theological concept, based on a literal reading of 1 Thessalonians 4. 17 that the faithful will be gathered up into the air to meet with the returning Christ. This belief, popular among certain influential fundamentalist strands of Protestantism, is part of a complex set of creeds related to the Second Coming and the condition of the world. The chapter places Perrotta's representation of grief and religious extremism in the wider context of 'Rapture' culture in the contemporary United States. Perrotta, like Maine and Gee, is theologically ambiguous about the source of suffering in his apocalyptic narratives. Is the universe simply indifferent to the human desire for order and mercy?

The persistence of spirituality, and in particular, of religious narratives, in a world after God and, indeed, after humanity is crucial to Chapter Four. Its subject, Margaret Atwood's 'MaddAddam' trilogy, is set in a world in which members of a remnant of mankind, including an initially solitary storyteller, remember the destruction of the world that they knew. These survivors, as grief-stricken as Perrotta's 'leftover' souls, encounter a peaceable, unworldly community who are not quite human. The 'Children of Crake' are keen to know about their creator, the geneticist who carefully and coldly brought about the end of the world. Atwood's sequence of novels, published across a decade, is characteristically genre bending, synthesizing elements of, for example, classical mythology, biblical allusion, Gothic horror and Modernist invention in her satirical form of speculative fiction. The chapter will pay particular attention to Atwood's complex critique of the relationship between art and religion.

Chapter Five turns to questions of mobility and agency. Post-apocalyptic terrain is typically not densely populated, but its cracked black-top roads, free from fast-moving traffic, are positively busy with ambulatory figures: itinerants, drifters and nomads who pace these ruined environments. The chapter focuses on McCarthy's *The Road* and Crace's *The Pesthouse* and addresses the relationship between post-catastrophe walkers, the 'promised lands' that they may seek and the wider relationship between apocalyptic presentiments and the mysteriously countercultural deed of taking a hike. What kind of destination do they hope to reach and is there any 'end', in a conventional sense, to their wanderings at the end of the world?

Chapter Six examines the apocalyptic turn in Young Adult (YA) fiction. Two tough, smart young women wander the ruins of the land that used to be America; one, an ingenious hunter with an instinct for survival, named Katniss Everdeen, hides out in a city situated somewhere in the Rocky Mountains, known only as the Capitol, the wealthy metropolis that reigns over the 12 Districts of Panem; the other, Tris Prior, stigmatized for her complex, nonconformist identity, survives in a post-apocalyptic Chicago. Elsewhere, a similarly defiant, problem-solving but amnesiac teenager named Thomas wakes up in a subterranean prison structured like a maze. These characters share much in common but never meet because they are the central protagonists of separate twenty-first-century dystopian, post-catastrophe narratives. Katniss, the rebellious but conflicted narrator of Suzanne Collins's 'The Hunger Games' sequence, Tris of Veronica Roth's 'Divergent' and Thomas, the central protagonist of James Dashner's *The Maze Runner* might become great allies or sworn enemies with their shared contempt for authority. They are all, however, also extraordinarily marketable. The chapter explores the representation of apocalyptic rites of passage in relation to debates about surveillance, commerce and the politics of rebellion.

The conclusion focuses on Emily St John Mandel's *Station Eleven* (2014), a novel that both parodies aspects of our catastrophe-fixated times and celebrates the beauty of the present, flawed world. The Travelling Symphony, a group of touring musicians and actors, walks across a largely deserted landscape performing Shakespeare to the disparate, tiny settlements that now constitute civilization. What makes survival worthwhile? How will human achievements be remembered, if at all? Contemporary apocalyptic fiction tracks the contradictory desires for self-destruction and survival that haunt human beings. The end of the world is, oddly, a rich beginning for narrative.

2

'God rains over everything': Two floods

When narrating catastrophe, twenty-first-century journalists frequently deploy a rather anomalous choice of soubriquet: even in a relatively secularized, liberal news culture, the whole gamut of disasters including flood, famine, plague, war, earthquakes and tsunami are frequently described as 'biblical'. This deceptively simple term, however, is one that radically divides communities: believers who regard the Bible as a continued source of revelation and sceptical thinkers who appreciate the historical and aesthetic legacy of scripture. Newspapers that have no specific religious alignment continue to draw on this sacred idiom: following the floods that submerged large parts of New Orleans in 2005, one report in the British paper *The Guardian* reflected that 'Hurricane Katrina was billed as a biblical storm [...] and it prompted an exodus of biblical proportions'.[1] The motif, in an era of relative biblical ignorance, has global mobility, a phrase ready to apply to all disasters: 'Japan counts death toll after biblical scenes of destruction', stated *The Guardian* in March 2011; 'Texas explosion: Biblical scene of destruction on Waco's doorstep', proclaimed a similar headline in *The Independent* newspaper in April 2013.[2] The adjective is a cheap way of conferring meaning on everyday horror, an ironic assertion of scale in a world divided between those nations where death and destruction are aestheticized as elements of popular entertainment and others, for whose citizens such desolation has become a daily reality. The epithet 'scenes of biblical destruction' has mutated into a journalistic cliché, one that generates an instantly recognized iconography of suffering, and which is also successful at promoting sentiment. Such representations can be gruelling to witness but somehow they also keep events at a safe distance. We are quick to forgive ourselves necessary emotional detachment when misery that takes place *somewhere else* swiftly becomes the hazy stuff of memory.

Opportunist news headlines are not the only form of popular narrative to appropriate the apocalyptic aura of scripture. Twenty-first-century fiction also draws on biblical lexicons to tell ostensibly secular stories of incalculable loss and trauma; sometimes such allusions to Judeo-Christian apocalyptic are explicit and playful: *Kingdom Come* (2006), J. G. Ballard's final novel, is one of his many surrealist catastrophe narratives, but its title is an allusion to a line in the Lord's Prayer, versions of which appear in two of the synoptic gospels (Matthew 6. 9–13; Luke 11. 2–4). 'Your kingdom come' is the second petition in the act of supplication that Jesus teaches as an alternative to ostentatious or 'babbling' public prayers ('when you pray go into your room, close the door and pray to your Father, who is unseen', Matthew 6. 6). Ballard's ironic invocation of God's kingdom is an estranging device: the term is ambiguous in the New Testament and Jesus is never precise in his statements that are variously interpreted as assurance of territorial liberation, supernatural redemption or ethical transformation. However, the promise of a kingdom still to come is rooted in the Jewish belief in a future Messiah, a rule of justice, righteousness and mercy. Ballard's novel, a dream–logic satire of advanced capitalist culture, trades on a white noise, cultural awareness of the traditional prayer as a counterpoint to contemporary obsession with material wealth and comfort. The narrative blends middle-class ennui with acts of terror in shopping malls and the rise of a new form of media savvy fascism; the characteristically deadpan narrator approvingly describes one anonymous suburban town, somewhere 'vaguely south-west of Heathrow' as 'a place where it was impossible to borrow a book, say a prayer, consult a parish record or give to charity [...] the town was an end state of consumerism. I liked it'.[3] Religious impulses, however, have not quite evaporated in Ballard's nation of history-free, churchless supermodern 'non-spaces', to borrow Marc Augé's phrase.[4] One character describes the bizarre altars of consumer goods displayed outside shop windows as 'prayer sites': 'The Metro-Centre is a cathedral, a place of worship. Consumerism may seem pagan, but in fact it's the last refuge of the religious instinct. Within a few days you'll see a congregation worshipping its washing machines' (*KC*, p. 252).[5] Shopping, in this world, is a ritual, a religious end in itself, and the Metro-Centre, topped with a dome, becomes home to a barely conscious cult. A vivid, hellish apocalypse of sorts takes place as this cathedral of consumption 'devour[s] itself, a furnace consumed by its own fire' but there is the dark promise of another 'even fiercer republic' that will 'open the doors and spin the turnstiles of its beckoning paradise'.[6] There is a curious biblical connection between Ballard's last and first novels: *Kingdom Come* is marked by New Testament eschatology and the provocative surrealism of his debut, *The Drowned World* (1962), in which a future London, alongside the rest of the Western world, has been submerged by the waters of solar-ray melted polar ice caps, echoes two foundational disaster narratives in the Jewish–Christian tradition: Kerans, Ballard's protagonist, is compared with the original exiled patriarch; as he heads away from the remnants of civilization into the dense jungle, he becomes 'a second Adam searching for the forgotten paradises of the reborn sun'.[7] The most sustained apocalyptic allusion, however, is to the story of a great world-destroying flood and the salvation of Noah.

The concept of a destructive, God-willed ending is most commonly associated in the popular imagination with the Revelation. Yet early in the very first book of the *Tanakh*, the Hebrew Bible, Genesis, the book of beginnings, sacred to both Jews and Christians, a violent end is decreed against life on earth. In the biblical account, narrated in Genesis 6–9, a great flood is ordained by God who is angered by humanity's propensity for sin ('I will destroy man whom I have created from the face of the earth [...] for it repenteth me that I have made them' [Genesis 6. 7]). Although this story concludes with restoration and the promise of a new beginning, it is a troubling narrative and one that remains a source of inspiration for catastrophe-themed art. The peculiar contemporary resonance of the biblical flood, one that seems to anticipate the destructive consequences of climate change, might seem counterintuitive since the first book in the canon is associated in the popular imagination with a narrative of creation. However, the flood, a source of artistic inspiration for apocalyptic artists of the past, including John Martin's *The Deluge* (1834), is a pervasive, saturating presence in contemporary culture. Darren Aronofsky's *Noah* (2014) is an epic Hollywood adaptation that weaves together different elements of mythology with themes of sin, violence and mercy, rewriting certain

elements of the narrative including Ham's rebellion against his
father. A BBC television drama, *The Ark* (2015), similarly recre-
ates the biblical setting, but places greater emphasis on intimate
family dynamics. It also adds another son who does not appear
in Genesis: Kenan is the dutiful, awe-struck youngest child who
eventually defies Noah and chooses to remain in the city that is
washed away by the flood. Both adaptations accentuate the wilful,
occasionally alienating presence of the apparently divinely inspired
patriarch.

A plethora of novels, written during the last thirty or so
years, including Timothy Findley's *Not Wanted on the Voyage*
(1984), Julian Barnes's *A History of the World in 10 ½ Chapters*
(1989), Jeanette Winterson's *Boating for Beginners* (1985) and
The Stone Gods (2007), Michèle Roberts's *The Book of Mrs Noah*
(1987), Geraldine McCaughrean's *Not the End of the World* (2004)
and Sam Taylor's *The Island at the End of the World* (2009), rein-
terpret aspects of the flood narrative.[8] Will Self's *The Book of Dave*
(2006) rewrites the biblical deluge as a future event that may simply
be the hallucinatory projection of the titular taxi driver/prophet,
a damaged man energized by drunken fury and the beginnings of
psychosis. Self's novel, full of linguistic invention and grotesque
behaviour, homages Russell Hoban's post-apocalyptic *Riddley
Walker* (1980) in its satire of revealed religion and slavish obedience to self-justified authority, especially patriarchal piety that uses
ostensibly divinely inspired texts as grounds for social control. The
future island community of Ham is a punning allusion both to
Hampstead Heath and to the son of Noah, punished by his father
with a curse that was to be visited on his son, Canaan (Genesis
9. 20–7).[9] Margaret Atwood's *The Year of the Flood* (2009), the
second novel in her 'MaddAddam' trilogy, features a character who
names himself Adam One, a post-apocalyptic first man, and the title
itself alludes to the deluge described in Genesis.

This chapter focuses on two twenty-first-century novels by
David Maine and Maggie Gee that participate in this tradition of
rewriting the biblical deluge. Both are named *The Flood* and their
uncanny doubling is further underlined by the fact that they were,
coincidentally, both published in 2004. In Gee's *The Flood*, a version of present or near-future London has become a 'watery city', 'a
city sliding under the sea' after two years of near constant rain; this
provisional, hypermodern Venice is already partially submerged,

on the threshold of disappearing into an aquatic nowhere.[10] Maine's iteration of the flood, published in the United States as *The Preservationist*, is a more direct retelling of the biblical story, one that maintains the historical setting and that draws specifically on the English translation of the Catholic Douay Bible (1582–1609). Both novels fuse a contemporary reading of disaster, loss and grief with elements of biblical narrative. They also, in radically different ways, address the possibilities of life after the end. The chapter places these novels in critical conversation both with each other and with the originating biblical narrative. Are these novels apocalyptic only in the modern sense of representing world-ending disaster or might they recuperate the primary sense of *apocalypsis* as a mode of disclosure in which something once hidden is brought to light?

The biblical account of the flood is disturbing and more ambiguous than its surprising popularity in children's hymnody, toys and comic wall-friezes might suggest. As Maggi Dawn observes, the 'gentle and comic reading' of the ark, defined by 'the image of pairs of animals being loaded onto a [...] boat and sailing happily away to sea' runs counter to the 'elements of horror' that are a crucial aspect of the story. She cites the devastating tsunami of Boxing Day 2004 as an example from recent history that might illuminate the scale of destruction evoked in the Genesis account.[11]

Jürgen Moltmann, a theologian who is particularly concerned with the relationship between catastrophe and hope, notes that this shadowy story involves a very distinctive kind of struggle: not with 'different gods, and not even as a struggle of the One God against evil' but as 'a conflict in God himself'. In this sense, Moltmann suggests, 'the Creator revokes his resolve to create'.[12] The biblical narrative begins with grief: God mourns because his creation has become utterly corrupt: 'And God saw that the wickedness of man was great in the earth, and that every imagination of the thoughts of his heart was only evil continually' (Genesis 6. 5). However, one man, Noah, 'a just man and perfect in his generations' finds 'grace in the eyes of the Lord' (Genesis 6. 9, 8). This story of a worldwide flood is neither unique nor wholly original; indeed, scholars suggest that 300 accounts of great deluge exist in different cultures.[13] The Noah narrative is preceded by stories from Mesopotamia including the epic of Gilgamesh; it also finds parallels in Greek mythology in a story told by Plato of a man named Deucalion who, with help from Prometheus, builds an ark to escape a flood sent by Zeus.

There are a vast number of theological interpretations of the biblical story – literalist, allegorical, mythic – but a common strand emphasizes both God's righteous anger at human hatred and his final change of heart that results in a restoration of creation:

> I will not again curse the ground any more for man's sake; for the imagination of man's heart is evil from his youth; neither will I again smite any more every thing living, as I have done. While the earth remaineth, seedtime and harvest, and cold and heat, and summer and winter, and day and night shall not cease (Genesis 8. 21–2).

Walter Brueggemann offers a distinctive theological response to the difficulties represented in the story. He suggests that the narrative's vital drama can be articulated in a single question: 'Can God change his mind?' His interpretation stresses that the God of this narrative is 'fully a person who hurts and celebrates' and 'rather than a captive of old resolves' he can 'change his mind' both 'to abandon what he has made' and 'rescue that which he has condemned'.[14] Finally, in Brueggemann's reading, 'what distinguishes God in this narrative from every other god and every other creature is God's deep grief' and this form of sorrow 'enables God to move past his own interest and to embrace his creature-partner in new ways'.[15] By contrast, many modern fictional interpretations of divine action in the Genesis account tend towards the subversive and playful. Barnes's 'stowaway' narrator, for example, finally revealed to be a woodworm, an 'unclean' animal not welcome on board, describes the holy boatbuilder as 'a monster, a puffed-up patriarch who spent half his day grovelling to his God and the other half taking it out on us'.[16] The deity is described, without reverence, as 'a really oppressive role model' and the post-catastrophe covenant is also regarded with scepticism ('A pretty hollow contract, if you ask me [...] Noah probably realized that he had God over a barrel') (*AHOTW*, pp. 48, 52). This wry reinterpretation is not simply a rejection of Judeo-Christian theodicy but also a critique of authorial power.

David Maine's *The Flood* has a much more richly ambivalent relationship with its source material; the novel occupies the threshold between belief and scepticism as its characters wrestle with the meaning of the world-ending deluge. It also draws on a range of narrative modes including tragicomedy, quest tale and family saga; the conflict between generations, signaled in the Genesis narrative by Noe's anger with Ham, whose son Canaan he then curses, is another form of catastrophe. *The Flood*, Maine's debut novel, is also the first of his three audacious rewritings of stories from the Jewish canon; it was followed by *Fallen* (2005), an account of the first biblical family told with an inverted chronology that begins with the death of an elderly Cain and moves backwards, chapter by chapter, until the moments after Adam and Eve have disobeyed God; *The Book of Samson* (2006) is a vivid, unsanitized retelling of the ancient Israelite judge, retaining the violence of the biblical story. Maine's approach to sacred narratives is neither constrained by ersatz reverence nor dominated by showy contempt for the text. His first novel, despite its emphasis on loss and the destructive potential of nature, also features moments of sublime surprise: before the rain begins, Japheth watches the vast menagerie of animals, 'thousands of critters' that have been gathered for the forthcoming journey. The youngest son, normally taciturn, bears witness to the strangeness of the event, the diverse mass of life with a kind of earthy awe:

> I know when I'm in the presence of something mightier than myself. It happens during thunderstorms and earth tremors and clear nights with no moon, and here it's happening again right in front of me. I'd be stupid to say otherwise.[17]

Japheth also finds an odd sense of communion with his fellow creatures as he listens to the uncanny 'sound of a couple of thousand bodies waking up and stretching' and realizes that they are 'not so different from me. Or you' (*TF*, p. 83). However, the novel does not reimagine the Genesis story as a proto-environmentalist treatise in which Noe is effectively the first green activist. One reviewer of *The Flood* notes Maine's refusal either 'to modernise or sentimentalise the story' despite the 'enticing opportunities to draw metaphorical parallels with our own time'; so the 'impregnable faith' of Noe might have heighted a parallel with fanatics 'around the world who claim God is on their side', but 'Maine disdains all these metaphors, instead telling a story that cannot be read simply. No one knows Yahweh's reasons for making the flood'.[18]

The Flood offers neither the theological recuperation of, for example, Brueggemann nor the caustic incredulity of Barnes's understandably vexed narrator. Maine's novel reads as a type of fictional commentary on the biblical text, one that pays attention to the specifics of the Genesis narrative including its setting, theological claims and plot. The novel has a tripartite structure ('Clouds', 'Rain', 'Sun') to reflect the world immediately before, during and after the deluge. This novelistic division of time, emphasizing the elemental experience of duration rather than a *kairotic* sense of eternity, is matched by its attention to the interior life of its characters. A number of the chapters begin with epigraphs taken from the biblical account; these citations give a scriptural frame to the subsequent action. The opening chapter, for example, sets up the narrative with a verse about the central protagonist's spiritual status rather than one anticipating the destruction to come: 'But Noe found grace before the Lord' (Genesis 6. 8). This allusion to divine favour, however, finds a compelling counterpoint in the vivid, earthy way in which the patriarch, 'roughly six hundred years old', is introduced, urinating as he stares out at the horizon. This anticipates a novel that fuses transcendent events with mundane reality; the book is replete with bodily detail: when God speaks, with news of the forthcoming destruction, Noe 'felt his bladder loosen, and hot urine stream down his thigh' and he experiences a sense of despair that 'chewed through him like a maggot' (*TF*, pp. 6–7). *The Flood* does not question the biblical Noe's standing as one who hears God (though multiple interpretations of the origins of this divine voice remain open), but neither does it euphemize his anger or authoritarian behaviour. He is not a modern man, disdains challenges to reason and deals with his wife and family in a high-handed fashion. However, unlike other critical rewritings of the narrative, he is not simply represented as a dictator; for one thing, he commands no respect or power over people outside his family. Although the novel has a certain loyalty to the structure and many details of the Genesis account, there is also much embellishment. For example, one chapter begins with a quotation from Genesis 6. 11 ('And earth was corrupted before God, and was filled with iniquity') and narrates an episode in which crowds gather to mock and taunt the boatbuilder. In a significant departure from the biblical narrative, Noe offers his mockers the opportunity to join him ('You can still repent. There is room for

you in the boat'; places on the boat 'cannot be bought' but are
open to those 'with a pure heart', *TF*, pp. 73–4). The skirmish
also gives voice to the damned, who are largely omitted from the
biblical text. These figures are not romanticized: indeed, many of
the men and women who mock Noe are represented as brutal and
malicious, some of them ready to sell their children as prostitutes.
However, among the contemptuous voices are plausible challenges
to Noe's creed: the evidence, speculates one cynic, is that Noe's
God has 'forgotten' him; another theological wit surmises that
'God threw Adam out of Paradise for eating an apple. Or so your
story says. Does that sound like someone you should put your
faith in?' (*TF*, p. 73). Although Noe's prophecy is ultimately vindicated, Maine is careful not to make the leap of faith a self-evident
choice; his character is virtuous in relation to the traditions of his
professed religion, but his version of Noe is also short-tempered,
impulsive and autocratic. In another revision to the biblical narrative, during the time of the flood, Maine's Noe, already familiar
with divine voices, argues with God 'in a fever dream of salvation and exile, of God and Hell' (*TF*, p. 123). The chapter skil-
fully appropriates other elements of the Jewish scriptures and
the conversation pastiches, in particular, the terror and grief
narrated in the book of Job. The 'holy man of Uz' loses his live-
stock, children and, finally, his health, following a wager between
God and the adversary (named Satan in some translations). Job
refuses to curse God but, following the frustrating counsel of his
self-righteous friends, he eventually utters a desperate prayer ('I
cry unto thee, and thou dost not hear me: I stand up, and thou
regardest me not', Job 30. 20). God eventually answers 'out of
the whirlwind' and reminds Job of their relative positions in the
universe ('Knowest thou the ordinances of heaven? canst thou set
the dominion thereof in the earth?' Job 38. 33). These apocalyptic
utterances are reimagined in Noe's delirious conversations with
a shape-shifting figure whose responses resemble both God and
the 'adversary' from the Job narrative. In response to Noe's query
regarding the nature of a creator who would abandon a man who
has 'done all' that he was asked, the voice replies: '*An unreliable
one, perhaps*' (*TF*, p. 125). The narrative is equivocal about the
source of Noe's visions, in both health and delirious sickness; it
is more interested in the ways in which individuals interpret the
experience of suffering.

The most revealing perspectives, however, come neither from confrontations with Noe's unbelieving enemies nor from his long, dark night of the soul; they are instead articulated by his extended family. Maine's retelling is split between eight narrators: the chapters focalized through Noe are told in an omniscient voice, typifying his status as one who (believes) he hears the voice of God. The remaining seven narrators (Noe's wife, three sons and three daughters-in-law) tell their own stories. This polyphonic structure differs from the originating biblical narrative with its focus on the patriarch's dutiful response to God, the flood and the eventual restoration of creation. These additional voices open up alternative views of the visionary's character: his wife, for example, who is nameless in the Genesis narrative retains her gendered anonymity ('Does he even know my name? Don't bet on it […] I'm the wife now, no more nor less'), but has an acerbic take on her domineering husband (she nicknames Noe 'Himself') and his predilection for unquestioned oration (*TF*, p. 9). Bera, married to Noe's dutiful eldest son, Sem, was part of a distant tribe who worshipped other gods; despatched to the south to bring back 'breeding families of every beast in creation', she does not wholly reject the faith of her new family but is nevertheless irritated by the spiritual complacency of their assumption that 'God will provide' (*TF*, p. 38). In the same chapter, Bera undergoes a form of conversion experience as she becomes a surrogate nurse to two abandoned children; she registers the ability to breastfeed as a miracle. However, in describing Yahweh to an acquaintance, she acknowledges that this deity is 'fond of riddles and double meanings, and things are seldom clear' (*TF*, p. 51).

Of Noe's three sons, Cham (Ham in most English translations) is the least convinced by his father's form of monotheism: as the narrative begins he is recently married and living at a distance from his family; when confronted with the news of Noe's revelation by his brother Sem, he teases their shared sense of devotion: 'Our father […] has a special relationship with Yahweh, it's true. Most of the time I think the old boy likes to tell God what he's doing wrong' (*TF*, p. 32). This mild disrespect is proleptic of Cham's later decisive and disastrous confrontation with Noe, inspired by the mysterious episode in Genesis 9. 21–7 in which the patriarch becomes drunk from the wine of his own vineyard. The biblical account indicates that Noah 'lay uncovered' in his tent and is seen by Ham; his brothers, however, on hearing the story avert their eyes and cover their father with a garment. The mystery of the story lies in Ham's punishment when it is strangely transferred by Noah to the next generation ('Cursed be Canaan!' Genesis 9. 25); Ham's son, according to Noah, will be the slave of his cousins. Maine's adaptation of this puzzling element of a story already abounding in loss and disaster embellishes the drama with Noe's drunken episode taking place outside and his nakedness also reveals an erection. The event is rewritten as an oedipal struggle: Cham mocks his ageing father and Maine also gives his dissenting protagonist a moment of ironic foresight in which he hopes that when future generations are 'singing the old man's glorious history, they don't forget to include *this* little episode' (*TF*, p. 202). Maine reflects the biblical narrative in the disquiet of Cham's brothers and Noe's subsequent cursing of his son. However, he also, in another divergence from Genesis, gives Cham a vivid interior life and a rationale for his dissent. After the decisive break with his father, Cham observes that his family are guilty of religious narcissism: 'a sense of their cosmic insignificance is one thing they most definitely do *not* have' (*TF*, p. 219). As Cham and his brothers are sent off in different directions to restart civilization, he reluctantly repeats words of gratitude for their children ('Yeah. Praise Yahweh'). His confession to the reader is indicative of a very hesitant theology in which he acknowledges that the God in whom he has been raised to believe is 'a master craftsman [...] but unlike most such He's short on respect for the things He builds and a touch too eager to reduce them to dust' (*TF*, p. 224).

Cham's disillusionment with monotheism is complicated by his alienation from his father. His wife, however, is a more articulate counterpoint to her father-in-law. Ilya is represented as both rational and passionate when she offers an open-minded theological reflection on the flood:

> It seems to me that Yahweh has a thing or two to answer for. But I'm the first to admit, there's a lot I don't understand [...] perhaps through understanding Yahweh's creation, I can understand Yahweh. At least a little. Perhaps by understanding Him I'll better understand His motivation for destroying so much of the beauty He had wrought. (*TF*, p. 236)

Ilya is one of a number of figures in the narrative to challenge, silently or otherwise, Noe's straightforward acceptance of the disaster as the will of an angry creator; she embraces uncertainty, an approach that now characterizes post-secular approaches to traditional stories of suffering. Ilya is a spiritual sceptic, haunted by 'the memories of those poor drowned unbelievers', and one who questions why she, rather than they, were saved. These questions, however, receive no divine response (*TF*, p. 122). The horrors of the flood itself, narrated across fourteen chapters, are rendered most intensely from Ilya's perspective. She observes that the 'frightening thing wasn't so much the rain or the flood [...] But what left me truly cold, genuinely afraid, was Noe's reaction to it all. Which was, in a word, jubilation' (*TF*, p. 113). Noe's apparent delight at the loss of life is not part of the biblical account; his gloating is something that Maine adds. At this point, Ilya becomes the moral centre of the narrative and counter-voice regarding the nature of the catastrophe. Ilya is appalled by the deaths that she witnesses and says to her husband 'only a man's god would show love for his creation by destroying it' (*TF*, p. 119). Her challenge to a certain strand of monotheism anticipates contemporary suspicion of an apocalyptic mode that seems to relish suffering as a necessary corollary of redemptive change.

Ilya is not, however, given the last word. After the death of Noe's wife, three families of Noe's children disperse to begin new tribes, and Mirn, married to Japheth, reflects on his quip that the events of the flood and their survival will, at least, become a 'Hell of a story for the grandkids' (*TF*, p. 258).

> Of course people will tell *some*thing, it was the end of the world after all. A story like that won't be forgotten. But things will get added and left out and confused, until in a little while people won't even know what's true and what's been made up [...] The least we can do, J. and me, is get as much of it right as we can (*TF*, p. 258).

This may be a playful allusion to biblical source criticism since J (for 'Jahwist') is regarded by scholars as one of the sources of the Pentateuch. Mirn also speculates about Noe's words on the meaning of the deluge. Did he say 'God reigns over everything' or 'God rains over everything'? (*TF*, p. 158). The difference between these two theological positions, she claims, makes an enormous difference to the kind of stories that will be told regarding loss, suffering and survival. Maine's novel, despite its realist orientation, also shares a metafictional self-awareness with Barnes's *A History of the World in 10 ½ Chapters*: it is about the politics of storytelling. Narratives, it accepts, will be repeated, passed on and embellished; this is particularly true of disastrous events in which lives are lost. Yet it is important to know what kind of story is being told.

Maggie Gee's version of *The Flood*, though strikingly different in setting to Maine's novel, is similarly concerned with the ethics of storytelling, particularly about loss and grief. Gee's multi-genre novel embraces satire, ecological warning and Dickensian celebration of a diverse, mutually dependent, multicultural metropolis. It is also a bold attempt at modern, elemental myth-making in which the world will meet its much foreshadowed end 'not in fire, but water' (*F*, p. 318). There is no obvious Noah figure: Gee's novel is not a straight rewriting of the Genesis story with a range of counterpart characters. However, the role of prophet is split between a series of characters: the violent preachers of One Way take the tyrannical aspects of some iterations of Noah; Kilda, an unlikely teenage seer, anticipates both the flood and the heavenly transfiguration of life after the world has ended; Davey, a television astronomer/astrologer, attempts to warn the world and is not listened to; May, the oldest character in the novel, is burdened by familial regret and loss but seeks to save her wayward son from his worst tendencies. All these figures embody aspects of the biblical figure.

The novel is also replete with allusions to water: characters are frequently soaked with the floodwaters; one character is described as a kind of 'tsunami'; others are able swimmers and so on (*F*, p. 90). This waterlogged motif differs from Gee's second novel, *The Burning Book* (1983), which meditates on nuclear apocalypse, a displaced, technologized version of hellfire. The citizens of Gee's waterlogged urban landscape are torn between a dread of death and a suspicion that finality is always deferred; when the sun starts to shine, some citizens believe their shifty government's promises that the crisis is over – a kind of *faux* covenant, a parody of God's promise to Noah that the world will never again be destroyed. One reviewer commented that the novel constitutes 'not so much apocalypse now as apocalypse again and again and again'.[19] The opening part of *The Flood's* framing narrative – 'Before' – in which a nameless speaker evokes a heavenly 'strange place […] A city hovering over the darkness

[...] A place which holds all times and places' (*F*, p. 7) – signals that the novel does not adhere to the logic of standard realism; instead, an alternative ontology, one that draws on discourses of transcendence interrupts a story of ordinary disaster. The 'earthly city', we infer, no longer stands, though its fate is not made absolutely clear. In her Derridean reading of the novel, Sarah Dillon reminds us that 'biblical apocalyptic narratives [...] both confront and diffuse the threat of total destruction, since they describe, reveal, or predict cataclysmic events but only and always with the structural guarantee of a postcataclysmic continuance, be it in this world or the next'.[20] Dillon observes that the novel 'is told from a temporal location after the end of the world, after the flood that the novel's title promises' and that from the 'very outset [...] the novel consoles the reader with the impossibility of remainderless destruction, with the apocalyptic triumph'.[21] Does this literary magic allow Gee to evade the realities of human suffering? A dreamlike, semi-sequel to a number of Gee's other metropolitan fictions, *The Flood* echoes the tone of Ballard's 'visionary present' narratives. Gee's postmillennial London is recognizably like the early-twenty-first-century world in which it was written, though transfigured by defamiliarizing names: it is part of a world at war in which 'armies were raised, weapons stockpiled' and world leaders (Presidents Bliss and Bare) attempt to convince citizens that security lies in overseas military adventure; one political advisor observes that the 'common enemy will unite' people and prove a useful distraction from the floods that have already encompassed The Towers, a high-rise estate 'where everyone lived who could do no better; the old, the mad, the poor, newcomers' (*F*, pp. 8, 38, 165). Gee's fictional city is in a liminal state, one in which interminable rains and global conflict perpetuate apocalyptic anxiety, but ordinary life persists: office workers wade through flooded streets 'with bags and brief-cases on their heads' and, in an echo of Ballard's Dr Kerans living on a top floor in the ruins of the Ritz, Gee's wealthiest characters are ferried to the Opera House in 'gilded gondalas, lit at the prow and stern by blazing flambeaux' whilst others drown in their scores on more mundane forms of public transport (*F*, pp. 135, 137–8). Gee explores a capital that is both full of hierarchical division and replete with coincidence and connection across class, race and religion.

A religious cult, 'The Brothers and Sisters of the One Way' ('One Way, One Truth, One Path. Open your hearts and come home'), preaches that the end of the world is imminent; a number of Gee's most desolate characters become members of the movement – Dirk, a convicted murderer; Moira, a disillusioned and lonely former academic; Kilda, an alienated teenager (*F*, p. 24). The novel's intertextual relationship with the biblical flood is underlined when, early in the narrative, the group's preacher begins a public rally by quoting a version of Genesis 6. 13 ('God said to Noah, "The loathsomeness of all mankind has become plain to me, for through them the earth is full of violence, I intend to destroy them, and the earth with them"', *F*, p. 30). The preacher, Bruno, is also fascinated by Revelation and the idea of last days: his interpretation privileges ferocious judgement of those who he believes to be guilty.

The One Way cult that claims 'to unite Jews and Christians and Muslims because they all shared the same sacred texts' seems to offer a utopian alternative to religious conflict (*F*, p. 35). The reality, however, is less auspicious since their scriptural interpretation is not only authoritarian and exclusive, but also used as a sanction for violence against anybody they perceive as enemies, including dissenting members. Their apparent (though debatable) reverence for 'the Book' is also significant in a narrative that is frequently concerned with how meaning is manufactured and disseminated. For Bruno there is 'only' one book, Revelation, and of that book there are only a select number of pages that he truly takes seriously (*F*, p. 18).

Many of Gee's characters are part of a culture of book-making and reception – authors, publishers, critics, students – and the narrative is flooded with images of texts, read or forgotten, nascent and old: wandering in the ruins of the Towers, May, the matriarch of the White family, is represented as 'the last reader, at the end of the world' (*F*, p. 215). Books are represented as a source of solace and meaning (*F*, p. 188). May, 'a reader of real books, not papers', is afraid of losing an auratic object, her 'leather-bound book' of Tennyson's poems (*F*, p. 176). May's life of struggle is alleviated by her encounters with poetry and Greek mythology. Dirk White, May's violent son, was taught by his mother to read a 'lifetime ago, but it took forever and you never saw him reading' (*F*, p. 180). Delorice, sister of the man murdered by Dirk, a precocious reader as a child ('you was always reading', her sister comments [*F*, p. 168]) and now a success in the publishing business, imagines a popular title that her company expects to sell half a million copies 'spill over the side-streets, infect the libraries, infest the bookshops' (*F*, p. 35). Multiple textual forms festoon the narrative including, finally, a storm of yellowing 'Protect and Survive' leaflets that are rained, uselessly, across the city. The drama of the narrative is partly based on rival literacies: fundamentalism versus aestheticism; poetry versus prose; political expediency versus justice.

The novel might seem narrowly self-reflexive, but it uses the figure of the reader and the material object of the book as a way of addressing bigger questions of meaning. Dillon describes such self-reflexive literary returns as 'the recursive procedure' of Gee's novel, a kind of strategy that she suggests, via M. H. Abrams, 'replicates that of Revelation, which "represents the present and future by replicating or alluding to passages in earlier biblical texts." '[22] *The Flood* is fascinated by the idea of apocalyptic returns, repetition and, perhaps, resurrection. At a simple level, a number of characters, including some who died, return from many of Gee's other novels to play their part in her narrative of a deluge. One such character is the freelance, gentleman scholar, Harold Segall, on the verge of completing an apparently endless volume on the mysteries of time, first mentioned in *Light Years* (1985). Harold embraces a mystical form of physics and believes that 'nothing could ever be lost': 'All that ever had been, still was' (*F*, pp. 90–1). This view 'allowed for no past or future, only a single infinite structure. A hall of time from which the moments opened, a mansion of many sunlit rooms'. The image reminds Davey, pop science presenter, of a biblical motif, learned in childhood ('*in my father's house are many mansions*', *F*, p. 91). These words are a promise from Jesus to his disciples, an inclusive form of eschatology (John 14. 2). Harold is 'fascinated by simultaneity' and understands time not as linear sequence but as a single moment:

> At any one point in time, the thousand flowerings of event – the murders and weddings, mud-slides and military coups, the earthquakes, torture sessions, shy first kisses [...] all of them gathered on the same string of time (*F*, p. 205).

In one of the novel's most distinctive, layered set-pieces, Harold attends a staging of *Madam Butterfly* with his wife, Lottie, his stepson, Davey, and Delorice. The conversation turns to the resurrecting powers of art: Madam Butterfly dies every night but also comes back to life every night with each new performance: 'No one ever dies', claims Harold. 'Good moments, like this one, go on for ever' (F, p. 141). There are echoes in Harold's idiosyncratic world view of both the tragic, Nietzchean understanding of eternal recurrence and the alternative, Christian understanding offered in T. S. Eliot's *Four Quartets* (1936–43), about the (im)possibility of redeeming time.

The penultimate chapter witnesses 'the whole glittering city' 'vanish' despite one character's belief that such fear is 'ridiculous' (F, p. 134). The event that precipitates the tsunamis that will drown civilization is far beyond human control: neither President Bliss and his neo-liberal, colonial endeavours nor the countries he blames or even the failure of governments and corporations can cause or prevent the coming end. The threat is a universal accident: 'Usually the planets lie well-spaced, they are plot-able, predictable as novels [...] But every so often the pattern fractures' (F, p. 261). Gee playfully draws on the language of fiction and pits science against art but both these human constructions are not enough to resist the stark power of cosmological change. The 'near-earth object that careens towards us' in Gee's novel echoes two Hollywood movies of the 1990s – *Deep Impact* (1998) and *Armageddon* (1998) – in which life on earth is threated by an 'extinction level event' of an enormous asteroid that is finally defeated by muscular human intervention (indeed, one of Gee's characters dismisses warnings of the oncoming disaster as 'a cliché from a [...] movie' [F, p. 268]). The narrative resists such spectacular formulae or platitudes; there is no human saviour in this novel. Gee's prose is transfigured into a hymn-like form of poetry as civilization ends. However, death and destruction, the end of life, does not have the final word. Even the last lines of the principal narrative allude to the possibility of rebirth in an image that fuses motifs of evolution and rebirth:

> three thousand generation of humans
>> stiff and damp from their spell underground
>> pushing up alive from the flood-washed catacombs
>> pulling themselves to their feet like apes (F, p. 320).

The novel synthesizes two alternative ways of thinking about the end(s) of life: the motif of eternal recurrence is twinned with a destabilizing hope of resurrection. At the end of the narrative – in the post-apocalyptic epilogue – the dead seem to rise from the drowned world. The world narrated in 'After' matches that in 'Before': this is no ruined world but, rather, 'the paradisiacal spatial and temporal space before the story, where all differences are erased [...] and the living are reunited with the dead'.[23] Instead of a tiny elect who are saved whilst the mass of humanity drowns in a sea of judgement, Gee rescues all her principal characters, just and unjust alike. The novel itself becomes a kind of literary ark. The city at the end of the novel resonates with Christian eschatology and in particular Revelation's vision of the heavenly city, home to the Tree of Life ('In the midst of the street of it, and on either side of the river, was there the tree of life, which bare twelve manner of fruits, and yielded her fruit every month: and the leaves of the tree were for the healing of the nations', Revelation 22. 2). Gee's heavenly version of Kew Gardens is a place of 'perpetual summer' and rest – where, as the final line of the novel indicates, 'we come, to lie down at last' (F, p. 325). It is quite different from, for example, Dirk's early vision of heaven: 'a mount of blood and gold and glory, a place where his enemies will burn like straw'. This typically self-serving, violent piece of apocalyptic might not be surprising for such an aggressively repressed figure, but it is worryingly close to the theological outlook of respectable fundamentalists (F, p. 23). For Adam Trexler, however, Gee's *The Flood* is a warning: 'This is not purification, but a stained, bloody, horrific disaster [...] the novel denies the revelatory function of the apocalyptic narrative, as well as its escapism, returning the reader to a sense of real loss'.[24]

Gee may be combing what one character in a David Lodge novel names 'the eschatological wreckage' of Christian thought for a comforting image of the end.[25] The disparity between those who take a sceptical perspective on the prophecies of religious texts and the communities who regard them as divinely ordained creates a curious atmosphere for literary writers who engage with disaster, trauma and threats to continued human existence. In their rewritings of the foundational Judeo-Christian mythology of ruin, obliteration and eventual redemption narrated in Genesis, Gee and Maine offer alternative interpretations of suffering. Gee's conceit of a transfigured London, green and egalitarian, full of joy and peace, is a radical alternative vision to the dystopian post-apocalyptic fiction that dominates the contemporary landscape. Similarly, Maine's narrative is one of recovery and resistance. Neither novel sanitizes their biblical sources; indeed, both use these ancient stories as a way to critique the injustices of the present.

3

'Sudden departure': Rapture writing

In a pre-credit death sequence of the American television series *Six Feet Under* created by Alan Ball (a 2004 episode named 'In Case of Rapture'), a devout woman mistakes a host of floating blow-up sex dolls, accidentally cut loose from a delivery truck, for the bodies of believers ascending into heaven, gathered up to meet Jesus. In her excited confusion, and perhaps anxious that she will be left behind, the woman jumps from her car and is immediately struck and killed by another vehicle. A moment of bathos in which religious impulse collides with absurdity anticipates the sceptical but sympathetic tone of Tom Perrotta's novel *The Leftovers* (2011). This uncanny novel, set in Mapleton, New York State, a small town that is prosperous to the point of blandness, begins months after an event known as the 'Sudden Departure', a 'Rapture-like phenomenon' in which millions of people 'at the same time, all over the world' disappear without trace, never to be seen again.[1] The novel is focalized through one middle-class family, all of whom have ostensibly escaped this inexplicable, possibly supernatural, event: Kevin Garvey is a successful entrepreneur who has retired early and has become a semi-reluctant community leader as mayor of Mapleton; his wife, Laurie, is a life-long agnostic not 'raised to believe in much [...] except the foolishness of belief itself', but whose cheerful scepticism is shattered; Tom, a freshman in college, attempts to assuage repressed grief, first through hedonism and subsequently in discipleship to a charismatic spiritual teacher; his sister, Jill, a smart high school senior has lost all sense of purpose; both children are increasingly alienated from their family (*TL*, p. 9).

The Leftovers is a post-apocalyptic text but one that has few of
the signifiers readers might anticipate: the suburbs in which it is
set remain comfortable and prosperous; hunger exists only where
it already defined everyday life; the sky has not turned a perma-
nent and oppressive slate grey; the ordinary business of education,
government bureaucracy and holidays have resumed; cannibals
do not roam the street; transgenic creatures, in which human
DNA has been spliced with that of a pig, do not pursue luckless
victims. Yet everything has changed. Perrotta is not specific about
how many million people disappeared on 14 October – the subsequent television adaption (2014-) offers the more precise statistic
of 2 per cent of the world's population, approximately 140 million souls – but it is clear that everybody has lost somebody: if not
a child or close family member then a friend or teacher. This is,
in other words, a text that magnifies the quotidian experience of
what it names 'the invisible haze of stale grief and chronic bewil-
derment', but then gives it intense focus by concentrating on one
small town and, in particular, on a single family (*TL*, p. 30).[2] The
novel was, coincidentally, published in the same year in which
Harold Camping, the late doomsday preacher, confidently predicted that biblical prophecies regarding the end of the world
would be fulfilled.[3]

Both *The Leftovers* and 'In Case of Rapture' appropriate a strand
of Christian eschatology known as premillennial dispensationalism, an understanding of biblical 'end-times' prophecy developed
by a nineteenth-century founder of the radical Plymouth Brethren
movement that has become uniquely influential in contemporary
American fundamentalist churches. This form of theology gained
ground in the United States in the wake of the Civil War and, as
Michael Northcott notes, it made particular sense to evangelical
preachers 'who saw ever more proofs that the millennium of peace
was ever further from being realised [...] Instead of the progressive march of humanity towards the kingdom, which Jonathan
Edwards had foreseen, the dispensationalists saw a downward spi-
ral of cataclysms'.[4]

For millions of Americans, the classification of a contemporary catastrophe as 'biblical' has a much more literal signification
than in sensational news headlines or subversive, avant-garde fiction: for these believers natural disasters and international conflict
fulfil the coded prophecies of scripture and are read as signs of

Christ's imminent return. In *American Apocalypse* (2014), a history of the rise of Christian Fundamentalism ('best defined as radical apocalyptic evangelicalism'), Matthew Avery Sutton proposes that the strand connecting the variety of such groups in the United States is that, since the nineteenth century, they have 'believed that the world was going to end. Imminently. Violently. Tragically.'[5] Confidence that the Bible's so-called end-times prophecies are an accurate portrayal – associated primarily, though not exclusively, with premillennial dispensationalism – is not a rarity, found only on the extreme fringes of the church. Avery Sutton cites a 2010 Pew Poll that '41 percent of all Americans (well over one hundred million people) and 58 percent of white evangelicals believed that Jesus is "definitely" or "probably" going to return by 2050'. A more recent poll, also quoted, reveals that many Americans read the Bible 'in order to learn about the future'. 'We now live', he observes, 'in a world shaped by evangelicals' apocalyptic hopes, dreams, and nightmares'.[6]

These ideas have relatively little influence outside the United States. However, one index of the cultural ascent of this kind of dispensationalist, fundamentalist Christianity in America is to be found in the extraordinary popularity of a series of fantasy novels, though its creators or sections of its readership may not appreciate the generic label. *Left Behind* (1995–2007), co-authored by Tim LaHaye and Jerry B. Jenkins, is, in short, a fictional version of premillennial dispensational theology: the sixteen-book sequence envisages events pertaining to the Second Coming foretold in the Bible – primarily from the book of Revelation but also from other New Testament epistles, elements of the gospel narratives and a number of the Jewish prophetic texts including the books of Isaiah and Daniel – taking place in the contemporary world. The sequence of events, for those who embrace a premillenialist understanding of end-times, begins with the ascent of the faithful, living and dead, into the skies to join Christ and is followed by a period of 'tribulation' that will witness the rise of an anti-Christ and a time of oppression for those souls who are left on earth because of their lack of faith but who come to accept Jesus. These events are a prelude to Christ's return, a millennial kingdom and a final victorious battle against Satan and his followers. The first of these phenomena is known as the 'Rapture' and is derived from the Latin word *raptus* that signifies 'a carrying off'. The vital proof

text for this doctrine is found in one of Paul's epistles to the early
church:

> For the Lord himself will come down from heaven, with a loud
> command, with the voice of the archangel and with the trumpet
> call of God, and the dead in Christ will rise first then we who are
> alive and remain shall be caught up together with them in the
> clouds to meet the Lord in the air. And so shall we ever be with
> Lord (1 Thessalonians 4. 16–17).

This event is represented in *Left Behind* when millions of people
suddenly disappear into thin air, leaving only their clothes – and
non-believers – behind. A group of LaHaye and Jenkins's characters, including an airline pilot whose devout wife is among the
missing, a previously half-hearted pastor and a sceptical journalist,
realize that the prophecies of scripture are true and band together
to form a 'Tribulation Force' that will commit to telling the world
the truth and resisting the Anti-Christ.

The novels embody a conservative view: Americans are called
to not only embrace Christ as their saviour, but also return to
old-fashioned, traditional 'family' values.[7] The sequence has sold
close to 70 million copies – not including the various derivatives
such as YA spin-off novels, a controversial computer game and a
number of film adaptations – so it is difficult simply to dismiss the
phenomenon as a subcultural backwater.[8] For Jennie Chapman,
who offers a nuanced, non-judgemental appraisal of a sequence
in which she finds 'much to criticize', *Left Behind* constitutes a
particular challenge for academics who are resistant to addressing
the specifics of religious practice in America – 'especially "irrational," "excessive," "antidemocratic" religion' – without easy
contempt or a failure to understand. The world view embodied in
these novels is, Chapman notes, 'one that is often egregiously out
of step with the liberal, progressive, tolerant values that many in
academia hold dear'.[9] *Left Behind*, she argues, is unusual amongst
'the majority of bestselling popular novels, whose ideological
operations are often covert and subtextual' because it 'proudly
wears its weltanschauung on its sleeve'.[10] The sequence's fierce
critics, including many Christian theologians, as well as secular
liberals and those of other faiths, regard the books as aesthetically poor, ideologically reprehensible or theologically suspect.

However, Chapman also maintains that it is a mistake to miss the sophisticated readerly strategies and acts of interpretative agency demanded by *Left Behind*. Similarly, Amy Johnson Frykholm argues that in order to understand the place of the highly specific eschatological beliefs in America that they should be interpreted 'as a fluid part of the broader culture, not as the realm of isolated believers'.[11]

Left Behind is a divisive cultural phenomenon but it has ignited a wider fascination in twenty-first-century North American culture with end-times imagery that crosses sacred–secular boundaries. Seth Rogen and Evan Goldberg's *This Is the End* (2013), for example, is a crude, self-referential comedy of divinely ordained catastrophe in which a variety of Hollywood actors play versions of themselves as the world is destroyed in a cataclysmic battle between God and the Devil. The film not only trades on the big screen fascination with spectacles of destruction, but also draws on the prophecies of the Revelation of Saint John and deploys much vulgar humour, similar in tone to Kevin Smith's (e)scatological comedy, *Dogma* (1999). The Canadian novelist and visual artist, Douglas Coupland, a long-term explorer of 'life after God', frequently returns to dispensationalist imagery. He quipped that the amoral behaviour evoked in his comic tech-*noir* novel *Jpod* (2006) surreptitiously described a post-rapture world in which only the damned had been left behind, and both *Generation A* (2009) and *Player One* (2010) also allude to the concept, mixing profane comedy with spiritual aspiration. The latter text, originally delivered as the 2010 CBC Massey Lectures – described by one reader as a 'collage novel' – includes a glossary of neologisms, similar to those that bordered the pages of *Generation X* (1991).[12] One of these witty, odd entries is for 'Rapture Goo': 'The stuff that gets left behind. The fact that the only thing that really defines you is your DNA. Jesus gets your DNA. That's all he gets, roughly 7.6 milligrams of *you*'.[13] Coupland's fusion of religious prophecy with biological reality typifies his interest in the collision of alternative world views in an accelerated technological era. The final chapter of *Generation A*, narrated by the questing Harj, uses the concept as figurative of metamorphosis:

I began my trip as a lost soul [...] Somehow the group of us killed Superman. We entered the Rapture. We cut away those bits of ourselves that had become cartoons. And we turned the world back into a book.[14]

This conscious splicing of popular culture with an image of transcendence from biblical narrative is typical of Coupland's oblique but persistent fascination with mutations of the sacred. In September 2012, Coupland contributed to a 'Museum of the End of the World' for Toronto's *Nuit Blanche* festival, a single night of apocalyptic art, with his *Museum of the Rapture*, a 'site-specific installation interrogating life and death and things in between'; the work, an uncanny tableaux of lonely figures, projected images and everyday objects, was installed in an underground car park beneath Toronto City Hall.[15] These isolated figures in a 'pretty gothic' display are, in Coupland's words, those who have been ' "left behind," so to speak'.[16] Experimental art is not the only form to appropriate the Rapture. Michael Grant's six-novel, YA 'Gone' sequence (2008–13) begins with a similar narrative premise to *The Leftovers*: everybody over the age of fifteen disappears in a single instant from the town of Perdido Beach. It is also a rapture-like event and Grant not only trades on the religious implications of the sudden disappearance, but also connects it with other tropes of horror and apocalyptic fiction.

Perrotta's novel reads as a sceptical, but not crudely satirical, response to *Left Behind* and other dispensationalist narratives. How would a community respond if the Rapture or a rapture-like event took place? What does the merciless finality and senseless nature of the departure signify about the human capacity for agency? One critic, responding to the HBO television adaptation of the novel, suggests that Perrotta's take on those who are 'left behind' might belong to the 'science fiction subgenre of "alternate history," perhaps, but more fully to the speculative apocalypticism that includes such things as Cormac McCarthy's *The Road* and the television drama *Lost*. *The Leftovers*, he suggests, asks a specific set of questions about the nature of the end of the world: 'What if the apocalypse will not be some sudden, violent, catastrophic event but is rather an already-happening, slowly-burning, utterly indeterminate, multicausal, and complexly systemic psychological event?'[17] Although Perrotta, raised in the Roman Catholic tradition, is clear that he is 'not a religious person', the fascination with fundamentalist phenomena in *The Leftovers* is anticipated by its immediate precursor, *The Abstinence Teacher* (2007), a novel that also explores conservative piety in suburbia. Perrotta thinks of the disappearances of this traumatic event

> not as a theological concept but as a powerful metaphor for getting older, for living with loss and mystery [...] *The Leftovers* takes place in a world that looks exactly like the world we live in now. It's not about how we survive when there's no food and no clean water, but how we endure when everything we believed has been, if not obliterated, then seriously challenged.[18]

A crucial difference between *The Leftovers* and LaHaye and Jenkins's series is that the characters in Perrotta's novel live in a world in which *Left Behind* exists. The world is divided between those who believe the stories to be, at best, violent fantasies and true believers for whom the sequence embodies a realistic, if speculative, interpretation of future events. The 'sudden disappearance' of Perrotta's novel is, in part, a metafictional commentary on a culture already saturated with stories of damnation and salvation. As the novel begins, Laurie is struggling with a radical break in her sceptical world view. Before the apocalyptic 'catastrophe' that took place a year before the prologue – a year in which 'the survivors had absorbed the blow and found, to their amazement, that they were still standing' – she was one of the 22.8 per cent (according to a 2015 survey by the Pew Research Center) who identify as agnostic, atheist or 'nothing in particular'.[19] This sceptical minority has risen considerably in recent years, but remains very small compared with the combined 76.5 per cent of Americans who describe themselves as belonging to a faith.[20] The Garvey family do not embrace even vestigial Christianity and the children have been taught that uncertainty is the most credible position: '*We're agnostics*, she used to tell her kids [...] *We don't know if there's a God, and nobody else does, either. They might say they do, but they really don't*' (*TL*, p. 9). It is tempting to read Laurie as a kind of proxy for the reader of sceptically oriented literary fiction. However, the narrative begins with a crisis of non-belief: Laurie is wrestling with the idea of the Rapture, a concept that she had first encountered during her college years in an Intro to World Religions class when the 'phenomenon [...] seemed like a joke to her' (*TL*, p. 9). Her only post-college encounters with this set of prophecies are mediated by second-hand experiences of LaHaye and Jenkins's bestselling novels: when she witnesses 'someone reading one of the Left Behind books in an airport or on a train' Laurie feels a 'little twinge of pity, and even a little bit of tenderness, for the poor sucker who had nothing better to read, and nothing else to do, except sit around dreaming about the end of the world' (*TL*, pp. 10–11). Perrotta draws on a paradigm of liberal exceptionalism; Laurie's sentimental (and reproachful) response enables an illusion of superiority and difference: Laurie believes that she, unlike these less enlightened individuals, transcends American apocalyptic paranoia. Although premillennialism is enormously influential, Laurie represents a sceptical community (one that might, incidentally, include many mainline Christians as well as atheists and people of other faiths) for whom the 'murky' theology of dispensationalism ('Armageddon and the Antichrist and the Four Horsemen of the Apocalypse') is simply so much 'mumbo jumbo' (*TL*, p. 10). Significantly, Laurie's revulsion is rooted in a barely suppressed elitist, class-based aesthetics as much as in ethical sensibilities: the populist narrative of the Rapture

> felt like religious kitsch, as tacky as a black velvet painting, the kind of fantasy that appealed to people who ate too much fried food, spanked their kids, and had no problem with the theory that their loving God invented AIDS to punish the gays (*TL*, p. 10).

This conveniently cartoonish view of the millions of Americans who embrace aspects of premillennialism echoes Chapman and Frykholm's analyses of the cultural politics that inform the critical rejection of *Left Behind*. Laurie's spiritual contempt is intensified as an ironic prelude to the devastating phenomenon of the 'sudden departure':

> The biblical prophecy came true [...] People disappeared, millions of them at the same time, all over the world. This wasn't some ancient rumor – a dead man coming back to life during the Roman Empire – or a dusty homegrown legend, Joseph Smith unearthing golden tablets in upstate New York, conversing with an angel. This was real. The Rapture happened in her own hometown [...] God's intrusion into her life couldn't have been any clearer if He'd addressed her from a burning azalea (*TL*, p. 11).

The 'sudden departure' is a dividing event, a temporal rupture that does not destroy civilization but still changes everything. It is unaccountable according to the logic of cause and effect. Perrotta is more interested in the surviving remnant than in discovering an originary cause for the 'rapture'. The ontological astonishment that Laurie – and many of her fellow sceptics – experiences resonates with Slavoj Žižek's commentary on the slippery philosophical category of the 'event'. For the Marxist–Lacanian thinker, an event is 'something shocking, out of joint, that appears to happen all of a sudden and interrupts the usual flow of things; something that emerges seemingly out of nowhere, without discernable causes, an appearance without solid being as its foundation'. He also suggests that a creedal leap of faith is 'evental' in that it has a circular logic that is not dependent on causes ('it is only when I believe that I can understand the reasons for belief').[21] Perrotta connects Laurie's experience both with American religious history in his allusion to the founder of the Church of the Latter Day Saints (popularly known as Mormonism) and to biblical narrative. The 'burning azalea' is an echo of the blazing bush out of which God speaks to Moses (Exodus 3). However, the event that shatters Laurie's open-minded, cool rationalism is not represented as an unambiguous, self-evident theophany. Indeed, Perrotta makes a bold narrative decision in affirming ambiguity (in fact, silence) regarding the reasons for the 'sudden departure'. Neither science nor religious discourse can provide a satisfying account of the rapture-like event. One high school teacher is fired for speculating that 'the Sudden Departure was a natural phenomenon, a kind of global autoimmune reaction, a way for the earth to fight off the infection' (*TL*, p. 340). His ecological perspective is articulated in a way that seems tactless rather than constructive and, by the time that the novel starts, it is outmoded since human life seems more contingent and fragile than ever before. However, for early twenty-first-century readers of the novel it is likely to resonate more strongly than belief in a coming supernatural end. Nevertheless, Perrotta's novel is not interested in exploring causes: whether the Anthropocene, divine judgement or natural events precipitated the 'departure' is less significant than the emotional consequences of bereavement. Similarly, the narrative does not focus on the theological rationale for Laurie's conversion. Her movement from scepticism and suburban comfort to reluctant but intractable belief tracks an anxiety about the future

of middle-class belonging and, tacitly, about the institutions of marriage, family and work in which America's self-image is rooted.

The Leftovers uses a readily recognized element of the popular apocalyptic imagination to critique national identity. The official motto of the United States, inaugurated in 1956, is 'In God
We Trust' – the dictum first appeared on printed currency a year
later – yet the constitution enshrines an absolute division between
church and state. In which god, if any, do Perrotta's citizens 'trust'?
The event might be expected to be welcomed by some Evangelical
churches, but this is, in a sense, a very inclusive, post-traditional
'Rapture': the roll call of the disappeared is not solely (or even primarily) Christian, but includes 'Hindus and Buddhists and Muslims
and Jews and atheists and animists and homosexuals and Eskimos
and Mormons and Zoroastrians' (TL, p. 12). This 'random harvest'
is not what conservative believers in a premillennial dispensation
expected: 'The whole point was to separate the wheat from the chaff,
to reward the true believers [...] An indiscriminate Rapture was no
Rapture at all' (TL, p. 13). The novel again deploys a popular biblical allusion: the separation of the wheat (which is to be saved) from
the chaff (tossed on the 'unquenchable fire' with a 'winnowing fork')
is a stark, violent image offered by John the Baptist in anticipation
of Jesus's ministry (Matthew 3. 12). In the microcosm of Mapleton,
the impact of the 'rapture-like event' on mainline religion is primarily traced via the Reverend Matt Jamison, former minister of the
Zion Bible Church. Jamison's post-event disillusion mirrors Laurie's
conversion: he was a man of faith, once widely regarded as 'a decent
guy' who has 'lost his bearings' because, like other committed
Christians he is 'deeply traumatized' and 'tormented by the fear that
Judgment Day had come and gone, and he'd been found lacking'. As
with any number of real-world traumatic events that might reason-
ably be expected to shake the faith of devout believers, 'some people [...] had responded with redoubled piety'. The one-time minister,
by contrast, moves 'in the opposite direction, taking up the cause of
Rapture Denial with a vengeance'. Jamison becomes a new kind of
preacher, dedicated 'to proving that the people who'd slipped their
earthly chains on October 14th were neither good Christians nor
even especially virtuous individuals' (TL, p. 41).

The novel's reception frequently emphasizes its allegorical use
of biblical prophecy. One reviewer argues that The Leftovers pays
'sporadic lip-service to its eschatological theme, this was never

really a Rapture novel [...] Here, the spooky prologue is just a con-
venient allegorical disaster to usher in a time of emotional tribulation among individuals: it stands in for 9/11, tsunami or pandemic,
as the reader sees fit'.[22] Indeed, one of the problems with the genre
of speculative apocalypse might be that it facilitates an easy iden-
tification with any kind of future loss. However, the trauma of the
terrorist attacks on the Twin Towers of the World Trade Centre in
New York on 11 September 2001 is the novel's defining point of
reference. Indeed, Perrotta evokes 9/11 in addressing the media representation of the 'sudden departure': 'the hysterical monotony of
the TV news – the obsessive repetition of the same few basic facts,
the ever-rising tally of the missing, interview upon interview with
traumatized eyewitnesses' certainly seems very familiar to readers
used to the repetitive drip feed of twenty-first-century news cycles
(*TL*, p. 119). However, Tom Garvey, a young adult for whom the
terror attacks on New York would be memories from childhood,
thinks that 'the coverage felt different from that of September
11th, when the networks had shown the burning towers over and
over'. A crucial difference is that because 'October 14th was more
amorphous, harder to pin down [...] the media was never able to
settle upon a single visual image to evoke the catastrophe' (*TL*,
p. 120). 9/11 is ineradicably associated with horrifying images of
the destroyed North and South Towers. A new date of fear and
grief in the world of the novel, 14th October, has no memorable,
easily reproduced and circulated icon. The (dis)continuities with
9/11 and the subsequent 'War on Terror' are strengthened by the
observation that after the mysterious disappearances there simply
'weren't any bad guys to hate, which made everything that much
harder to get into focus' (*TL*, p. 120).[23]

Perrotta does not deploy the trope of a common enemy as a
way of drawing together his disparate community. There is no anti-
Christ, no devil seeking to lead a one-world government, against
whom Kevin can lead a bold, American fightback. Although there is
no clear antagonist – and no group is scapegoated for the 'sudden
disappearance' – the narrative features two shadowy religious cults
that flourish specifically as a result of humanity's abrupt existential
crisis. These new religious movements are represented, in different
ways, as dangerous, manipulative and seductive. Both groups – the
Guilty Remnant (GR) and the followers of a charismatic healer
nicknamed Holy Wayne – have a direct impact on the Garvey family.

The GR is a radical, separatist millenarian sect: they have taken a vow of silence, dress in white, walk in same-sex pairs and, more idiosyncratically for a religious cult, they constantly smoke cigarettes. Laurie Garvey's friend, Rosalie Sussman, whose only daughter is among the disappeared, is an early convert. Before joining the group she explains that the group's counter-intuitive cigarette smoking is 'a sacrament', something to be endured during the 'seven years of Tribulation after the Rapture' (*TL,* p. 22). Rosalie is also persuaded that no anxiety is needed regarding one's health since the final judgement will take place long before any of these dutiful, if reluctant, born-again smokers can develop life-threatening disease. On Christmas Day – a festive event not celebrated by the GR because it 'BELONGS TO THE OLD WORLD' – the group silently watches a PowerPoint sermon that states 'WE SMOKE TO PROCLAIM OUR FAITH' (*TL,* pp. 459, 463). Within a year of driving her friend to the group's headquarters (gifted by a wealthy property developer), Laurie, the former sceptic, has also left her family life behind to become a member of the GR. Laurie's gradual leave-taking of her middle-class family life, a slow unravelling of her gentle, progressive beliefs, inverts abrupt trauma of the 'sudden departure'. The group's arresting soubriquet connects with the novel's wider concerns regarding culpability and survival: Rosalie longs to see her daughter again and is persuaded that Jen's disappearance signifies her belonging to the elect; she is emotionally vulnerable and her decision to affiliate with the group, who show her kindness, offers her a shred of hope that she will be reunited with her daughter. Laurie has no ostensible motivation but she, like others, is in a state of existential shock and suffers a form of survivor's guilt; she is burdened by the fact that her bourgeois existence, and secure family life, might continue as if nothing had taken place. *The Leftovers* limns the quotidian difficulties of life after traditional concepts of security and the human ability to maintain a happy vision of an earthly future are shaken.

The specific theology of the GR is difficult to determine; like many counterpart 'real-world' millenarian or doomsday groups, they are significantly clearer about their vision of the future (in human terms, it will be very short) and activities of which they disapprove (work, marriage, consumerism, friendships, dancing, conversation, not smoking and so on) than any particular ethical creed. The term 'cult' is emotive and potentially inaccurate, but the GR seems to fulfil most sociological criteria associated with this form of religiosity: it involves total commitment to the group including emotional and physical separation from family, friends and work; personal desires and objectives are abandoned entirely to the will of the group and its leaders; marriages and friendships are repudiated, as are ordinary freedoms of expression; finally, personal finances are eventually transferred to the group, including property.

Although the GR is ostensibly a Christian group, Laurie discovers that the son of God does not figure very strongly in their teaching: the group is not 'big on spelling out its creed; it had no priests or ministers, no scripture'; it believes in 'the inherent sinfulness of humanity, and the certainty of the Final Judgment – while completely ignoring the figure of Jesus himself' (*TL*, p. 475). In lieu of oral communication, devotees hand out business cards: 'WE ARE MEMBERS OF THE GUILTY REMNANT. WE HAVE TAKEN A VOW OF SILENCE. WE STAND BEFORE YOU AS LIVING REMINDERS OF GOD'S AWESOME POWER. HIS JUDGMENT IS UPON US' (*TL*, p. 16). The group members are secessionists and actively oppose civic power: they refuse to pay taxes, stage sit-ins at a local school and engage in a variety of acts of civil disobedience. One member is killed during a botched police action at the group's shared home. This skirmish echoes the Branch Davidian cult and the Waco siege that ended with a conflagration and a number of deaths in 1993. Kevin, as mayor, is reluctant to confront the group, particularly after his wife joins their ranks. However, the novel stages a number of tense encounters between members of the GR and other citizens of Mapleton who have not been converted to their cause.

The novel's principal narrative begins three years after the disappearance with a very American event: a town parade of commemoration. Although the pageant is both sombre and secular, the 'first annual Departed Heroes' Day of Remembrance and Reflection', to mourn and to celebrate the disappeared, it is indicative of the ways in which American civic religion is embedded in public ritual (*TL*, p. 30). The event is popular but it also generates a very American kind of discord as some citizens claim 'that the secular commemoration [...] was wrong headed and possibly blasphemous' (*TL*, p. 30). The position of religion in American public life is contested, even in a post-apocalyptic era. Every act of commemoration needs its public face: Nora Durst, who 'lost her entire family on October 14th [...] in what was widely considered to be the worst tragedy in all of Mapleton', embodies the town's grief; indeed, within the economy of Perrotta's microcosm she incarnates the sorrow of a world in mourning (*TL*, p. 44). Her address, a celebration of mundane reality that she, like many others, has lost ('God bless us, the ones who are here and the ones who aren't. We've all been through so much') sounds like the kind of commemorative speech that might be given at a place of public mourning for the victims of a terrorist act or natural disaster (*TL*, p. 67). The speech is silently, but effectively, interrupted by twenty or so adherents of the GR, including Laurie, who form a line and hold up a 'jagged row of letters that spelled the words STOP WASTING YOUR BREATH' (*TL*, p. 65). Nora responds to the disruptive act (a combination of performance art, political protest and pious censure) in a moment of unwarranted generosity by asking police officers to allow their silent protest. Nora's gesture resonates with American understandings of liberty enshrined in the 1791 Bill of Rights to defend, inter alia, freedoms of speech, assembly and religious expression. *The Leftovers* engages with the social problems that arise in a world where such freedoms may be inconvenient for those in power: Kevin, the reluctant civic leader, and the Chief of Police are tacitly encouraged to curb repressive powers, even against a group that may wish to see the downfall of the 'old world'. An ideal of the republic is upheld because a grieving woman refuses to capitulate to a logic of confrontation or violent repression.

A later confrontation takes place on Christmas day as Kevin, in solitude, is watching *It's a Wonderful Life* (1946): this screening of Frank Capra's melancholy film about an aspirant angel, a good man contemplating suicide and the vicissitudes of small-town American life in a time of crisis underscores Perrotta's off-kilter apocalyptic aesthetic. In Malpeton, a twenty-first-century iteration of Bedford Falls, celestial beings endowing a renewed sense of hope are not evident and Kevin is 'feeling a little too much like George Bailey himself, with no guardian angel in sight' (*TL*, pp. 495–6). However, Laurie and her roommate, pseudo-heavenly messengers with a far less benign or humanist lesson than Capra's Clarence, are sent to the Garvey household to bear silent witness to the forthcoming judgement. Their half-hearted attempt to remind Kevin of this ominous future fails and the odd trio share a silent, but intimate, meal. The dinner – an improvised feast replete with American comfort food (Campbell's Chicken Soup, salami, coffee, Hershey's

Kisses) – is a form of secular communion, one sufficiently liberal to include two members of a radical sect and a representative of municipal order. The meal is also a counterpoint to the objectives of the GR whose 'one essential mission […] was to resist the so-called Return to Normalcy, the day-to-day process of forgetting the Rapture, or […] treating it as part of the ongoing fabric of human history, rather than the cataclysm that had brought history to an end' (*TL*, p. 474). This insistence on the imminence of judgement combined with strategies of civil interruption and peaceful – if chilling – protest might suggest that the GR is a fusion of America's history of dissenting religion and political engagement. There are echoes of both Puritan belief (the emphasis on inherent sinfulness and the dread of a coming judgement) and Transcendentalist rejection of ordinary society (the withdrawal into separate, apparently self-sufficient communities). However, the activities and endgames of the group are gradually revealed as considerably darker; in a smart twist both the reader and Laurie discover this reality late in the narrative. A subplot involves the murder of two members of the group, widely assumed to be committed as hate crimes against the sect. However, the narrative eventually discloses that these murders have been committed as secret rituals by the GR. Friendships, normally discouraged by the group's hierarchy, are nurtured with the intention that pairs – sometimes lovers – will eventually enter into a kind of suicide pact, in which one person shoots the other. This is the conclusion of Laurie's narrative: she is expected to kill Meg and, though she cannot complete the murder, her friend takes her own life. Perrotta does not bring easy resolution to this plot: Laurie does not wake up to the reality of what is, in effect, a death cult and return to her middle-class life, but departs, in a dark car, with other members of the GR. This plot connects with a dark history of religious martyrdom in which death is regarded as preferable to life and as a shortcut to eternal salvation. In an additional twist, the secretive murders and suicide are unresolved; the apocalypse of disclosure is granted only for the reader who is reminded, by Perrotta, that separatist religion is not always simply a peaceable withdrawal from everyday life.

Laurie is not the only member of the Garvey family to abandon family life and join a new religious movement. Tom, disorientated by a nameless grief that is a constantly evolving 'mosaic of loss', struggles as a freshman in college, fails his courses and eventually drops out after attending a healing meeting (*TL*, p. 123). The novel narrates his near three-year discipleship of Wayne Gilchrest – 'Holy Wayne' – via retrospective narrative. This subplot begins with the bad news: the guru has been arrested for a variety of crimes against his female followers including allegations of rape 'as well as tax evasion'; broadcasters describe 'the spectacular downfall of the self-styled messiah' and his public disgrace echoes a number of late-twentieth-century religious scandals (*TL*, p. 111). Holy Wayne is a rather different figure from the austere GR: when Tom first encounters him 'in an overheated church basement' on a 'frigid March Saturday' as a reluctant inquirer, alongside approximately twenty others, he is simply a modest, 'grieving father' who appears to have a miraculous gift for absorbing the emotional pain of others (*TL*, p. 150). Tom's conversion experience follows an articulate, personal talk – more like a vivid confession than an orthodox sermon – and is mediated via a moment of physical intimacy in a 'strong embrace'. Tom and a fellow member of his college fraternity who also joins the movement describe the experience as one of 'gratitude that spreads through your body when a burden gets lifted, and the sense of homecoming that follows' (*TL*, p. 167). This affective transfiguration is an echo of the 'sudden departure', but the 'homecoming' is a form of rapture that seems to bring joy to the body rather than an abrupt disappearance from incarnate existence. The encounter is transformative but ultimately misguided: whatever the reality of Gilchrest's ability to heal, he eventually proves to be an abusive, ego-driven manipulator and, after getting one of his teenage disciples pregnant, he eventually confesses his crimes and abandons many thousands of followers. Tom is left to care for the mother of this child, initially believed to be a miraculous, potentially messianic figure. On the road to Mapleton – the only place that Tom, hesitantly, thinks may welcome the child – they disguise themselves as members of yet another cult-like group. The Barefoot People differ from the severity of the GR and the messianic fervour of Holy Wayne: they embrace wild hedonism and reject both convention and footwear. They are an echo of the 1960s hippie radicals and the attendant sexual revolution, but it is also clear that their own freewheeling theology is frequently selfish and exploitative.

In a review of *The Leftovers*, Stephen King – a novelist who is not unfamiliar with either the quiet horrors of suburbia or speculative dystopias – describes the novel as a 'troubling disquisition' on, amongst other things 'the unobtrusive ease with which faith can slide into fanaticism'. Perrotta, he argues, observes 'that in times of real trouble, extremism trumps logic [...] Read as a metaphor for the social and political splintering of American society after 9/11, it's a chillingly accurate diagnosis.'[24] King's own novel, *Under the Dome* (2009) has much in common with *The Leftovers*: it also features an initially inexplicable event – the sudden descent of an invisible barrier around the perimeter of a small New England town – on an otherwise unremarkable October day that might also read as an allegory of opportunistic and authoritarian post-9/11 moral panic. Both focus on life in small towns; experience of a shattering event narrated via the domestic; alternative voices vying for control; reason versus irrationality; liberty versus oppression. The shared early autumnal setting of the novels suggests a sense of ending, of things drawing to a close. Kevin's counterpart in *Under the Dome* might be Dale Barbara, a former captain in the US army and an Iraq War Veteran. However, Kevin actually has more in common with Big Jim, King's chief antagonist. Both are lawmakers and men who are looked to during a time of crisis: one reluctantly and the other with a desire for power. Where Kevin holds even limited authority with a degree of ambivalence, Jim pursues it ruthlessly; Kevin is respectful but sceptical about religion, whereas Jim uses biblical teaching and credulous belief to enforce his own will. Both *The Leftovers* and *Under the Dome* respond to the apocalyptic anxieties perpetuated by the war on terror and are especially concerned with the exploitation of fear. Perrotta's novel, however, is somewhat more sanguine about the exercise of bureaucratic or governmental power. Kevin is, at worst, ineffectual, but Big Jim embodies a muscular, undemocratic force that is ready to manipulate the distress and insecurity in order to ensure his own continued power.

The self-aware, uncomfortable relationship that Perrotta's traumatic narrative has to its eschatological antecedents recalls Robert McGill's assessment of Douglas Coupland's *Girlfriend in a Coma* (1998): Coupland's premillennial parable, he argues, is 'not apocalyptic' but rather is 'a response to apocalyptic literature'.[25] Where Coupland deployed a range of genre conventions – dream-vision, angelic visitors and miraculous reversals of time – Perrotta's narrative remains more precisely within the bounds of realism (or, at least as realistic as is possible for a novel whose premise is the sudden disappearance of millions of people into thin air). The saved remnant, the band of survivors or, depending on one's perspective, the damned souls left behind is rather bigger than in most post-catastrophe narratives: 98 per cent of the world's population – around 5.5 billion people – do not disappear. The novel is a study in grief and an acknowledgement of American fascination with 'end-times' prophecies; it is also an exploration of the seductive rhetoric of fanaticism as a response to loss and a sense of powerlessness. This is a kind of new agnostic narrative: phenomena that exceed rational explanation are not dismissed or exposed as a hoax, but neither are they represented as signs to be followed into blind obedience to cult leaders or authoritarian politicians.

Perrotta's novel offers an ironic perspective on the nineteenth-century apocalyptic theology that, in various displaced forms, saturates contemporary American culture. Eschatological thought is impoverished if it is understood merely as a quartet of readily rationalized ideas associated with closure – an abrupt death, a dismissive judgement and a fantasy of heaven or hell, one that diminishes into a dismal fantasy of reward or punishment. This vulgarization is particularly tempting for what Frank Kermode famously names 'end-determined' fictions. Mark Knight, who draws on Jürgen Moltmann's 'theology of hope', has argued, *pace* Samuel Beckett, that 'eschatology articulates something other than a violent endgame'; such an eschatological vision is 'aware of our past suffering and the material needs that continue to surround us, [it] commits itself to imagining a future in which the whole of creation might be resurrected and made new'.[26] The denouement of *The Leftovers* is partly an anticlimactic parody of such renewal and partly a cautiously optimistic sign of things to come. As the different narrative strands dovetail, Tom Garvey arrives home in Mapleton and secretly leaves the baby daughter of Holy Wayne on the threshold of his family's home, where he knows the child will be cared for. Nora, still deep in grief and about to flee town, arrives at the Garvey household and encounters the child: 'The baby in her arms was a complete stranger, the way they always are when we meet them for the first time, before we give them names and welcome them into our lives' (*TF*, p. 808). Kevin and Nora are figured as surrogate parents in a pastiche nativity tableau. A novel of catastrophic grief ends with a different kind of quiet apocalypse, one in which new life is celebrated.

4

'In the beginning, there was chaos': Atwood, apocalypse, art

The 'end of the world', as conventionally imagined, is not noted for its convivial qualities. However, Margaret Atwood's post-catastrophe landscapes offer a certain chilly hospitality to storytellers. In *Oryx and Crake* (2003), the first part of her dystopian 'MaddAddam' trilogy, Atwood, a pioneer in politically acute and scientifically inflected fictions, speculates a near-future reality in which the world is, it would seem, home to one solitary human being who is also, in his author's terms, a 'word-guy', a reluctant but lifelong teller of tales.[1] This melancholy last-guest-at-the-party is a lonely soul once named Jimmy, whose temperament and hopes for the future are less than persuasively sanguine. The unfortunate survivor is, by training and vocation, a storyteller who, with the limited creative options available to arts graduates in a hypercapitalist era, half-heartedly traded his aptitude with words for a career in advertising. A gift for narrative, whether he likes it or not (and Jimmy most emphatically does not like it), is ultimately revealed as a primary reason for his continued survival in the inauspicious environment, already ruined by pollution, of the world after civilization's final collapse. As the novel opens, from the limited sanctuary of a tree, Jimmy, who now thinks of himself exclusively under a new soubriquet, the icy and lonesome 'Snowman' (a slightly corny but tenacious pun on 'no man'), looks out over the desolate, depopulated and despoiled earth to remember the world before the species-destroying catastrophe that produced this horrifying solitude.

The memories of Snowman-Jimmy are not bathed in a warm glow of nostalgia: the pre-catastrophe era was one of endemic exploitation, social anomie and vast social divisions based on financial fortune. In this near-future vision of North America, the wealthy live in gated compounds run by powerful corporations such as HelthWyzer, the ethically dubious company for which Jimmy's father works in genetic experimentation; everybody else inhabits the violent and deprived Pleeblands. The environment is polluted, human rights have all but evaporated and animals are the subject of appalling experimentation as a source of prolonging youth for the wealthy or as a means of providing cheap, addictive and unwholesome food such as the grotesque but very popular ChickieNobs, a deeply unpleasant meat product generated via genetic experimentation. In short, the world to which Jimmy returns in flashback – a narrative device used throughout the trilogy – is too hauntingly similar to elements of present reality not to disturb potentially complacent contemporary readers. Katherine Snyder, writing of Atwood's pre- and post-apocalyptic worlds, notes that 'the future as imagined in dystopian speculative fiction must be simultaneously recognizable and unrecognizable, both like and not-like the present' and for the 'cautionary' element of such narratives to work 'we must see the imagined future in our actual present and also recognize the difference between now and the future-as-imagined'.[2] Atwood's fiction deftly moves between disparate eras, but her estranging technique, rich in allusion, satire and ethical nuance, undermines readerly comfort in the idea of dystopia as a distant or improbable future.

Jimmy is troubled by the spectres of diverse endings including the everyday catastrophe of his parents' marriage (and, more specifically, the unresolved disappearance of his mother); the failure of his own relationships, in particular his long-time obsession with the mysterious Oryx, a woman he may first have encountered via internet pornography and who later returns as Crake's lover and scientific collaborator; and, ultimately, the apparent demise of humanity. During the pandemic that all but destroys humanity, he recalls that 'street preachers took to self-flagellation and ranting about the Apocalypse, though they seemed disappointed: where were the trumpets and angels, why hadn't the moon turned to blood?'[3] This, incidentally, is the only use of 'apocalypse' or any other term derived from *apocalypsis* in the entire trilogy. However, the sequence has an apocalyptic logic, in both its destructive and its revelatory senses, that was foreshadowed by Jimmy's unhappy childhood: he was frightened by his parents' arguments, but also 'felt compelled to listen. If there was going to be a catastrophe, some final collapse, he needed to witness it' (OC, p. 65). This is proleptic of the 'final collapse', on a global scale, to which Jimmy becomes the primary witness. His mother became increasingly disenchanted with the nature of her husband's genetic research. Significantly, in one flashback, Jimmy remembers a confrontation in which his mother described research on porcine brain tissue in the language of religious taboo: 'You're interfering with the building blocks of life. It's immoral. It's … sacrilegious', she claims. The scientist, however, counters that 'there's nothing sacred about cells and tissues' (OC, pp. 64–5). A debate about what might be considered to be 'sacred' – life, community, art or a shared history of the planet—is fundamental to Atwood's trilogy.

No twenty-first-century post-collapse, post-catastrophe novel, with the possible single exception of Cormac McCarthy's *The Road*, has inspired as much critical interest as *Oryx and Crake* and its successors. There are, however, two substantial differences between these two popular visions of catastrophe: first, Atwood's trilogy is ultimately unambiguous about the anthropogenic causes of her eco-catastrophe, whereas McCarthy's narrative is oblique and, indeed, shows no real interest in establishing why its world is an infertile place of ruin, decay and starvation. The second distinction is central to the focus of this chapter. *The Road* is a model of linguistic economy as all forms of communication (conversation, story, art) either have been lost or are gradually, irrevocably fading; words disappear as the concepts they once described no longer have referents in reality and names seem to have evaporated; the everyday commerce in ideas, friendly insults and phatic greetings have diminished. McCarthy's novel is pitted with missing apostrophes, a conscious grammatical deviation that embodies the erosion of narrative and its possibilities. The apocalyptic outlook of Atwood's sequence is scarcely less desolate – this is, after all, a world in which the majority of human beings have succumbed to an act of bioterrorism – and in which 'the air smells faintly of burning […] the ashy but greasy smell of a garbage-dump fire after it's been raining'.[4] However, Atwood's narrative style and apocalyptic idiom are, in many ways, radically different from the austere, concise vocabulary of *The Road*. The trilogy is a riot of neologism, word play and hybridized ideas; when the world ends, Snowman-Jimmy and his eventual successor, Toby, create rich, bizarre stories about it; acts of naming do not stop and neither does art. Even books, in rudimentary form, make a tentative return by the end of the sequence in *MaddAddam* (2013). Jimmy has no orthodox faith, but, in attempting to remember the kind of basic World Religion lessons he received as a school child, he recalls the concept of a mantra. For the sceptical last man, this is not a way of contacting divinity but of preserving a disappearing reality: his desire to 'hang on the words' is a kind of godless prayer intended to preserve 'the odd words, the old words, the rare ones' (*OC*, p. 78). This curious act of linguistic consecration anticipates the desire of the anonymous father in *The Road* who attempts to remember things that have perished and who exhorts himself to 'make a list. Recite a litany. Remember'.[5] However, the post-collapse America of *The Road* is one in which names and art seem to have become irretrievably a thing of fading memory. In Atwood's world, story and even print culture might have a future. This chapter focuses on Atwood's representation of storytelling in her end-of-the-world trilogy with another long-standing human activity: the practice of religious belief. What are the ethical and aesthetic implications of the human proclivity for narrative? Do all acts of storytelling tend towards trickery and deception rather than revelation?

Snowman-Jimmy is a type familiar to readers of the broad family of genres associated with apocalyptic endings: he is a contemporary iteration of the 'last man', popularized by Mary Shelley's 1826 tale of Lionel Verney – another citizen of the twenty-first century, though one dreamed up either by Shelley or, if you accept the conceit of her preface, by an ancient prophecy of the Sibyl, painted on leaves and found in a cave.[6] Although, in another echo of Shelley's narrative, humanity has succumbed to a pandemic, the ruined world that Jimmy inhabits is one created not by an act of God. The devastation is, instead, wrought by a man with god-complex: the would-be species slayer goes under the soubriquet Crake, a long-standing avian alias created during adolescence as part of a secretive online game named *Extinctathon*; his given name is the more mundane Glenn, and he is Jimmy's oldest friend, though their relationship has always been unequal and rooted in Glenn-Crake's desire to manipulate those he deems to be weaker. This mischievous zealot, who is privately possessed of a particularly misanthropic world view, brings about the sudden demise of the human race by manufacturing a very popular pill ('BlyssPluss') that is ostensibly designed simultaneously to promote sexual desire, provide invincible protection against 'all known sexual diseases' and 'prolong youth' (*OC*, p. 346). If things seem to be too good to be true, particularly in dystopian fiction, it is because they always are. The eponymous Crake – a characteristically brilliant scientist whose high ideals are matched only by his penchant for species destruction – tells Jimmy, now his marketing man and dupe – that the product has another, covert function: it will irreversibly sterilize all of those who capitulate to the seductive sales pitch. However, this clandestine act of population control is not the real endgame: the pill also contains a disease designed to precipitate the end of humanity. Crake almost succeeds in his genocidal objective to kill all but one of his fellow *Homo sapiens*. In Karen Stein's memorable brace of epithets, Crake is both 'trickster-scientist and postmodern Prometheus', a figure who 'crosses boundaries, disrupts the social order, and embodies contradictions'.[7] Promethean figures, those who seek the secrets of human origins and consequently risk the punishment of other gods, abound in twenty-first-century popular culture. Two recent films, for example, engage with aspects of the myth of the Titan of Greek mythology: Ridley Scott's *Prometheus* (2012) follows the mission of the titular ship into deep space to discover an alien species who its financial backer believes created human life; Alex Garland's *Ex Machina* (2015) focuses on the creation of artificial intelligence that is virtually indistinguishable from human life. Its inventor also invokes the name of the Titan to describe his actions. Crake, in Stein's reading, is part of the same Promethean literary tradition as Mary Shelley's Victor Frankenstein; both are young scientists, brilliant but arrogant and unable to connect 'reason [...] and emotion'; both tamper with nature to catastrophic effect in their different bids to create human life and 'set themselves above ordinary people'.[8] Atwood's ethically wayward, delinquent–genius always intended to spare one person as a guardian for his new world: this role is given to Jimmy, whose gift for narrative and appreciation of empathy curses him to be the guardian of Crake's new world.

It is a paradox of 'nearly every apocalyptic text', argues James Berger, that 'the end is never the end'; the apocalypse, he notes, 'resembles the end, or explains the end', but in most apocalyptic narratives 'something remains after the end'.[9] This is true of *Oryx*

and Crake in which even the last (Snow)man's solitude is not absolute. For one thing, he is tracked by transgenic beasts: Wolvogs,
Rakunks and Pigoons, synthetically produced in laboratories and
freed after the apparent extinction of their creators, are hungry and
living prey is scarce. The threat of becoming lunch for a nightmarish
animal – for example, pigs whose DNA is mixed with human stem
cells originally intended as a way of producing spare organs – is,
however, less disconcerting than the other figures, who emerge from
the trees, and speak to the tree-dwelling, ostensive last human. The
Crakers appear in the first few pages of *Oryx and Crake*, though
their true origin and identity are veiled in the early sections of the
novel. They are represented as childlike: guileless, vulnerable and,
with uncanny song-like questions, they apprehensively catechize
Jimmy about their shared world. Atwood's warning against technoscience, particularly in its most destructive, unethical forms, may
culminate in Crake's Promethean act of creation. The Crakers might
also be read as future humans in another sense, one not dependent
on fears about gene experimentation or bioengineering. These meek
creatures who seem destined to 'inherit the earth' – or what remains
of it – represent generations of the not-yet-born, human beings
who did not bring about the fall of civilization, the basis of which
always appears to be worryingly precarious in speculative fiction.
They, like all children, are a biological product of their ancestors –
Crake's genetic experiments brought them into being – but they are
also inheritors of other human traits, including, it would seem, an
instinct for storytelling.

Just as Maggie Gee's May White in *The Flood* (2004), haunted
by grief and regret, feels herself to be 'alone [...] the last reader, at
the end of the world', Atwood's Jimmy might be the last storyteller,
a man burdened with narrative, an isolated figure but not quite
alone.[10] Indeed, this putative last man has an audience – literally
those who hear or listen – for the stories that he would rather not
tell. These gentle post-humans, a new species specifically created to
succeed humanity by the architect of its final destruction, look to
Snowman as a kind of pastor, one whose ministry must be rooted
in fable; they wish to hear, in particular, stories of their now absent
creator: 'Snowman, please tell us about the deeds of Crake' (*OC*,
p. 117). *Oryx and Crake* features parallel narratives: one is a flashback *de*creation narrative, told in omniscient voice, of the world
that Jimmy knew and how it came to die; the other is the improvised

creation myth that Snowman-Jimmy recounts to the 'children of Crake'. This isolated figure is not, it turns out, the only human being left on the polluted planet; the species is depleted, but Atwood finds other people, a number of whom are, in a self-consciously novelistic fashion, coincidentally connected to Jimmy, and who, like him, somehow escaped the plague, and are now endeavouring to survive at the end of the world; Toby and Ren, in particular, take on the mantle of storytellers in two sequels, *The Year of the Flood* (2009) and *MaddAddam* (2013). As Calina Ciobanu puts it, the first of these sequels 'gives us a "last women" narrative that serves as [a] counterpoint' to Snowman-Jimmy's story.[11]

This sequence of novels is saturated with alternative manifestations of creativity, not all of them emblematic of humanist aspirations to beauty: diaries, music and libraries of disregarded books vie, for example, with violent pornography and a variety of voyeurisms. However, Atwood also engages with forms of expression that aspire towards transcendence: the main narrative of *The Year of the Flood*, for example, is punctuated by the eschatological sermons and hymns of an eco-religious group, God's Gardeners, that expects global catastrophe. In one interview, conducted between the publication of the second and third novels in the sequence, Atwood proposed a highly pragmatic view of spirituality:

> I think that religion is one of those things that are probably built in, like art – like the brain pattern that makes you feel sad when you see somebody crying in a movie. It may just be part of being human. It's not a question of whether people are going to have religion or not, so then it becomes a question of 'What kind are they going to have?' [...] It's a question of how people are using it and to what ends. Are they using it to increase their own affluence or to further their military or political aims? [...] Or are they using it to achieve a relationship with a numinous world that they can't point to as existing in solid objects? What is the hammer being used for? Is it being used to build a house or to murder a neighbor?[12]

For Shannon Hengen, the 'addition of thought from the discipline of religious studies represents the greatest peculiarity, and the greatest contribution of [Atwood's] recent work' because she searches for a concept of moral responsibility and a ground for

mutual dependence that also recognizes human vulnerability in
what Hengen calls 'ancient, enduring spiritual belief'.[13] Jimmy,
she notes, is a protagonist who 'values and knows many words',
but his vocabulary is deployed 'in the service of dubious persua-
sion' (manipulating women for himself and consumers for the
products he is employed to promote). His apparently abundant
lexicon is, however, bereft of 'words for God, truth, goodness or
justice'.[14] Crake views religion with contempt; it is a kind of parody of certain psychoanalytic understandings of the persistence of
piety as infantile neurosis. He sees the rationale of the religious as
grounded in 'misery, indefinitely deferred gratification, and sexual
frustration' (OC, p. 348). Atwood, by contrast, does not represent 'religion' as if it were a singular, monolithic phenomenon. The
Year of the Flood introduces a diverse range of unconventional
cults that thrived during the last days before the pandemic: the
eccentricities and sometimes comical minor theological differences
that distinguish these 'battling' groups, such as the Lion Isaiahists
and their rivals, the Wolf Isaiahists, echoes the parody of messianic expectation of Monty Python's The Life of Brian (1979) (YF,
p. 47). The novel also explores the vast differences of interpretation and praxis that are possible within Christianity: the 'rich people religions', including the Known Fruits and the Petrobaptists,
self-serving churches that are very comfortable with worldly
wealth and environmental devastation, are contrasted with the
eco-friendly, inclusive 'Green theology' of God's Gardeners (YF,
p. 47). Theism is not always understood as a benign influence on
environmental politics. Christianity, in particular, is sometimes cas-
tigated as a root cause for current ecological turmoil. This view
argues that church teaching on the dominion of humanity over and
above the rest of creation perpetuates an estrangement between
people and the land they inhabit, as well as the other creatures with
whom they share the planet. In A Political Theology of Nature
(2003), Peter Scott quotes Lynn White's stark claim, made almost
fifty years ago, that 'we shall continue to have a worsening ecological crisis until we reject the Christian axiom that nature has
no reason for existence save to serve man'. This 'contribution to
the disgracing and subsequent mastery of nature', perpetuated by
the creation story of Genesis 1, is part of a bigger, more complex
story of theological understandings of the relationship between
human beings and ecology.[15] Stewardship, another word used

to describe human dominion or responsibility, has rather more positive connotations, but it is regarded with a degree of suspicion. To take one famous example, James Lovelock, author of the 'Gaia hypothesis', dismisses the concept of stewardship as 'sheer hubris'.[16] This blunt assessment of a dominant religious view is cited by Richard Bauckman in a study that calls for a much more nuanced and deeper engagement with ecological issues than superficial – and frequently self-serving – ideas based on one element of the Judeo-Christian creation narrative. For Bauckman, humanity's undertakings 'are bound to be misunderstood and abused unless the fundamental solidarity of humans with the rest of creation is recognized as their context'.[17] However, theological voices are heard amongst those who are committed to fighting against environmental degradation. 'Global warming is the earth's judgment on the global market empire, and on the heedless consumption it fosters', claims Michael Northcott.[18] This ethical assessment, rooted in an eschatology that is oriented towards a countercultural liberation of the earth and its people, is part of a rather too long suppressed recuperation of deep tradition of protest and resistance to consumer culture. Yet this is by no means the prevailing view in the West. For example, the results of a 2008 survey conducted by the Pew Research Center for the People & the Press about the occurrence and causes of global warming, analysed by its forum on Religion and Public Life, indicated that only 31 per cent of white Evangelical Protestants believe that climate change is a result of human activity, compared with 47 per cent of the population as a whole (an alarming statistic in its own right).[19] In this sense, Atwood's parodies of the more complacent elements of contemporary religious practice are often worryingly close to reality.

One distinctive element of the post-collapse, MaddAddam universe is that forms of spirituality abide in a world where technoscience, with almost every other human achievement, has collapsed. From one perspective, resurgent 'religion', in any form, may signify regression to a childlike state of ignorance and naïve credulity. Yet the post-apocalyptic setting of the narrative presents a world in which any rigid line between secular and sacred traditions has been obscured. There is an ambivalence about the potential of spirituality as a source of ethical commitment: for example, God's Gardeners are represented as rational mystics, committed to care of the planet including their fellow creatures; however, some of the sect's adherents may also help to precipitate the 'waterless' deluge orchestrated by Crake-Glenn.

In Atwood's 'Burning Bushes: Why Heaven and Hell Went to Planet X' (2010), an essay that takes in religion, SF and the narrative impulse, the author speculates about the origin of our dependence on stories.[20] 'Are they the result of nurture', she enquires, 'or are they built in, hard-wired into the brain in template form' in a way that will cause 'stories to generate semi-spontaneously' if the right 'switch is turned on'?[21] Atwood also raises two related narrative problems that are particularly relevant to the 'MaddAddam' sequence: she asks if 'narratives are a means to enforce social control or a means to escape from it' and to what extent 'the use of "story" as a synonym for "lie" is justified, and if so, are some lies justified?' (IOW, p. 41). Her vivid title alludes to an episode in the Jewish scriptures in which Moses encounters the voice of God in the form of a bush that is on fire but which, miraculously, does not burn up (Exodus 3. 1–21). This foundational incident, in which the voice of God says 'I AM THAT I AM, or possibly I WILL BE WHAT I WILL BE' is, notes Atwood drily, 'not something that a Jane Austen heroine would be likely to encounter' (IOW, p. 44). However, equivalents of Moses's auditory experience of theophany occur in SF and forms of speculative writing without destroying their internal consistency. In fact, Atwood's fiction anticipates her literary criticism: one of the final chapters of Oryx and Crake alludes to the Exodus story. Snowman-Jimmy decides to make use of the narrative as a way to explain his absence to the Children of Crake: he understands that he will 'need to tell some lies' and decides to say that he encountered their creator in a 'burning bush', in part to avoid being specific about his physical appearance (OC, p. 417). The stories that Snowman-Jimmy concocts for the Crakers are, superficially at least, deceptive, but the three novels display a significant ambivalence about the human desire both to tell and to hear such 'lies'. 'Orthodox stories of any kind always try to eliminate their competitors', notes Atwood (IOW, p. 42). How long will it be before the mild Crakers start to dispute the meaning of Snowman-Jimmy's narratives of their creator?

One of the ways in which humanity distinguishes itself as a species is in its capacity for creating objects and stories that have an oblique relationship with the real. Oryx and Crake is, in part, a novel of ideas that focuses on a long-standing debate regarding the value, or otherwise, of art. Jimmy and Crake are set in opposition throughout the first novel: as teenagers, for example, the two boys play a bizarre game named *Blood and Roses* in which competitors contest 'human achievements' against 'human atrocities'; the list of massacres, cruelty and genocides is put into battle with, for example, Homer, Tolstoy, ecclesiastical architecture and medical advances (*OC*, pp. 90–1). This 'wicked game' haunts Snowman-Jimmy as he endeavours to find a reason to live and to think well of his, apparently, vanished species: however, not only did the 'Blood' player normally win, the atrocities are easier 'to remember' than the achievements (*OC*, p. 91).

'When any civilization is dust and ashes', claims Jimmy in a flashback to his undergraduate days, 'art is all that's left over. Images, words, music. Imaginative structures. Meaning – human meaning that is – defined by them' (*OC*, p. 196). This passionate defence of 'art' as a kind of transcendent remainder, a consolation of lost faith, is indicative of the novel's sceptical exploration of humanism and its limits. Crake rejects his friend's liberal thesis and offers the view that art is simply another adaptation, a phenomenon that 'serves a biological purpose' in propagating the species. Indeed, the novel, for all its fascination with the politics of catastrophe, is also a caricature of the late capitalist abuse of art. In the dystopian, bureaucratic and consumer-led world that Atwood evokes before Crake's day of reckoning, art is either neglected or exploited. Snowman-Jimmy's interior life in the post-apocalyptic reality is frequently referred to in textual terms: in his frazzled consciousness, for example, fragments of the literature that he once prized emerge 'from the burning scrap-book in his head' (*OC*, p. 11).

One strand of Jimmy's pre-collapse memories is focused on his time as a student. The university at which Jimmy studies, Martha Graham Academy, is a caricature of contemporary attitudes to art. Literature, painting and film are all readily instrumentalized, turned into servants of the market. A loss of investment in art for arts' sake has created an environment in which students, such as Jimmy, pursue courses in Problematics (essentially a form of marketing), and the institution now has openly 'utilitarian aims'. The original motto (*Ars Longa vita Brevis*) has been joined by the more nakedly capitalist and faintly desperate strapline 'Our Students Graduate With Employable Skills' (*OC*, p. 220). Jimmy makes a particular study of self-help books as his undergraduate thesis and

becomes particularly fond of those books that are becoming obso-
lete. Symbolically, Jimmy later gets a job at his alma mater 'going
through old books and earmarking them for destruction while
deciding what should remain on earth in digital form'. He loses
the position because of his inability 'to throw anything out' (*OC*,
p. 283). Culture is being disposed as a symptom of a deeper vandal-
ism and deliberate amnesia.

The 'MaddAddam' sequence is particularly focused on anthro-
pological questions about the purpose of story (as an adaptive
advantage, for example) and, not surprisingly, a range of critics
engage with the function of narrative in Atwood's post-apocalyptic
world. Andrew Hoogheem, for example, draws on the 'evocriti-
cism' of Brian Boyd's *On the Origin of Stories* (2009) to read *The
Year of the Flood* (the books, coincidentally, were published in
the same year). However, he also asserts that Atwood's 'ambivalent, sardonic, and ultimately fond portrayal of religion transcends
the explanatory capacities' of the current evocritical – or Literary
Darwinist – paradigm.[22] The trilogy is both a constellation of competing tropes appropriated from a vast range of cultural sources
and work of metafiction that explores the texture of a whole body
of previous writings. J. Brooks Bouson, for example, emphasizes the
generic diversity of the first instalment in the sequence which, she
notes 'embraces castaway-survivor narrative [...] the detective and
action–thriller novel [...] and the romance story'.[23] Similarly, for
Coral Ann Howells, the first novel is a 'transgeneric construction' –
a blend that includes 'satire, wilderness survival narrative and
castaway narrative, tragic romance triangle, and the quest to the
Underworld' as well as its more obvious use of dystopian motifs.[24]
She argues that *Oryx and Crake* is not only a 'text about the future',
but also 'weighted with literary legacies from the past', including a
'postmodern version of the transcendent metanarrative' offered in
Genesis of Adam and Eve's defiance of God, the fall and the exile
from the Garden of Eden.[25] Indeed, the entire three-novel sequence
is freighted by a concern with the ethics of storytelling. Although
Bouson stresses the generic and structural complexity of the novel,
she also asserts that *Oryx and Crake* is unambiguous in its didactic
morality: 'A cautionary tale written to inform and warn readers
about the potentially dire consequences of genetic engineering'.[26]

One of the 'consequences of genetic engineering', amongst the
Pigoons, and Wolvogs, is a new form of human being. However,

these figures do not simply emerge from the dubiously named Paradice Dome guided by their reluctant teacher. They also bear the trace of textual history and, though initially illiterate, they are very much literary beings. The name 'Paradice Dome', for example, the place in which the Children of Crake were given life, is a ludic rewriting of a canonical rewriting: Milton's paradise, from which Adam and Eve are exiled, is a Puritan epic that interprets the fall narrative of Genesis 3 and Howells suggests that, in turn, 'Atwood offers a revision of that myth for a post-Christian world'.[27] In *Oryx and Crake*, a new species, supposedly free from the failings and limitations of their progenitors, is similarly exiled but not as a result of their own transgression; they, in an echo of Milton's Adam and Eve leaving paradise, walk through a natural landscape with a new world 'all before them', but they are yet to experience the kind of sadness or lack of their literary predecessors.[28] The Miltonic echoes of Atwood's universe are even more explicit in *Year of the Flood*, especially as articulated in the theology of a man who styles himself as Adam One, a postmodern preacher for whom 'the Fall of Man was multidimensional' (*YF*, p. 224). This 'fall' from grace is, however, translated into scientific terms:

> The ancestral primates fell out of the trees [...] Then they fell from instinct into reason and thus into technology; from simple signals into complex grammar and thus into humanity; from firelessness into fire and thus into weaponry (*YF*, p. 224).

In many ways, the prelapsarian identity that Adam One evokes is the condition that Crake, an avowed disbeliever, aspires to for his new creation. The sequel also reveals that the scientist covertly engaged with members of the religion, though his purposes were rather different from those envisaged by Adam One and his followers. Crake's post-human community also bears a kind of family resemblance to the Eloi, the childlike future humans of H. G. Wells's *The Time Machine* (1895): they are represented as similarly innocent and bereft of both knowledge and aggression; like the Eloi, they are vegetarian and vulnerable to predators. Wells's guileless characters, living in rural England approximately 800,000 years in the future, are quarry for the stronger and more inventive Morlocks, chthonic beings who emerge at night to prey on their helpless rivals. Similarly, the Children of Crake have no way of comprehending the pitiless aggression of the so-called Painballers, violent criminals who, brutalized from their experience in a violent game show that doubled as a form of incarceration, have also survived the epidemic. In Wells's novel, the anonymous time traveller is horrified to realize that both species are descended from *Homo sapiens*: the gentle, unintelligent Eloi are descendants of a leisured elite and the spider-like subterranean-dwelling Morlocks are inheritors of the exploited nineteenth-century working classes. Wells's ambivalent social critique is a fin de siècle cautionary tale: inverting the predatory/prey relation between wealthy and poor via an alienating, time travel device encourages a middle-class readership to think about the cost of their own decadent leisure. Although his narrative imagines a distant future, its crucial visionary resources are in the mythic past: the lush future London initially resembles a recreated paradise, an echo of Eden before the fall. The species designations are also biblical borrowings: Morlock is a slight reworking of Moloch, the name of a Cananite god who demanded child sacrifice (see, for example, Leviticus 18. 21); 'Eloi' translates as 'My God' and, in the Gospel according to Mark, is one of the last words of Jesus on the cross: 'Eloi, Eloi, lema sabachthani?', which means, 'My God, my God, why have you forsaken me?' (Mark 15. 34). The name for this branch of Wells's post-humans implies that they have been abandoned by their creator; this is certainly true of the children of Crake whose originator appeared to stage-manage his own death by manipulating his erstwhile friend into shooting him and taking on responsibility for his creation.

Oryx and Crake have mythic identities both before and after what God's Gardeners refer to as 'the waterless flood'. The scientist and his lover escaped from the unhappiness of their own lives with fictional, projected selves by taking on names borrowed from other species; this estranging act of reclassification is a secular baptism that might be designed to allow the pair to shed self-consciousness, but which intensifies their human need for identity, self-assertion and narrative. After their death, Oryx and Crake become dual gods of the Crakers' curious cosmology, a mishmash of the Judeo-Christian tradition and many other spiritual sources that Jimmy tells the childlike creatures. The creator of these childlike, perfect beings was, ironically, a zealous anti-theist who, Jimmy acknowledges, 'would surely be disgusted by the spectacle of his own gradual deification' (*OC*, p. 118). Indeed, Crake, the anti-theist, has become a peculiar god who sees both free will and worship as twin curses. The Crakers are theoretically free from the spiritual impulses that have dogged *Homo sapiens*. Yet they wish to know their creator and seek out Jimmy-Snowman to tell them stories of their origin. '"In the beginning," intones the hesitant bard–preacher, "there was chaos"' (*OC*, p. 117). This oral narrative borrows from non-identical twin scriptural sources in its echoes of the first words of both the Gospel of John ('In the beginning was the Word', 1. 1) and Genesis, the book of beginnings ('In the beginning God created the heaven and the earth. And the earth was without form, and void; and darkness *was* upon the face of the deep. And the Spirit of God moved upon the face of the waters', 1. 1–2). Jimmy knows that his listeners will ask to be shown 'a picture of chaos' since 'all the stories begin with chaos' (*OC*, p. 118). This account, however, is an act of reverse creation, a destruction of chaos that was not merely an empty world 'without form', but one busy with people who 'were full of chaos themselves' who indiscriminately kill both each other and 'all the Children of Oryx', the name that Jimmy gives to non-human animals, in homage to the mysterious Oryx, the woman with whom he was infatuated.

The storytelling develops into a form of call and response. The Crakers are 'fond of repetition' (they learn in very similar ways to the species that they were designed to replace) and, not coincidentally, Jimmy thinks of these frequently reiterated phrases as a 'liturgy' (*OC*, pp. 117, 119). It is also a ritual exchange: Crake's children want a story that they pay for with the gift of a fish, an odd trade between words and things. These acts are a formal rite that is becoming foundational in a nascent society. Jimmy, as storyteller, is aware that successful narrative, even one that embraces supernatural reality – gods creating entire sentient species from coral; language emerging from an egg – is dependent on 'internal consistency'(*OC*, p. 110). The links that he makes between his own imagined cosmology and more banal, sometimes aberrant, forms of storytelling (for example, criminals in the dock and his own misadventures with deceit) reveal an anxiety about the nature of narrative.

Jimmy's improvised cosmology both anticipates and unconsciously echoes the creation account given in the first of Adam One's interpolated sermons in *The Year of the Flood* (pp. 13–15).[29] 'Remember the first sentences of those Human Words of God: the

Earth is without form, and void, and then God speaks Light into being', intones Adam One (*YF*, p. 13). The Gardeners embrace evolutionary theory without anxiety about the literal truth of 'the Human Words of God' ('we have never felt it served a higher purpose to lie to children about geology', *YF*, p. 13).

In terms of narrative sequence, Adam One and his co-religionists do not feature in depth until *Year of the Flood*, but, it is revealed, they were on the fringe of Jimmy's world and, perhaps, awareness. The sequel reveals that two of his girlfriends, Brenda (Ren) and Amanda Payne, who have cameo appearances in *Oryx and Crake*, spent part of their childhoods and teenage years as part of the radical eco-community. Retrospective rereading, in the light of *Year of the Flood* and *MaddAddam*, might suggest that Jimmy was intuitively appropriating ideas that he briefly encountered years before. In her skilful knitting together of a fragmented world, Atwood links the Children of Crake, Snowman-Jimmy's extemporized genesis story and the theology of Adam One.

Crake intended that his post-human children's programming would mean that they evolved without the need for symbolic thinking: storytelling, mythology and religion would be redundant and without the vestiges of *homo narrans*, the new humans would be free of the emotional lives that, in the geneticist's view, perpetuate territorial conflicts, desire and war. Perhaps not surprisingly, this man of technology who has little time for empathy other than as a mode of survival, is also profoundly suspicious of artistic endeavours: '*Watch out for art*, Crake used to say. *As soon as they start doing art, we're in trouble.* Symbolic thinking of any kind would signal downfall, in Crake's view' (*OC*, pp. 419–20).[30] Significantly, his taxonomy of this 'downfall' includes 'inventing idols': consciously or otherwise, Crake, like the God of Moses, is against the worship of graven images.

Although there are few signs that the so-called Children of Crake have made an evolutionary shift towards violence, not even to defend themselves, they are susceptible to the experience of desire. Ralph Pordzik, drawing on Lacanian vocabulary to address the 'posthuman future', notes that the Crakers 'gradually become aware of their very own variety of lack [...] No matter how many words Snowman adds to the signifying chain, no matter how often he tries to rectify a mistake or white lie by modifying his tales, the Crakers always get the hang of it and want him to enlarge upon details'.[31]

Anxiety about what Pordzik names the Crakers' 'uncertain ontogenetic status' might explain their decision to build a 'scarecrowlike effigy' of Snowman-Jimmy when he is absent (*OC*, p. 418).[32] For Pordzik, this idol-fashioning event marks the Crakers' 'return to the bosom of the human family [...] by distinguishing absence from presence and thus reintroducing into their discourse a new essential dichotomy.'[33] In truth, Crake's meticulous planning is a parody of providence, his beatific vision of a world inherited by peaceable beings dependent on a violent piety that is able to rationalize genocidal violence. The scientist also believes that belief itself is a matter of neurology, 'the G-spot in the brain'; God, for Crake, is merely 'a cluster of neurons' rather than a transcendent reality or prime mover (*OC*, p. 186). In a separate flashback in *Year of the Flood*, Crake argues that God and immortality are both a 'consequence of grammar':

> As soon as there's a past tense, there has to be a past before the past, and you keep going back in time until you get to *I don't know*, and that's what God is. It's what you don't know – the dark, the hidden, the underside of the visible, and all because we have grammar [...] God is a brain mutation, and that gene is the same one birds need for singing (*YF*, p. 377).

His attempt to eradicate this orientation towards the divine, however, fails and Jimmy recognizes that the eugenic experiment has not resulted in distrustful beings who trust only what they can see, touch, taste and smell. Instead, the men and women are 'conversing with the invisible' and have 'developed reverence', and though they have not yet become idolaters of 'graven images', this too has changed by the end of the novel (*OC*, pp. 185–6).

Anxieties about the purpose, freedom and potential signified by different forms of 'symbolic thinking', particularly those that crystallize in art and religion, are central to the whole trilogy. Singing and dreams are two things that even Crake understands are not wholly explicable signifiers of human identity. He recognizes that music, particularly the sound of the 'human' voice (however that unstable term is defined), cannot simply be eliminated. '*We're hard wired for singing*', he acknowledges (*OC*, p. 411).

Song becomes a recurrent motif in the trilogy: the unnerving singing of the Children of Crake, somehow 'beyond the human level,

or below it' and simultaneously both 'old' and 'newborn', is aesthetically overwhelming for Jimmy and 'forces too many unwanted
emotions upon him' (*OC*, p. 122). Singing seems to transcend time
past and present and to belong in an eternal realm to which the
last man feels he cannot belong. After all, songs have frequently
been used to express mystical longings as well as quotidian sensuous desires. One reviewer describes the very structure of *The Year
of the Flood* 'as a hymnal praising the saints of natural science' and
notes that it anticipates 'the biblical tone' that informs a vital strand
in the trilogy's conclusion in *MaddAddam*.[34]

Individual songs (that might also be read as poems) punctuate
the principle narrative of *Year of the Flood*. They serve a number of
structural and thematic purposes: as a counterpoint to Jimmy's delirious and tentative storytelling of a world that once was in the first
novel, they set out an alternative vision to the dystopian, consumerist society of the fictional world we already know to be doomed;
they also, perhaps deliberately, interrupt the narrative coherence of
the novel. Atwood uses the hymns to remind us that we are in a textual world that itself is dependent on other texts. Although the lyrics were written by Atwood, the text uses a conceit that they belong
to a religious community and are attributed on the pages in which
they appear to *The God's Gardeners Oral Hymnbook*. The hymns
fuse reverence for creation and the saints who venerate nature and
God; the theology is frequently panentheistic, emphasizing both
immanence and a radical interpretation of incarnation. 'When God
Shall His Bright Wings Unfold', for example, imagines the creator
taking a variety of avian forms and condemns those who hunt birds
for sport (*YF*, pp. 446–7). In her acknowledgements, Atwood indicates that her 'clearest influence' is, not surprisingly, William Blake,
a poet who combined rebellion with heterodox reverence. However,
she also cites *The Hymn Book of the Anglican Church of Canada
and the United Church of Canada* and, perhaps more surprisingly,
John Bunyan (*YF*, p. 517). The Puritan allegorist might, in fact, be
a significant presence in the trilogy as a whole: like his *Pilgrim's
Progress*, the sequence fuses wit, fearful visions and a moral interpretation of life that is simultaneously both complex and frighteningly clear-cut.

The hymn book appears in print, but emerges from a culture
that is hostile to writing. Indeed, the God's Gardeners are suspicious of writing and insist on the authority of oral narrative: it is

a phonocentric tradition that values speech above writing. These ideas are foregrounded by Jimmy's reluctant but tenacious acts of storytelling in the first novel, but they become crucial in *The Year of the Flood*. The novel begins with the words of an Edenic hymn ('The Garden') and ends with a group of characters hearing, for the first time, the other-worldly music of the Children of Crake. The printed word has rivals in oral culture. One narrator, a former girlfriend of Jimmy's named Ren, speaks via a diary and remembers that her religious teachers, 'the Adams and the Eves', regarded writing as dangerous:

> *Beware of words. Be careful what you write. Leave no trails.*
>
> This is what the Gardeners taught us, when I was a child among them. They told us to depend on memory, because nothing written down could be relied on. The Spirit travels from mouth to mouth, not from thing to thing: books could be burnt, paper crumble away, computers could be destroyed. Only the Spirit lives forever, and the Spirit isn't a thing (*YF*, p. 7).

Does Atwood's trilogy take the idea that writing, and the printed word in particular, are both politically 'dangerous' and, equally, in danger of disappearing? The sequence as a whole certainly registers the transience of human structures and the fallibility of culture. The focus on acts of storytelling culminates in *MaddAddam*. Toby, another member of God's Gardeners, succeeds the delirious and later deceased Jimmy-the-Snowman as the Crakers' teacher–priest; she is particularly conscious that the stories she tells will shape the future of these vulnerable creatures. She thinks about the mythology that she was taught by one of her mentors in the movement, Pilar, another 'Eve', about the afterlife: she is able to balance her own religious doubt with an appreciation of the emotional significance of such narratives: 'People need such stories [...] because however dark, a darkness with voices in it is better than a silent void' (*MA*, p. 154).

Toby becomes a mentor, in particular, to one of the younger Crakers, named Blackbeard, and teaches him about the shape of stories. He becomes a narrator of the novel and his storytelling acuity emerges, in part, because of a traumatic encounter, fittingly enough at the place of his origin. Blackbeard is devastated when he encounters the decaying bodies of Oryx and Crake, the twin gods of his universe. He is confronted with an unpleasant material reality that is incommensurate with the cosmology that he has been taught by Snowman-Jimmy and Toby. Instead of the 'beautiful', supernatural creator and guardian of creation 'like the stories', the pair are 'many smelly bones [...] they were dead ones, very dead ones and all fallen apart' (*MA*, p. 359). This moment of uncanny, corporeal revelation – a Gothic encounter with a repressed event – might herald an accelerated end to the Crakers' guileless faith. However, the epoch of disenchantment is, at the very least, deferred because Toby, the skilled storyteller, makes a distinction between the bodies as mere 'husks' and a higher reality in which Oryx and Crake now have 'different forms' in which they are 'good and kind' and 'beautiful' as in the stories. The surprising element of this incident is not Blackbeard's initial sense of ontological shock, but the speed with which he is able to move from literalist to symbolic thinking. He understands, in a simple way, the distinction between everyday history that includes the disappointing truth that those we love eventually become 'many smelly bones' and mythology, a form of narrative that transfigures quotidian detail into something that appears richer.

MaddAddam is self-conscious about its status as a book, a material object designed to resist the ravages of time and to be shared with future generations. As the novel ends, Toby has taught Blackbeard not only how to read and write, but also how to create books. Indeed, one review describes the final novel as 'an exposition of how oral storytelling traditions led to written ones and ultimately to our sense of origin'.[35] The so-called Children of Crake are shifting from a predominantly oral culture to a literate one; they are, in short, becoming a 'people of the book'. The production of a book contradicts the phonocentric principles of God's Gardeners but suggests an evolution and emphasizes the significance of cultural memory. Toby, he says, 'gave warnings about this Book that we wrote':

> She said the pages must not get wet, or the Words would melt away and would be heard no longer, and mildew would grow on it, and it would turn black and crumble to nothing. And that another Book should be made, with the same writing as the first one. And each time a person came into the knowledge of the writing [...] and the reading, that one was also to make the same

Book, with the same writing in it. So it would always be there for us to read (*MA*, p. 386).

For Ciobanu, 'if MaddAddam does gesture toward "a thing of hope" at the end of the world [...] it is through writing, which presupposes a tomorrow that will bring with it those who will read the words written today.'[36] The final sentence of the trilogy, following Blackbeard's celebration of the dead – 'Now we will sing' – invokes both a shared future ('we will') and the persistence of art as an expression of community (*MA*, p. 390). In a sense, this is an unconscious refutation of their own creator's bemused contempt for art and a rejection of violence. The spirituality of Atwood's sequence is complex, contradictory and ambivalent, but Mark Bosco argues that it can be placed in the 'long line of oracular literary texts in Western culture' that include both the books of Daniel and Revelation, Jewish and Christian texts that 'express the expectation of an imminent cosmic cataclysm in which God will destroy the ruling powers of evil and raise the righteous to life in a new messianic kingdom'.[37] In these terms, *Oryx and Crake* is not merely a secular, satirical appropriation of end-times prophecy, but a text that is determined by what Bosco names an 'eschatological question about endings'.[38] Atwood is not a theologian – nor is she a 'believer' in any orthodox sense – but her narrative is deeply embedded in the same kinds of enquiry as theology.

Atwood's sequence uses the horizon of a feared imminent catastrophe to examine anxieties about writing, memory and story; the novels examine the ways in which narratives are communicated and diffused across time and space. Atwood self-identifies as an 'absolutely strict agnostic' but her thoughtful distrust of certainty is not simply a blank denial of spiritual possibility; indeed, this ambivalence fosters in her fiction a rich engagement with the persistent idea of holiness.[39]

5

Empty roads: Walking after catastrophe

In *A Philosophy of Walking* (2009, 2014), Frédéric Gros advocates the joys of a rudimentary, creaturely activity that is emphatically 'not a sport'.[1] To walk, he argues, might constitute a 'rebellious' form of freedom in which the 'micro-liberations' of accelerated modern life (the choices that characterize a consumer economy) are revealed to be 'dependencies'.[2] Is walking always character-istic of such agency? We might ask where those unable to walk fit into this Romantic defence of the aimless, unmotivated peripa-tetic. The future imagined by post-catastrophe narratives – a time when anxieties about shopping are less pressing than, for example, avoiding death from hypothermia – is frequently defined by a kind of enforced, continual motion. This movement, in contradiction to the accelerating tempo of early twenty-first-century culture, is often slow (unless, say, hasty escape from hungry cannibals is necessi-tated) and motivated by something other than the circulation of capital. However, it is rarely the kind of purely liberating endeav-our celebrated by the political philosopher. Apocalyptic landscapes are, in short, normally witnessed by characters at walking pace, but without a joyful spring in the step. This chapter focuses on two journeys by foot across alternative future versions of ruined, post-collapse America: Cormac McCarthy's *The Road* (2006) and Jim Crace's *The Pesthouse* (2007). These visions of catastro-phe imagine epochs in which twenty-first-century technologies of transport have been abandoned and human mobility is radi-cally circumscribed. They are also novels in which contemporary subjectivities are fundamentally revised: in *The Road* even names have disappeared as language deteriorates and concepts evaporate. The central protagonist of McCarthy's novel, an unnamed father, undertaking a very long walk to the possible greater warmth and safety of the coast in desperate and exceptionally dangerous circumstances accompanied by his young child, reflects that 'there's not a lot of good news on the road'.[3] The chapter thinks about the relationship between post-catastrophe walkers, the 'promised lands' that they may seek and the wider relationship between apocalyptic presentiments and the mysteriously countercultural deed of taking a hike.

Contemporary post-apocalyptic film and television narratives are busy with walking tropes: for example, in the Hughes Brothers' film *The Book of Eli* (2010), a kind of post-apocalyptic version of John Bunyan's *The Pilgrim's Progress* (1678–84), a man bearing a prophetic name undertakes an archetypal journey westwards across an America that, decades earlier, has been ruined by nuclear war; this single-minded expedition echoes traditions of the frontier and the screenplay playfully draws on the iconography of the Western genre. The narrative is similarly fraught with violence, but its motivation rather differs from both conventional notions of Manifest Destiny and motifs of revenge. Eli (Denzel Washington) is undertaking his hazardous walk to deliver what might be the last remaining Bible to an archive of all human achievements and endeavours housed on Alcatraz Island. A less funereal form of walking is central to Edgar Wright and Simon Pegg's *The World's End* (2013), in which an ill-advised nostalgic pub crawl by a reluctantly reunited group of school friends seems to precipitate Armageddon; one protagonist, terminally resistant to the pressures of adult responsibility, continues the walk between pubs after the world's end.

For North Americans, the ordinary act of going for a walk has long been regarded as a spirited form of dissent. In his cultural history of 'this first and principal way of American native and colonial locomotion', Joseph Amato emphasizes the significance of walking in a variety of protest movements. Walking, he argues, 'has symbolic connotations in a society that rides. It stands for [...] the people's historic way. Taking to one's feet adds solemnity, humility, and an air of sacrifice to one's cause.'[4] He cites, for example, peaceful marches against the Vietnam War and, more recently, the American invasion of Iraq and the economic policies of the G8 nations. This tradition can be traced as far back as the nineteenth-century nonconformist American Romanticism of Henry David Thoreau. In 'Walking' (1862), a digressive defence of travelling by foot that has become a touchstone for eco-criticism, Thoreau castigates those who have capitulated to the insidious logic of a sedentary era. The sometime teacher, advocate of civil disobedience and occasional 'sojourner in civilized life' claims that he could only 'preserve' his 'health and spirits' if able to 'spend four hours a day at least [...] sauntering through the woods and over the hills and fields, absolutely free from all worldly engagements'.[5] This perambulatory diligence was so contrary to the inactive posture of the day that it became positively countercultural. Thoreau's mentor, Ralph Waldo Emerson, famously complained that 'civilized man has built a coach, but he has lost the use of his feet'.[6] The success of capital and new technology did not produce a renewed vitality in humanity but an epidemic of sitting down.

Thoreau offers a bathetic image of a bustling economy that has, ironically, produced bodily stasis: he imagines 'the mechanics and shopkeepers' cooped up in their places of work for hours on end 'sitting with crossed legs, so many of them – as if the legs were made to sit upon, and not to stand upon' (W, p. 262). The horrors of this enforced desk or workshop-bound life prompts Thoreau to confess that such lynchpins of the American trade 'deserve some credit for not having committed suicide long ago' (W, p. 262). By contrast, he reveres those rare, nonconforming figures who display 'a genius for SAUNTERING'. According to Thoreau's idiosyncratic etymology, this unhurried practice is 'beautifully derived from idle people who roved about the country' and claimed to be 'going a la Sainte Terre, to the Holy Land'. An alternative meaning, however, he notes, is 'sans terre', signifying one who is 'without land or home [...] but equally at home anywhere' (W, p. 260). This leisurely mode of mobility, whatever its linguistic origins, is, in Thoreau's eyes, a dissident act, in which 'every walk is a sort of crusade, preached by some Peter the Hermit in us, to go forth and reconquer this Holy Land' (W, p. 260). Walking, in these terms, is not simply rebellious; it is a form of resistance against the inactive nature of the emerging commercial imperative. Thoreau celebrates the freedom of leaving everything behind. He disdains the purely recreational walk ('Our expeditions are but tours') and declares that even the shortest of walks be undertaken 'perchance in the spirit of undying adventure, never to return' (W, pp. 260–1). His take on walking fuses a gospel-like revelatory idiom with political ideals of liberty:

> If you are ready to leave father and mother, and brother and sister, and wife and child and friends, and never see them again – if you have paid your debts, and made your will, and settled all your affairs, and are a free man – then you are ready for a walk. (W, p. 261)

In homiletic mode, Thoreau's words specifically echo Christ's injunction for his followers to leave everything behind in order to follow him (Luke 14. 25–7). The emphasis on the 'free man' not only is gendered language typical of the era, but also bears the trace of American Romantic investment in a certain kind of masculinity: independent, practical, solitary and cerebral. This version of free walking remains enormously influential, but, as with Thoreau's liberal approach to the inspiring ideas of the past, contemporary interpreters have found ways of moving beyond it. Rebecca Solnit, activist, essayist and impressively unpredictable thinker, has pursued a robust revision of nonconformist attitudes to mobility that acknowledge a debt to Thoreau. In *Wanderlust* (2001), a strikingly personal history of walking and 'also a polemic against industrialization, privatization of open lands, the oppression and confinement of women, suburbia, the disembodiment of everyday life and a few other such things', Solnit reflects on her ambulatory adventures as part of the anti-nuclear movement.[7] Peripatetic protests, in this case, are a speculative attempt at forestalling the end of the world. One of Solint's recent hiking routes takes her across 'a headland just north of the Golden Gate Bridge studded with abandoned military fortifications'. The trail, via the 'exuberant, riotous green' of the hills also affords the strange sight of an 'odd collection of objects and cement buildings' that 'were part of a Nike missile guidance system' and encourages her reader to 'think of the ruin as a souvenir of the cancelled end of the world'.[8] She associates these remnants of the Cold War with memories of demonstrations in a nuclear test site in Nevada during the 1980s. In a transgressive deed or form of 'civil disobedience' on 'an unprecedented scale' she and her fellow protestors walked on 'the off-limits side' at the test site, 'an act of trespass resulting in arrest': 'We bore a kind of bodily witness to

our convictions, to the fierce beauty of the desert, and to the apocalypses being prepared nearby.'[9]

Solnit's progressive, democratic walking practice is a defiant
alternative to the dominant mode of gas-guzzling, future-denying
culture of the present. Concepts of American identity in the era of
global capital are frequently defined by ideas of mobility and speed.
In short, the most popular narratives of freedom in the United
States are associated with the open road and burning gas in a fast
car. Walking narratives have a certain subversive logic in American
culture, even if they are often ideologically complex and nostalgic
for certain 'authentic' notions of masculine identity. However, contemporary representations of the walker are not always hymns to
the salvific possibilities of hiking, sauntering or strolling. Douglas
Coupland's early fiction, including *Generation X: Tales for an
Accelerated Culture* (1991) and *Shampoo Planet* (1992), explore
the classic tradition of North American 'road' stories with car journeys criss-crossing Canada and the United States. Nevertheless, a
number of his protagonists also trek out into the American wilderness on foot, their search for revelation frequently frustrated.
Coupland's comic novel *Miss Wyoming* (2000) includes a spectacular misadventure in walking that is part parody, part homage to the
American myth of the freedoms of the open road. The neatly named
John Johnson, successful Hollywood producer on the verge of a
breakdown, experiences a near-death vision with apocalyptic implications. His epiphany may be generated by medication and television rather than any supernatural agent, but, hallucinatory or not,
the apparition triggers a transformation and this man of wealth
decides to abandon his privileged life in order to become a 'citizen
of nowhere'. John walks away from the cluttered, (sub)urban life
in order to embrace an ideal of American freedom embodied in
what he names 'the romance of the road': 'Adventures every ten
minutes ... No crappy rules or smothering obligations'.[10] John's
aspirations are an echo of the spiritual quest of Jack Kerouac's *On
the Road* (1957); the freewheeling world view of the Beat generation is rejected by John's oldest friend who plainly dismisses the
project: 'The road is *over* ... It never even *was*' (*MW*, p. 52). John's
initial foray ends in spectacular failure, embarrassment and a bad
case of diarrhoea in the desert. As the novel ends, despite his initial
humiliation, John and his new lover once again walk away from

both metropolis and suburb to rejoin the tradition of 'endless pilgrims' 'along the plastic radiant way' of America (*MW*, p. 311).[11]

Joshua Ferris's *The Unnamed* (2010), by contrast, is a disturbing story of a successful New York lawyer, Tim Farnsworth, whose contented, secure life is ruined by sporadic recurrences of compulsive walking that find no satisfactory physical or mental diagnosis and resist all forms of treatment. He is a man who becomes 'trapped [...] in the next step, the next step and the next step'.[12] Walking, in a story that has shades of Edgar Allan Poe's urban Gothic (especially the restless pursuit of his 1840 tale of urban anomie, 'The Man of the Crowd') and to the title and absurdist universe of Samuel Beckett's *The Unnameable* (1953), is far from the liberating, defiant activity celebrated by Thoreau and Solnit. Tim's pathological walking exacerbates his loneliness and estrangement from family and alienates him from any sense of community. His unwilled exploits become a grotesque parody of the nineteenth-century flâneur: the aimless journeys by foot are not associated with leisure. Instead, these bouts of uncontainable restlessness separate the protagonist from a secure, suburban domestic life and propel him into the wilds of an America tainted by environmental ruin; these abandoned edgelands suggest that a wealthy nation is in the midst of a catastrophe. He encounters flooded towns and houses charred by wildfire and witnesses a flock of birds falling from the sky: 'Disaster once confined to the west had migrated, a wayward animal confused by scrambled weather. Reservoirs were poisoned' (*U*, p. 104). *The Unnamed* is haunted by a kind of pre-apocalyptic mood in a double sense: it is focalized via a character who not only seems to be on the brink of a revelation – one that never quite materializes – but is also overwhelmed by a sense of incipient doom. The novel opens during 'the cruelest winter' in which schools have been shut for weeks and long lines form at groceries (*TU*, p. 3). This unsettling, faintly dystopian mood fuses repressed anxieties regarding climate change with a disturbed social order. During one of her depressing, heroic forays to find her itinerant husband, Jane's perception of the snow-furrowed landscape is interspersed with the language of ruination: 'The black trees all around her stood with their sharp naked branches like burnt-out dendrites' (*TU*, p. 11). This sentence, in particular, is resonant of the scorched, lifeless world evoked in Cormac McCarthy's *The Road* in which ash constantly swirls and the 'trunks of trees' that border a river valley are 'charred and limbless' (*TR*, p. 8).

One reviewer, who otherwise plays down the elements of *The Unnamed* that seem to prefigure catastrophe, nevertheless notes that it constitutes a 'kind of existential journey' that bears comparison with *The Road*.[13] Indeed, McCarthy's sombre novel, in which a nameless father and his young son attempt to survive an astoundingly inhospitable and desperate future, walking along 'ashen scabland' and 'shuffling through the ash', pushing a cart with a few meagre possessions, across the blacktop of a broken, usually empty road has become the exemplary twenty-first-century postapocalyptic quest narrative (*TR*, pp. 4, 14). The father carries a pistol and crude, whittled bullets: what might appear to be a belated version of the right to bear arms as a means of protection is also, ominously, represented as a source of self-destruction; the boy is told, in the event that he is kidnapped by one of the cannibal gangs, that he should end his own life rather than face something worse.

Michael Titlestad notes that the nature of the journey undertaken in McCarthy's novel is 'far from the ideals of freedom, self-discovery, even manifest destiny' that we have come to associate with the distinctively American chrontope of 'the road'; instead it 'has become a site of diminution, on which survival is the best one can hope for. Traveling has become detached from any higher purpose – it is motivated by the inexorable need to keep moving.'[14] The nation in which McCarthy's walking narrative unfolds is, like father and son, never named, presumably because in the future that it imagines national boundaries and governments belong to a hazily recalled past. Instead, the land that we assume to be a ruined former United States of America is referred to in a series of dismal epithets; the 'country' (a synonym in the novel for landscape rather than nation) encountered by the novel's two central protagonists is variously described, for example, as 'wasted', 'darkening', 'desolate', 'burntlooking' and 'bleak' (*TR*, pp. 4, 8, 16, 51, 140). Where the American interior traversed by Ferris's errant lawyer intermittently testifies to a coming end, in water or fire, *The Road* takes place in an era in which nature appears already to be spoiled beyond any hope of recovery; colour has drained from the land and each day is 'more gray [...] than what had gone before', resulting in a darkness that is 'like the onset of some cold glaucoma dimming away the world' (*TR*, p. 1). This ocular simile, used on the novel's opening page, in which fading sight is a metonym for global desolation, foreshadows a novel where acts of seeing are, by turns, disappointing and terrifying or, on occasion, both.

The civilization-ending catastrophe that also appears to have ravaged the ecosystem is left unexplained and represented as minimally as possible, witnessed rather plainly in flashback as 'a long shear of light and then a series of low concussions' and 'a dull rose glow in the window-glass' (*TR*, p. 54). The ash-laden, charred earth that has no hint of returning verdure or animal life might resemble the imagined landscapes of a nuclear winter; the reader is never told whether this uninviting, deathly world is the consequence of atomic warfare, the impact of a meteor or an anthropogenic environmental event. Some ecologically charged fiction such as, for example, Ian McEwan's *Solar* (2010) and Kim Stanley Robinson's 'Science in the Capitol' trilogy (2004–7), focus on human agency and folly as crucial elements of climate change. McCarthy's novel, by contrast, is far more concerned with effects than with causes. The road is deployed, via the fragmented memories of the exhausted, ailing father as the defining space in which the human catastrophe plays out. 'In those first years' following the unspecified disaster 'the roads were peopled with refugees shrouded up in their clothing' (*TR*, p. 28). This stark sentence might imagine a wrecked future, but it also resonates with a distinctively early twenty-first-century history in which thousands of people are forced out of their homes as a result of war, starvation and environmental crises. During their journey, the father and son encounter a fallen city that is 'mostly burned', its streets lined with cars, once a signifier of speed and freedom of movement, 'caked with ash'; trees and rivers are blackened and motionless (*TR*, p. 11). This charred topography is no place to dwell safely (the sparse population must contend with not only starvation and disease, but also the lurking threat of cannibal cults); survival depends on the ability to keep moving.

Walking is the main activity in *The Road*. It is the only way that the father and son might survive for any length of time. The word 'walk' and its cognates ('walked', 'walking') are used more than a hundred times in the novel's 300 pages. Indeed, this iterative style takes on the timbre of liturgy and the hike, punctuated by the son's candid questions, becomes a kind of embodied prayer, a discreet rebellion against the temptations of despair. The man is drawn to the possibilities of repetition as a survival strategy: as he walks, he recollects things vanished from the world and exhorts himself to 'make a list. Recite a litany. Remember' (*TR*, p. 31). The present participle of the novel's favoured verb of mobility, however, does not always have entirely positive connotations. The man is haunted by memories of his dead wife and in one flashback to the early days following the catastrophe she rejects his assessment of their situation: 'We're not survivors. We're the walking dead in a horror film', she claims (*TR*, p. 55). The nameless woman, still pregnant at the point of global crisis, refuses to become part of this 'horror film' – a world that she already knows via the relentless visions of the end mediated in popular culture – and eventually takes her own life. Her choice of soubriquet to describe their horrendous predicament resonates with another twenty-first-century exploration of post-collapse America: *The Walking Dead* (2010-), a post-pandemic, 'zombie apocalypse' television drama adapted from Robert Kirkman and Tony Moore's continuing comic book series (2003-), emphasizes an ambulatory motif. It also prompts a question: are either the infected or survivors the eponymous 'walking dead'?

Mobility is foregrounded in McCarthy's emblematic title, one that echoes a long American literary tradition of travel writing. For Diletta De Cristofaro, drawing on Bahktin, the 'eponymous road' is an 'anti-apocalyptic chronotope'.[15] She argues that although the 'narrative forward motion might initially appear to suggest the road as a chronotope for the flowing of time, in consonance with the Bakhtinian understanding', a more careful reading 'subverts the teleological' interpretation of this distinctively American space. Such a subtle rethinking emerges, she notes, because 'the road, strictly speaking, does not take the characters anywhere' and because the novel emphasizes 'the cyclical repetition of almost identical events', complicating 'the teleological sense of an ending and convey the idea that no significant change is possible for the man and the child after the apocalypse'.[16] Similarly, Peter Boxall suggests that the novel, and the spoiled world that it evokes, is defined by an absence of 'any forward momentum, any future orientation'. 'Where the idea of a road offers the prospect of direction', notes Boxall, 'the road here has thickened, coagulated, like the cold oleaginous sea that breaks leadenly on the novel's grey shore'.[17] He also identifies a plethora of broken technologies of travel that clutter McCarthy's denatured landscape (in particular, an abandoned train and, finally, a wrecked ship). These relics of an age of speed are, to be sure, melancholy reminders that our own age may be vulnerable to the ravages of time and nature and that the human ingenuity that wrought such industrial marvels is not a transcendent, abstract virtue; it too might atrophy or be overwhelmed by bigger forces of destruction. Yet even if the novel views a world stripped of the kind of velocity that shapes its current readers' everyday life, it is not without energy or motion. The father and son do not surrender to the horrors of the road and, though it would take a rather skewed reading to support a 'survivalist' interpretation of the novel, this masculine dyad are resourceful in the face of hardship. They scavenge for useful scraps of lost technology, decant tiny residues of oil from abandoned gas stations to fuel their slut lamp and occasionally alleviate their constant hunger with rare discoveries of tinned food.

'Barren, silent, godless' is the depressing trinity of adjectives used to describe the terrain encountered by the man as he plans a journey south with his young son because 'there'd be no surviving another winter here' (*TR*, p. 2). They embark on their gruelling excursion to the coast, which the father emphasizes is vital for their survival, to cling to the conditions necessary for existence that the cold of the north is likely to obliterate. They are driven on by the indistinct, shaky hope of a better life. Maps and memories of maps are a recurrent trope in the narrative: as the boy studies their fragile paper guide, his father remembers that 'he'd pored over maps as a child, keeping one finger on the town where he'd lived' (*TR*, p. 194). The pair consult a 'tattered oil company roadmap' now deteriorated to the extent that it is 'just sorted into leaves and numbered with crayon'; the son, born after an era of government, is confused by lines on their fraying guide that his father names 'state roads' – 'they used to belong to the states. What used to be called the states' (*TR*, p. 43). In one sense, the absence of fixed names intensifies both the nightmarish logic of the narrative and the sense that the journey is not simply another trip into the heart of America but a more mythic venture. Although locations are occluded in the text, denying the reader a feeling of secure orientation, the boy learns 'the names of town and rivers by heart' and, in an echo of his father's early cartographic fascination, he sits 'by the fire at night with the pieces of the map across his knees' (*TR*, p. 229). Ashley Kunsa suggests that 'withholding place names' is part of 'a provocative rhetorical move that forces the reader to imagine new possibilities'; in this reading 'the burned out landscape, strangely, is a new if unlikely Eden awaiting once again those perfect names.'[18]

Although the topography of their journey is ambiguous, some critics map the walk in precise terms: for Amy Hungerford, for example, the pair set off from Appalachia and head for the Gulf of Mexico.[19] Shelly L. Rambo is similarly specific in proposing that the blighted territory evoked 'is post-apocalyptic Tennessee'.[20] Indeed, a characteristic of McCarthy's earlier fiction is its geography: his first four novels, from *The Orchard Keeper* (1965) to *Suttree* (1979), are set in Appalachia; a number of subsequent novels move westward.[21] Rambo, drawing on Dana Phillips's reading of McCarthy's brutal (anti) Western, *Blood Meridian* (1985), suggests that the possibility, or otherwise, of redemption – 'the concept of repairing or restoring what is damaged' – might be figured in the novelist's work in regionalist terms as a conflict between 'southern' and 'western' approaches.[22] The movement southwards tacitly invokes the literary memory of figures such as Flannery O'Connor, whose work abounds with specifically Christian (if very violent) redemptive imagery. Rambo notes, however, that this 'trajectory' competes with an alternative regionalist interpretation: to read McCarthy 'as a western writer' means that 'nihilistic images prevail'. The southern orientation of the character in *The Road*, she argues, is a literal and figurative 'return "home" for McCarthy', one that sends 'him back into the familiar frameworks of religious vocabulary; probing the question of a redemptive ending is, in this sense, warranted'.[23]

The novel is haunted by theological language. There is a radical difference between this journey in an ostensibly 'godless' environment with little more than a faltering hope of survival, on a road in which the man surmises that there are 'no godspoke men' and Thoreau's lofty belief that 'leisure, freedom, and independence [...] are the capital' in the 'profession' of a walker that 'comes only by the grace of God' and that 'requires a direct dispensation from Heaven' (*TR*, p. 32; *W*, p. 261). However, the father and son are represented, even as the narrative begins, as travellers with a holy burden: they are 'like pilgrims in a fable swallowed up and lost among the inward parts of some granitic beast' (*TR*, p. 1). The epithet 'pilgrims' is used four times in the novel and always in relation to a death-bound journey, including one instance late in the narrative in which detritus of the old world ('Electrical appliances, furniture. Tools') has been 'abandoned long ago by pilgrims enroute to their several and collective deaths' (*TR*, p. 213). This curious piece of allegorizing, early in the novel, draws on a distinctively American history of dissident religious migration and on the biblical narratives that those same European 'pilgrims' read so attentively. The 'granitic beast' that is the post-catastrophe world is figured in an idiom similar to the 'belly of the fish' in which a prophet is said to have spent 'three days and three nights' (Jonah 1. 17). Jonah's gastro-aquatic hell was, at least, temporary, whereas the brutalized, American landscape, cautiously navigated by father and son, seems endless; cyclical time itself has dissolved, as the only indicator of seasonal change is an intensifying cold. The landscape has been polluted beyond recognition and no longer has signs of the numinous, but the father reads the son as an act of divine speech: 'He said: If he is not the word of God God never spoke' (*TR*, p. 3). This improvised incarnational theology spills into a kind of polytheism: in one of the few conversations with another human being, the father asks the elderly Ely, a kind of existentialist seer who claims that he was 'always on the road', to think of his son as 'a god' (*TR*, pp. 179, 183). Although the mysterious interlocutor rejects this unorthodox speculation, his own utterances are stippled with theological paradoxes such as 'There is no God and we are his prophets' (*TR*, p. 181). The name Ely might be an allusion to the biblical Elijah but this incongruous mystic has little by way of good news or encouraging counsel. His role in the narrative is like an absurdist echo of symbolic figures, such as Evangelist, Hopeful and Mr Worldly Wise encountered by Christian during his walk from the City of Destruction in Bunyan's *The Pilgrim's Progress*. *The Road* does not articulate the theological certainty of Bunyan's allegory of the Christian life. However, the journey of father and son, like that of the eponymous pilgrim, is not simply a fight for life but a pursuit of goodness in a world that seems to mock this idea as a category error.

One of the axioms in a novel that is distinctively litanic in its multiple repetitions is idea that the father and son are 'the good guys' (for example, *TR*, pp. 81, 108, 136, 145, 148, 298). It is a soubriquet with which the child needs to be reassured and with which he challenges his father when the older man behaves in a way that seems less than ethically justified. The collision between the boy's innocent desire to uphold virtue and the grubby compromises necessary for survival might encourage interpretations of the journey as something more than a flight from death. In an alternative approach to those who locate *The Road* as a biblical novel, Lydia Cooper reads the novel more specifically as a rewriting of one of the paradigms of quest narrative, the story of the Holy Grail.[24] She notes that an early draft of the novel was titled *The Grail* and suggests that McCarthy makes similar use of Arthurian mythology as T. S. Eliot's apocalyptic *The Waste Land* (1922). For Cooper, the novel's 'evocations of those motifs suggest the power of the grail narrative as a metaphor for an extended study on a world seemingly "wounded" and "wasted" beyond recognition, possibly beyond salvation'.[25]

The dream of reaching the coast might be a reworked Arthurian quest or an echo of Christian pilgrimage, but the eventual arrival at the shoreline is, ostensibly at least, a disappointment. There is neither a transfiguring vision in which the world's former beauty is miraculously restored nor a neat deus ex machina in which the pair find safe haven and a functioning community. 'Cold. Desolate. Birdless', the ocean is dull, freezing and bereft of life (*TR*, p. 230). The encounter with the coast and its predictably wrecked cities is disheartening and it might have provided the frame for a particularly bleak ending. The end, however, is deferred: the shared journey continues until the father, wounded and in a deteriorating, sometimes semi-delirious state, eventually dies. The son, however, does not succumb to despair or to self-destruction with the pistol. Instead, in an uncanny twist, as the boy grieves, he is approached by a stranger who says that he too is a father, with a wife, son and daughter; he also tentatively invites the child to join their family. In a narrative that is characterized by grim disappointment, death and cannibalism, it is difficult not to read this situation as sceptically as the dead father might once have done. Yet, against the grain of survivalist suspicion, the boy makes a leap of faith: after an improvised and solitary funeral rite he rises and walks 'back out to the road' (*TR*, p. 306). The end of the boy's narrative is not quite an end: he joins this family – a group he trusts will honour their promise to be 'the good guys' and, like him, to be 'carrying the fire' (*TR*, p. 303). The last image that McCarthy grants of the boy is a familial scene and a shift from a father–son relationship to a maternal dynamic: the child is gathered in an embrace and greeted as a kind of lost son ('I am so glad to see you'), but it is also one of prayerful remembrance (*TR*, p. 306). Significantly, in a

novel defined by its sense that there is no era to come, an indistinct
but expanding future is implied in the description of the woman
and child 'sometimes' talking 'about God' and the boy's continuing 'to talk to his father' (*TR*, p. 306). The road has not reached a
deadly limit and the journey, it is implied, continues for the boy. The
death of the father does not negate their shared act of walking as
resistance.

Jim Crace's ninth full-length work of fiction, *The Pesthouse*,
shares a number of tropes, ideas and anxieties with *The Road* and,
coincidentally, was published only a few months after McCarthy's
novel. 'This used to be America, this river crossing in the ten-month
stretch of land, this sea-to-sea. It used to be the safest place on
earth', states the omniscient narrator, with a hymn-like cadence, of
the ruined, post-technological world.[26] America's former, but lost,
status as 'the safest place on earth' is resonant of post-9/11 fears
about national security. *The Pesthouse*, like *The Road*, constructs
a future version of the American landscape peopled by anxious,
imperilled pairs of walkers; the novel begins with two men walking
across a hostile, dangerous landscape in search of the coast, and in
both texts walking is an act of resistance against despair. The novels
feature vicious aggressors and idiosyncratically spiritual figures: in
lieu of a single, self-styled godless prophet, in Crace's world there
is a whole community of eccentric believers. The so-called Finger
Baptists are a monastic order who run an enclave symbolically
named the Ark and view metal and human industry as the source of
humanity's fall from grace.

Although *The Pesthouse* is ostensibly less bleak than *The Road* –
an odd thing to claim, perhaps, given that Crace's novel begins with
'six or seven hundred, at a guess' souls dying from asphyxiation in
their sleep – both feature characters who display resilience against
the temptation of despair (*TP*, p. 1). Resistance is not, in fact, futile
but might be found in the slow pace of a long walk. Late in the
narrative, a character who has already survived an apparently
fatal disease, evaded asphyxiation by natural gas (a fate that befell
her family) and escaped a murderous gang of thieves, becomes an
advocate for walking. 'We've walked before', she reminds another
survivor and companion on a journey across a ruined, dangerous
landscape (*TP*, p. 190). Like *The Road*, in which 'walk' and its cognates appear so frequently as to resemble a litany, *The Pesthouse* is
similarly concerned with walking and walkers.

The novel looks backwards to imagine a future that resembles a premodern epoch: this retrospective gaze is informed by a number of sources, and Philip Tew, in an early response to the novel, notes that Crace drew on reports of the Lewis and Clark expedition to the west of 1804–6, authorized by President Thomas Jefferson. However, notes Tew, 'the expansionary and idealized notions of America' or any 'notions of manifest destiny' perpetuated in the rhetoric of the third president of the United States, are countered in the novel 'by reversing modernity's myth of irreversible progress'.[27] The post-technological, post-federal America of Crace's novel is no agrarian utopia, but the rural and coastal environments are very different from the blighted, ash-covered landscape of *The Road*. If nature and culture are permanently wrecked in McCarthy's nightmare future, there are more signifiers of hope in *The Pesthouse*.

The central male protagonist, Franklin Lopez, bears a moniker from an older America. Although cultural memory has all but evaporated, this nominal allusion to Benjamin Franklin, inventor, printer, entrepreneur, statesman, revolutionary and Founding Father is a reminder of the former country of rugged individualism and experimental reason. Similarly, his older brother, Jackson bears the surname of the seventh president of the United States. America, however, has become a place to abandon in favour of mysterious new promised lands to the East; Europe, once the point of departure for adventure in the West is now the unfamiliar place of promise. Urban life is little more than legend for Franklin, who talks, with delight, of 'grand old towns – *cities* was the word that he'd heard' and an era in 'the people of America had been as numerous and healthy as fleas' (*TP*, p. 97). In fact, the brothers' lupine surname (Lopez is Spanish for wolf) associates them with the narrative of Romulus and Remus and the mythical foundation of Rome. The name is a quiet suggestion that a new civilization might be inaugurated by one of these brothers of the wolf.

The image of the present world as future folk rumour is less austere than the civic ruins of Crace's derelict nation, but it is, nevertheless, an estranging vision of metropolitan vitality. In common with McCarthy's fable, it is never clear why civilization, as we know it, came to an end. However, the former 'safest' (and most powerful) 'place on earth' is represented as a 'carcass' that opportunists will abandon once they have 'picked' it 'clean' (*TP*, p. 10). This language of aggressive consumption has a muted political resonance and might suggest one of the reasons for the nation's fall from economic and technological superiority.

The novel mischievously inverts the tradition of locating America as the final destiny of those seeking refuge, justice and belonging, particularly in the myth of the West. One character reflects on the vague hope that the 'best future' is to be found 'beyond the ocean' and 'happiness was in the east. Wasn't that what everyone believed?' (*TP*, p. 167). Franklin, like his brother, begins the novel motivated by 'hopes of getting free from America' (*TP*, p. 13). Franklin displays his self-reliant credentials when he decides to 'put his doubts behind him and concentrate only on the journey' (*TP*, p. 80). His journey, from West to East, is a reversal of the classic pilgrim and frontier journey across the continent. It is also an echo of an earlier narrative of desert exile; Franklin, like Moses, becomes a reluctant rebel and leader of a small family group wandering across the land. Indeed the word 'exodus' is used to describe this cross-continent migration (*TP*, p. 103).

If decelerated, ambulatory movement shapes the narrative, it is also punctuated by significant moments of stillness and encounters with places of rest and recuperation. The titular dwelling place, a 'little boulder Pesthouse above the valley', is a rough, temporary abode for the sick and dying; the basic shelter is a place of exile for residents of Ferrytown who show symptoms of 'flux' – an 'unwelcome' and 'intermittent visitor' – associated with travellers and feared by the community (*TP*, pp. 19, 20). Crace imagines a world in which walkers are associated with both the hope of survival and feared as a source of disease. Early in the novel, Margaret, whose father has already died from the disease is sent to the crude hut, her hair shorn, to await a lonely, but inevitable, end. Franklin, limping, takes refuge from the rain and, despite the risks of infection, stays with Margaret through the long dark night of her fever. In one moment of striking tenderness, Franklin massages her feet as an act of healing; his tradition believes that 'diseases depart the body through the feet' (*TP*, p. 47). This moment, one of mutual embarrassment and bonding between strangers for whom physical contact, in ordinary circumstances, might be regarded with suspicion or as breaking sexual taboos, takes on an anomalous spiritual aura as a kind of reworking of the episode, narrated in all four canonical gospels, in which a woman anoints Jesus's feet with lavish perfume (Matthew 26. 6–13; Mark 14. 3–9; Luke 7. 36–50; John 12. 1–8). The makeshift bothy, a dwelling that is barely

distinguishable from its organic surroundings, echoes other con-
cealed locations in Crace's fiction. Like Jesus's cave in *Quarantine*,
for example, it is a zone of intimacy, one in which life encounters
the near presence of mortality. Margaret, who did not expect to
live, experiences a near miraculous recovery, but the novel, in a
sinister rhyme, couples resurrection with the sudden death of the
town from which she was banished. The shared grief of this exiled
daughter of Ferrytown and Jackson, whose brother also perished
in the settlement, fortifies their provisional bond and a new walking partnership is created.

The long-distance walk east is scarcely less dangerous in Crace's
novel than the southbound hike in McCarthy's chastening narrative. The reversal of the classic migration from east to west is
one in which survival is far from assured: the 'wayside going east'
is 'already littered with the melancholy camps and the shallow
graves [...] of those whose bodies couldn't take the journey' (*TP*,
p. 7). However, a significant difference is that the road is constructed
as a place of possibility as well as threat. Early in the novel Jackson,
full of masculine bluster, speaks of 'the wisdom of the road' that
dictates risks must be taken and that 'only the crazy make it to the
coast' (*TP*, pp. 8–9). This soubriquet, repeated a number of times,
reads to me rather like an excessively solemn tag for a spectacu-
larly violent Hollywood version of the novel. However, Caroline
Edwards describes these repetitions as the narrative's 'mantra'; we
might read this rhythmic, semi-comic reiteration as an equivalent
to the litanic qualities of *The Road*.[28] Later in the novel, surviving walkers continue on the road to the coast and encounter 'the
Dreaming highway', the remains of a near mythical road that is
supposed to lead to 'Achievement Valley and a prospect of The Last
Farewell' (*TP*, p. 38). These names also sound like parodies of the
nation's Puritan and Enlightenment eras. However, this reminder
of a lost world is also a conduit away from an apparently dying
nation. The shape of the road defies nature in the way that it 'hur-
tled forward, all symmetry and parallels' and is a trace of the era of
automobile travel and human ingenuity (*TP*, p. 94). This relic of the
open road is a kind of post-apocalyptic version of Percy Shelley's
sonnet–hymn to the death of empires, 'Ozymandias' (1818): a 'traveller from an antique land' describes 'two vast and trunkless legs
of stone' in a desert as all that remain of the tyrannical ruler (ll.
1–2). The 'dreaming highway' is a similarly ironic, and perhaps

melancholy, testimony to a fallen republic whose ideal of freedom ultimately depended on oil, cars and the dream of mobility.

Margaret's intuitive suspicion of this old road, nurtured by the folklore of Ferrytown, is vindicated. Bandits ambush the walkers and Franklin is enslaved; Margaret's escape to the bizarre refuge of the Ark, where she sojourns for months and nurtures an adopted child, is a significant digression in the pilgrimage to the coast. However, following another attack by violent outlaws, the unlikely couple are reunited: in this instance, Margaret becomes Franklin's saviour, and the journey resumes. However, in another parallel with *The Road*, the eventual arrival at the coast is something of a disappointment, the ocean a negative 'surprise' as it appears, to Margaret, to be 'leaden [...] and lacking in expression' (*TP*, p. 196). Franklin also experiences a moment of epiphany: the ocean is transfigured from a source of mysterious potential into 'an obstacle' rather than 'a route to liberty'. Their shared rejection of the world beyond brings about a renewed myth of America as a place of belonging, a place that Franklin, in an echo of his revolutionary namesake, believes in as a place of possibility: 'His dream was not the future but the past. Some land, a cabin and a family. A mother waiting on the stoop' (*TP*, p. 206). This image of agricultural and domestic harmony echoes, consciously or otherwise, the idealistic image of America as a 'sweet mother' in Jean Hector St John de Crèvecœur's *Letters from an American Farmer* (1782). Franklin's decision not to abandon the nation is coupled with another ambulatory motif in a dream that he shares with Margaret: 'I've dreamed of walking back onto our land, poor though it is, and taking care of Ma. Those are my biggest dreams' (*TP*, p. 228). Indeed, the end of the novel fuses a motif of stasis and stability with one of walking and return. The novel's final journey is a return west in a repetition of archetypal 'American' journey: Franklin, Margaret and their adopted child, Jackie, arrive at the Pesthouse, the place of the initial encounter in which the woman's 'eyes had almost closed for good' (*TP*, p. 250). The adults renovate the place whose original purpose was as a waiting room for death and render it a dwelling of possibility. The rediscovery of Margaret's 'lucky things in a cedar box' includes coins 'from a past when Abraham sat on his great stone seat and the eagle spread its wings' (*TP*, pp. 253–4). This fragment of America's history suggests an ideal of democratic belonging. Indeed, the final image of the novel is of Crace's unconventional holy family improvising a new life in the land 'that used to be America':

> The couple knew that they only had to find their strength. And then – imagine it – they could begin the journey west again. They could. They could imagine striking out to claim a piece of long abandoned land and making home in some old place, some territory begging to be used. Going westward, they go free (*TP*, p. 255).

We might read this domestic idyll, and the promise of westward movement, as a conservative gesture. However, the end of the novel credibly embodies what Edwards describes as the novel's 'pastoral post-apocalypticism – replete with its microtopian familial communities'.[29] The protagonists do not simply survive; they flourish in a land that is being nourished by the patterns of natural rebirth. It also an end that promises a future: one in which, despite their current domestic contentment, they will continue their journey on foot.

Franklin, Margaret and Jackie join a long tradition of defiant American walkers, sojourners in fact and fiction, from Thoreau and Solnit to Kerouac's Dharma Bums and McCarthy's beleaguered father and son. According to Frédéric Gros, walking facilitates a kind of transcendent alternative to the imposition of coercive social identities: 'The freedom in walking lies in not being anyone; for the walking body has no history, it is just an eddy in the stream of immemorial life'.[30] Walking is sometimes a matter of survival and a way of rediscovering our bodies and minds. However, more than that, it is also an act of rebellion against a variety of tyrannies including the insidious idea that speed is the true index of freedom.

6

Keep watching: Spectacle, rebellion and apocalyptic rites of passage

In Nick Hornby's comic–apocalyptic short story, *Otherwise Pandemonium* (2005), a fifteen-year-old boy buys a second-hand VCR player and accidentally discovers that it has the capacity, via the fast forward button, to show the future. In typically laconic fashion, Hornby's anonymous Holden Caulfield-like narrator witnesses a coming crisis and the end of the world as mediated by second-hand, already-obsolete technology. The world to which this time-traversing box of tricks magically gives him access (as well as, in a sneaky nod to *Back to the Future II* [1989], knowledge of the outcomes of forthcoming sports matches) is ultimately one of endless, terrifying news broadcasts, 'no *Buffy*, no sports, no nothing' like 'the days after 9/11, if you can remember that long ago', and then an apparently endless 'Time of the Static' when everything, including even network television, seems to be over.[1] He is, however, pleased to be able to tell the reader that the prophetic bit of audiovisual equipment helped him to get a girlfriend because 'knowing the world is going to end makes you a lot less nervous about the whole dating thing' (*OP*, p. 20). 'Otherwise Pandemonium' is a concise, self-conscious pastiche of rites of passage narratives, one that draws on adolescent anxieties, yearning and contempt for a dishonest and disappointing adult world. However, instead of simply becoming what he calls 'a Stephen King-type story [...] with a really fucking scary ending', it is partly a meditation on the speculative optimism of school days that he realizes are 'all about anticipation' (*OP*, p. 15). The anonymous narrator believes that the end is coming not because he has a sense of incipient political catastrophe from his everyday encounters with the world, in spite of a hazy memory of 9/11, but because he has seen it in filmed form. However, where the narrator is finally resigned to the coming future, a passive witness to what will be, other contemporary narratives, particularly YA fiction, locate teenagers as figures of agency and potential political change. Hornby's story, layered with allusions to pop culture including clairvoyant figures in King's Gothic fiction, televised vampire zombies, *The Catcher in the Rye*, *Friends*, *Sabrina the Teenage Witch*, *The Breakfast Club* and *The Little House on the Prairie*, is also oddly prescient of the focus on media and surveillance as fundamental to many recent apocalyptic narratives of teenage self-discovery. The world that comes after the end of the news broadcasts might mutate into any one of the ruined, dystopian landscapes of future America that have become so extraordinarily marketable in the last twenty years or so.

The post-apocalyptic and dystopian genres are often marked by poisoned, denatured landscapes, food shortages and ravaged futures, but they provide a fertile environment for YA fiction and its narration of the threshold between childhood and the responsibilities of adult life. Post-apocalyptic environments have long been a key part of novels aimed at a teenage readership and, as Kimberley Reynolds observes, 'very few children's books since the 1980s have offered anything other than dystopian visions of the future'.[2] Robert C. O'Brien's *Z for Zachariah* (1974) and Robert Swindell's *Brother in the Land* (1984), for example, narrate coming-of-age experiences in brutal post-apocalyptic worlds; young people on the brink of adulthood have no choice but to assert themselves in dangerous milieus in which there is neither legal protection nor saving guidance from benign guardians. These children have to become their own protectors when older mentors prove, at best, highly ambiguous figures whose motivations are equivocal. This chapter focuses on the representation of violent rites of passage in the first instalment of Suzanne Collins's 'The Hunger Games' (2008–10) trilogy in comparison with the opening volumes of Veronica Roth's 'Divergent' (2011–14) and James Dashner's 'The Maze Runner' (2009–11). Each of these narrative sequences invoke tropes of observation and spectacle – young people are required

to perform ingenious and frequently violent acts in order to survive, while an adult world, with a variety of ostensible and tacit
motivations, watches. Collins, Roth and Dashner's novels are set
in surveillance societies; a crucial part of their dystopian status is
communicated by a reliance on a technology of observation that is
designed to contain dissent. All three texts also revise aspects of the
traditional bildungsroman; many motifs of the self-development
novel, including romantic awakening and disappointment, loss,
exile, grief and return, punctuate recent dystopia. Indeed, in her
comparative reading of the 'rebellious subjectivities' of Collins's
and Roth's young female protagonists, Miranda A. Green-Bartreet
identifies Charlotte Brontë's Jane Eyre, particularly her early, tentative acts of resistance as a crucial 'predecessor to other young
female protagonists who desire independence'.[3] Similarly, in their
introduction to *Contemporary Dystopian Fiction for Young Adults*
(2013), Balaka Basu, Katherine Broad and Carrie Hintz not only
argue that 'YA dystopias recapitulate the conventions of the classic
Bildungsroman, using political strife and, environmental disaster
or other forms of turmoil as the catalyst for achieving adulthood',
but also assert that 'the ability of the protagonist to really envision
something new might [...] be circumscribed by the conventions and
forms of the *Bildungsroman* itself'.[4] In early episodes in each of the
novels discussed in this chapter, the central protagonist deliberately
crosses a line that simultaneously intensifies the visibility of their
singular, heroic status and makes them more vulnerable to attack.
The adult world is frequently represented as corrupt or compro-
mised, but the characters are still seeking to take on the responsibilities of maturity – often with the disclaimer that their era will not
succumb to the manifold moral failings of previous generations.
Critiques of YA fiction are frequently drawn into debates about
ethical commitment and the responsibilities of the author.[5] Brian
Jansen, discussing the slippery problem of 'postmodern ethics' in
relation to 'The Hunger Games', suggests that this challenge is one
'felt perhaps even more acutely in the study of the YA novel because
of a temptation (whether misguided or not) to view the genre as a
didactic, pedagogical, or "moral" tool'.[6] The chapter considers the
ethical implications of narratives ostensibly written for a teenage
readership that pivot on plots in which young people are subject to
horrific violence, exploitation and manipulation. It also addresses
alternative political readings of these dystopian–apocalyptic

stories: are they subversive or reassuring, quietly conformist fables disguised as rebellious social critiques?

'What kind of a world allowed people to let kids live like this?' This innocent but anguished question is part of the interior monologue of Thomas, the amnesiac central protagonist of *The Maze Runner*, but it has a wider resonance.[7] That the version of future earth of Dashner's series is so hostile and perilous should not be much of a surprise; it is part of a literary tradition in which adult authority is typically dangerous, despotic and deceitful. However, if a corrupted hierarchy is often to blame for the turbulent, horrific state of the world, the dystopian genre often displaces its focus on to a violent struggle between rival children. The trilogies by Collins, Roth and Dashner resonate with the anxieties of William Golding's genre-defining *Lord of the Flies* (1954) – a kind of *ur-text* for YA post-apocalyptic fiction – in which a group of schoolboys, survivors, during an unspecified time of war, of a plane crash on a remote island in the Pacific Ocean, capitulate to aggression, superstition and cruelty after their provisional attempts to run a peaceable, free society fail. Golding's novel is informed by debates about the relationship between nature and nurture and a theological disquiet about the proclivity of humanity, even in its ostensibly most innocent phase, for evil and, in particular, violence. Two children, the innocent but rational Piggy and the mystically inclined Simon, are killed as a number of the boys succumb to superstition, fear and territorial aggression. Order is restored only when colonial, military adult society, in the form of a British naval officer, arrives on the island and the children, none of them older than young adolescents, confronted with authority, return, shocked, to their previous states. Collins, Roth and Dashner also focus on young people – children and teenagers – who are trapped in isolated environments in which a ruthless logic of self-preservation prospers and are forced into aggressive, occasionally murderous encounters with their peers.

Collins's sequence has a global readership, but is informed by a number of specifically American anxieties. Its fictional nation, Panem, is a heterotopic near-future fascistic state that 'rose up out of the ashes of a place that was once called North America'.[8] The novel is inflected with questions about class, justice and the tacit violence of capitalist, competitive society: Panem has not experienced civil war in three-quarters of a century, but it supposedly maintains its peace and prosperity by annually forcing a number of children, primarily of its poorest families, to fight to the death. The series of environmental catastrophes that destroyed the former nation are enumerated in a yearly act of storytelling by the district mayor ('the disasters, the droughts, the storms, the fires, the encroaching seas that swallowed up so much of the land, the brutal war for what little sustenance remained', *HG*, p. 21). However, Collins's narrative, in common with both *The Road* (2006) and *The Pesthouse* (2007), is far less interested in the original causes of the old world's collapse than in the politics of the new order. The overt symbolism indicates concerns about the fragility of the nation's continued prosperity, status as a world power and the future of its foundational commitments to 'life, liberty and the pursuit of happiness' as articulated in the Declaration of Independence (1776). Indeed, as the trilogy develops, elements of a rebellion against the autocratic regime aim 'to form a republic', a system of democratically elected representatives, in the style of Panem's 'ancestors'.[9] Collins's imagined post-apocalyptic society makes strategic use of both ancient tradition and the nation's history. Although Panem is a society projected many decades in the world's future, its devious strategy of social control via entertainment resonates with concerns that date back to ancient Rome. The name puns on two terms – Pan American, suggesting a collective of nations based in the Americas – and the Roman satirist's Juvenal's phrase 'panem et circenses' – 'bread and circuses' or 'bread and games' (*M*, p. 221). This ancient epithet was used to describe government that ruled by distraction. The precise geography of Panem is not specified, but its Capitol – the centre of wealth and fiercely protected power – is located somewhere in the Rocky Mountains. Katniss Everdeen, the narrator of 'The Hunger Games' trilogy, is a smart and self-reliant sixteen-year-old hunter who emerges as a key figure in the long and bloody fight against oppression. Her charisma, resilience and rebelliousness are manipulated for political gain by both conservative and revolutionary forces, but she, and the narrative of which she is a part, defies dominant models of both femininity and adulthood to forge an alternative mode of living.

Divergent, like *The Hunger Games*, is narrated by a sceptical sixteen-year-old who, like Katniss, is subjected to state-authorized violence. Beatrice 'Tris' Prior lives in a future version of Chicago, now a semiderelict and isolated metropolis. This dystopian society has a family resemblance to Panem: for example, social stratification, as in the world of 'The Hunger Games', is strict but managed via tribal groupings that are divided according to four dominant personality types: Abnegation (characterized by selflessness), Candor (honesty), Dauntless (bravery) and Erudite (intelligence). Children of this quartet of factions are schooled together until the age of sixteen when they are tested by the authorities and, in a public ritual that echoes both Panem's 'day of reaping' and, more comically, the sorting hat from the 'Harry Potter' novels, must make a final choice about their future faction.[10] This choice is definitive – if a candidate fails to make the grade they risk ending up 'factionless' and destitute; the individual becomes part of an abject class, abandoned to eke out an existence on the fringes of society. At her aptitude test – a formalized, drug-induced trial via dream – Tris discovers that she has 'equal aptitude' for three of the factions (Abnegation, Dauntless, Erudite) and that she is a rare type of person 'called … *Divergent*'.[11] Such varied abilities, however, are not regarded as a stroke of amazing luck in Tris's society. The 'Divergent' status is a social curse, one that her compassionate assessor warns her not to tell 'anyone, *ever*, no matter what happens' (*D*, p. 23). Tris is already privately ambivalent about such rigid group identity and, before the aptitude tests that are supposed to be an indication of a student's likely tribal destination, she recognizes that it is 'Faction Custom' that 'dictate[s] even idle behavior and supersede[s] individual preference', but accepts that her peers 'can't defy the norms of their faction any more than I can' (*D*, p. 8). Those who conform enjoy relatively peaceful, prosperous lives. However, the ostensibly idealistic aims of the system conceal a manipulative hierarchy and power-hungry leaders who punish dissent and, in particular, who will not tolerate 'divergence', the rare idiosyncrasy of displaying multiple, apparently competing characteristics. The sequels reveal that the city has been quarantined from the rest of the nation as part of a failed utopian genetic experiment. Roth's narrative thrives on ambivalence regarding the individualist ethics of contemporary culture. Tris's realization that she is somehow different from her peers is typical of many pop culture narratives of self-discovery: Harry Potter, the bullied orphan, discovers that he is the son of murdered, magical parents and that he has inherited their powers; Luke Skywalker is told that he is not just a farm boy and that his yearning to leave his dull, dry planet behind in search of adventure is the work of a mystical phenomenon known as the force.

'Divergent' limns a rigidly hierarchical world: those who are part of the established factions live in relative comfort and with a degree of choice, provided that it conforms to their 'chosen' (and fixed) group identity. The city, 'a patchwork of new, clean buildings and old, crumbling ones' is not obviously post-apocalyptic and might be any early twenty-first-century north American metropolis in which there is both a figurative divide and geographical proximity between luxurious prosperity and grinding poverty (D, p. 23). By contrast, in 'The Hunger Games' the Capitol and the poorer Districts are much more disparate. Tris is a guide to the reader and describes the city's abandoned, disintegrating quarters as 'places where the road has completely collapsed, revealing sewer systems and empty subways [...] and places that stink so powerfully of sewage and trash that I have to plug my nose' (D, p. 24). These neighbourhoods are not abandoned but home to the city's underclass, 'where the faction-less live. Because they failed to complete initiation into whatever faction they chose, they live in poverty, doing the work no one else wants to do [...] they get food and clothing, but, as my mother says, not enough of either' (D, p. 24). The 'factionless' are the equivalent to the working-class people of the Districts in 'The Hunger Games'. Tris, unlike Katniss, already belongs to a relatively privileged elite. She risks losing the kind of security and stability that Katniss has never known. The leaders of Roth's world are covertly dedicated to preserving the social privilege of those who fit into pre-ordained categories and who willingly accept their fixed identities. This pseudo-utopianism has a high cost for the community of the 'factionless' whose hidden labour sustains the social advantages of the factions. Tris's awakening, in the first book at least, is primarily to the tacit violence of the system as it impacts on her own life and those of her friends and family. Her encounter with a factionless man early in the narrative is figured as one of threat; he is predatory and unpleasant. To 'defy the norms' of a faction is social death. 'To live factionless is not just to live in poverty and discomfort; it is to live divorced from society, separated from the most important thing in life: community' (D, p. 19). Although Divergent is fascinated by the dynamics of the outsider hero, its narrator is not immune to the allure of shared identity. Young members of her chosen faction have a distinct fashion aesthetic ('they are pierced, tattooed and

black-clothed') that sounds less like the future than an iteration
of retro, 1990s Gothic chic. Tattoos, in particular, become a vital
marker of belonging: the Dauntless woman who is Tris's aptitude
tester has 'a tattoo on the back of her neck, a black-and-white hawk
with a red eye'; the elaborate body art provides an opportunity for
Tris's inquisitive nature to emerge, a trait that is not associated with
the modest Abnegation faction (D, p. 11). Basu, for example, critiques the novel's ostensible defence of diversity by suggesting that
though Divergent 'appears to be positioned as a warning against
the seductive pleasures of being categorized and classified [...] the
novel tacitly promotes the ideals of correctable corruption, not the
product of a fundamentally misconceived idea'.[12] The politics of
individualism versus those of community are a long-standing feature of American debate – at least as old as Puritan settlement – and
Divergent echoes this long, unresolved dialectic.

James Dashner's series shares much in common with both 'The
Hunger Games' and 'Divergent', but 'The Maze Runner' has a more
ambiguous, secretive geography. The first novel is primarily set in a
subterranean, artificially created world known to its amnesiac, adolescent inhabitants as 'the Glade'. The invisible gods of the Glade
(nicknamed 'the Creators' by the boys) deliver food via a metal
elevator known as 'the Box' that regularly delivers new inmates,
similarly confused and stripped of memory. The forty or so, initially all male, 'Gladers', some of whom have lived in this strange
place for two years, have no clear memories of who they are or the
reasons for their incarceration. Even their given names – the only
personal detail that they clearly remember – are false. At the heart
of the Glade is an elaborate and shifting maze that may, or may not,
lead to an escape. The children are subjected to a series of complex,
life-threatening tasks whilst being watched by a distant, mysterious
and authoritarian elite who, like the leaders of the Capitol and the
Factions, claim their work is vital to the future security of the state.
It is ultimately revealed, in the sequels, that the 'real world' above
the man-made Glade was devastated by solar flares causing incalculable environmental damage. This natural catastrophe was followed
by an anthropogenic apocalypse: governments conspired to release
a virus in order to limit population; in the traditions of classic SF,
this experiment was far more lethal than its architects intended and
its effects turned the infected ('Cranks') into cannibals. The Gladers
are part of an experiment by a secret organization that is seeking

to find a cure for the so-called Flare: teenagers and children, many of whom appear to be immune to the virus, are taken from their parents at an early age and, their memories wiped, they are placed in stressful and sometimes deadly circumstances and observed by a group of adult scientists. At the end of the novel, when some of the group fight their way out of the Glade and defeat the apparently absurd, unsolvable Maze, a nameless 'Creator' tells the grieving, angry survivors that 'one day' they will be 'grateful for what we've done for you' (*MR*, p. 352). The self-justification sounds uncannily like the kind of rationale for physical abuse articulated by vicious schoolmasters in Victorian novels.

Thomas's appearance at the beginning of the narrative is swiftly followed by the arrival of another new Glader: this unscheduled delivery breaks the pattern by introducing, for the first and last time, a young woman into the exclusively male world. Her fellow internees treat Teresa, like Thomas, with suspicion. The two are interlopers whose presence in the narrative overturns the stability of the world they enter – the pair challenge the dominance of the oldest, strongest leaders ('the Keepers') and shake up the atmosphere of complacent despair that has settled on a culture. The pair discover that they are able to communicate via telepathy and realize that they knew each other in their pre-amnesia life. This uncanny element of the narrative implies a supernatural, Gothic dimension to the world of the Glade. However, this too is rationalized as their shared extrasensory perception, it is ultimately revealed, is the product of invasive technological tampering by scientists. The adult world has granted a temporary form of magical connection but with a twist: they can be controlled. The Gladers' regular public meetings – 'Gatherings' – to discuss ways of surviving and any new crisis are particularly reminiscent of the impromptu assemblies interspersed throughout *Lord of the Flies*. Like Golding's remote island, the Glade is a kind of carceral Eden – it is even referred to as a potential 'paradise' – in which the homosocial community is both constantly at threat and, provided the rules are followed, secure (*MR*, p. 197).

Each of these post-apocalyptic narratives deploy the folk-tale trope of exile from home: Katniss, Tris and Thomas are alienated from friends and family. The desire for a return to domestic stability has distinctive connotations for a post-9/11 American readership: Chuck, the youngest and most vulnerable in *The Maze*

Runner, is homesick for a place of which he has no secure or strong memories. Thomas's anger with an enemy he knows nothing about suggests a darker side to this nostalgia, and Chuck is figured as an emblem of the wrecked family unit that is sacred to the national imaginary. He 'hated the people who'd taken this poor, innocent kid from his family [...] He wanted them dead, tortured, even. He wanted Chuck to be happy' (*MR*, p. 192). In a disturbing association, unchecked desire for revenge is conflated with the future felicity of a child: 'I swear I'll get you home', Thomas promises the younger boy (*MR*, p. 193).

There is a crucial difference between Golding's relatively conservative, if cruel, narrative world and contemporary survivalist scenarios: the appalling circumstances and violent outcomes in twenty-first-century dystopias are not an accident. Adult characters in these fictions are neither primarily last-minute saviours of vulnerable young people nor shocked witnesses of their misery. They are, in fact, the initiators and architects of intentional suffering that is inflicted for a variety of deceitful versions of the 'greater good'. Sacrifice of children or adolescents, observes Susan Louise Stewart, 'is frequently woven into novels of dystopia [...] it is often what makes them dystopian narratives'. The dystopian ideology is 'even more reprehensible when the sacrifice results from adults' mistakes, benefits adults, or is enforced by adults'.[13] An economy in which children are either scapegoated or submitted to callous utilitarian experiment is fundamental to the societies imagined by Collins, Roth and Dashner. A question that haunts the reader of such dystopias is whether these worlds are either speculative visions that imagine far-future consequences of human behaviour or, most disturbingly, allegorical narratives that represent aspects of contemporary reality. Karl Hand, in a fierce and boldly theological–political interpretation of 'The Hunger Games', argues that to read the sequence as a future dystopia is a mistake: as contemporary readers, he observes, 'we know that young people are caught up in terror, war, genocide, slavery, and oppression, and we take some comfort in the fact that, unlike the citizens of Panem, we are not "entertained" by it.' For Hand, Collins's sequence is 'a self-directed satire. Panem is the present world, presented to us without our ideological obfuscation.'[14] This reading risks missing some of the trilogy's political uncertainties, discussed in more detail in this chapter's conclusion, but it also usefully implies that interpretative strategies are vital in YA fiction's status as a resource for social change.

'The Hunger Games' splits its post-catastrophe world between the two classic shapes taken in many future-vision fictions: one so devoid of technology, privilege and basic freedoms as to resemble the deep past; the other replete with ingenious technologies and post-human enhancements, but also lacking in true liberty. The first of these twin types of dystopia is embodied by the twelve official 'districts' in which the workers of Panem dwell. The people of most of these strictly demarcated neighbourhoods are frequently on the verge of starvation and rely on meagre rations from a parsimonious state to supplement their own strictly controlled earnings; trade and entertainment are also rigorously policed; daily life in these exploited regions resembles the appalling conditions suffered by rural and urban nineteenth-century working-class communities. However, by contrast, the Capitol, the decadent centre of Collins's dystopian dream resembles what Veronica Hollinger has named 'the endless endtimes of the future-present': a luxurious city in which excessive consumption and continuous, gaudy entertainments are paid for by a subjugated workforce who have no political rights, no basic freedoms and no representation; in other words, Collins's Capitol is not unlike the most prosperous parts of twenty-first-century civilization.[15] This fortress-like, metropolitan locus of authority exerts sovereignty over its districts, each responsible for a different form of work, including mining, fishing and agriculture. The number of districts echoes the original thirteen British colonies founded between 1607 and 1632, prior to the American War of Independence. The dictatorial system of Panem headed by President Snow – very much one of 'taxation without representation' – is also a reminder of a pre-revolutionary era in which a distant king controlled the lives of his subjects via economic subjugation.

Throughout 'The Hunger Games' sequence Katniss is figured as a resourceful problem-solver, a young woman who remains hungry for justice even after traumatic experiences that inflict physical damage and enduring psychological wounds. She is independent and, from the earliest pages in the narrative, is represented as an outsider, a skilled hunter who is ready to transgress social rules. In the opening chapter, Katniss deftly slips under the electrified fence that surrounds District Twelve, a mining province in the region once

known as Appalachia, in pursuit of food; the chapter tells the reader
that 'trespassing' in these fertile woodlands 'is illegal and carries the
severest penalties'; it also reveals that its heroine is both highly pro-
ficient with her prohibited bow and arrow and that she lives in an
oppressive world in which any hint of political sedition, even from
children, is contained with violence. She possesses both sardonic
wit ('District Twelve. Where you can starve to death in safety') and
a world-weary maturity that ensures she knows not to speak openly
'about the people who rule our country' (HG, pp. 6–7). The idea
of opposition to the ruling elite is also articulated in the novel's
first chapter: Katniss's friend and fellow hunter, Gale, believes that
'it's to the Capitol's advantage to have us divided among ourselves'
(HG, p. 14). In his ethically oriented reading of the sequence, and
this early transgression in particular, Jansen identifies Collins's
strong-willed narrator as 'a born crosser of borders in a number
of senses' and as 'a potent symbol of the schism between ethical
rules and an innate moral urge.'[16] This is an apt way to describe a
young woman who is ultimately required by the vicious laws of her
land to fight for her life and, after her own recognition that these
laws cannot be endured, becomes a revolutionary who uses her
skills to fight for freedom. In a sense, she becomes a youthful post-
apocalyptic embodiment of an older American revolutionary tradition: she goes a step further than Henry David Thoreau's peaceable
version of 'civil disobedience' and her own form of 'resistance' to
government is one that fights injustice in a literal sense; by the
third novel, Mockingjay (2010), Katniss has become a fully fledged
freedom fighter, a leading figure in the uprising against the corrupt
and oppressive dictatorial administration. She remains, however,
sceptical of all externally imposed authorities, particularly those
who treat individual lives as expendable in the name of a supposed
greater good or ultimate justice.

Spectacular sacrifice is the basis of public order, and a way of
repressing any thoughts of a future rebellion, in the dystopian
future America of Collins's trilogy: approximately seventy-five
years before the events of the first novel, a period in the nation's
history now known as the 'Dark Days' witnessed a popular uprising that resulted in a new 'Treaty of Treason' ostensibly designed to
'guarantee peace' (HG, p. 21). The titular 'Hunger Games' emerged
as the fascistic government's sadistic penalty against the prov-
inces: every district is required to send two children, a boy and a

girl, aged between twelve and eighteen as a 'tribute' to fight to the death in an enclosed arena, full of traps and treacherous devices planted by 'Gamemakers'; the manipulated environment also abounds with poisonous plants and animals that have been genetically modified to intensify their predatory instincts. This abhorrent event is no secret but the very foundation of modern Panem. The bloody annual contest is explicitly both punishment and reward – 'a time for repentance and thanks', one official piously suggests (*HG*, p. 22). The televised games are Panem's most successful instrument of political coercion: for the wealthy residents of the Capitol, the spectacle is a statement of the power of their class, an escapist narrative of vicarious violence and a reminder that their privilege is contingent rather than inherent; its continuation depends on the blood of the young, poor and vulnerable; for everybody else, they reinforce a sense of helplessness and discourage any thoughts of a second uprising. The mythology of Panem is one in which the 'shining Capitol ringed by thirteen districts [...] brought peace and prosperity to its citizens' (*HG*, p. 21). However, Katniss, and the novel of which she is a part, is savvy about the nature of frequently iterated, public narratives: shared histories ostensibly bind a community together whilst implicitly keeping subjects in their place. She already has every reason to resent the status quo: her father was killed in a mining accident, there is no form of support from central or local government and the family is close to starvation when she steps into the role of provider.

Questions of agency are central to both the bildungsroman tradition and twenty-first-century YA fiction: how can an individual assert their liberty in an era of oppression? Katniss not only tells her own story, but also takes control of it in highly risky fashion. *The Hunger Games* begins on 'the day of reaping' – an annual event in which the name of every child in the districts of Panem, aged between twelve and eighteen, is entered into a public lottery in order to select 'tributes' to compete in the bloody titular contest. The far from democratic system is stacked against the dispossessed members of the social order and encourages the poorest children to risk entering their names multiple times because each entry is rewarded with extra food. The brutal contest is outlandish and improbable even when judged by the bizarre standards of reality television. However, from another perspective this may not be entirely unfamiliar to twenty-first-century readers. We live, after all, in a world where refugees drown in the oceans, preferring to take a chance for freedom rather than accept starvation or tyranny at home, whilst the privileged world watches, indifferent, numb or scandalized but, apparently, powerless.

The seventy-fourth Hunger Games is the first 'reaping' for Primrose, Katniss's twelve-year-old sister, and against the statistical odds but in line with ruthless narrative logic, her name is selected. Katniss, who has already been introduced as a accomplished tracker – she trespasses in the wilderness on the perimeter of her town, fishes and has killed a lynx – bravely swaps places with her sister. This deed involves public proclamation ('I volunteer as tribute!' *HG*, p. 26) and is likely to lead to her death, since the victors are almost always from the wealthy districts. In *Divergent*, Tris Prior, like Katniss, instigates her story by making an unpredictable and hazardous decision in a public ritual. She shocks her family, part of the Abnegation tribe, by choosing Dauntless, swapping a way of life marked by near monastic self-denial for bold, self-assertive courage. This decision precipitates immediate physical risk – some Dauntless initiates don't even survive the journey to their new quarters, others are disqualified in the early weeks of training, one is partially blinded by a rival, another commits suicide – and the likelihood of lifelong alienation from her parents. Green-Barteet reads the 'defiant behavior' of Katniss and Tris as the cause of their becoming 'self-governing subjects' rather than 'remaining passive objects [...] controlled by their societies'.[17] These rebellious decisions by teenage women have bigger narrative consequences: they are not simply moments of personal crisis but the beginning of the end for two hierarchical, dystopian societies. The two narrators ultimately become part of larger dissident movements but they are also represented as complex, questioning protagonists whose sense of agency is frequently marked by an unwillingness to conform, even to those whose ethical or political objectives they might share.

In *The Maze Runner*, Thomas, like Katniss and Tris, is defined by his inclination for defying authority: he bristles against the assumed leadership of the Glade's initial top dog, alpha-male Alby, and refuses the older boy's handshake when he emerges, amnesiac and afraid, from the 'box'. This low-level lack of submissive behaviour anticipates Thomas's crucial moment of disobedience approximately a third of the way through the novel. When night falls in the Glade, the walls of the maze close, ostensibly in order to protect the boys from the creatures that stalk the labyrinth. The so-called 'Gladers' have made a strict rule that nobody is to leave the relative security of the clearing at night, and entering the maze itself, for anybody but one of the selected 'Runners', is forbidden. Thomas, however, breaks the rule when he realizes that two of his missing friends, one of whom is badly injured, will not be able to make it back through the stone doors before they roll shut. He risks the ire of the community – and likely nasty death by biomechanical beast – as a result of this impetuous act of transgression. He literally crosses a line – referred to as breaking 'the Number One Rule' – and makes himself both a hero and a villain to his new community (*MR*, p. 112). Thomas later discovers that his name, like those of his fellow internees, is indeed borrowed from a historical figure: his pseudonym comes from Thomas Edison, the American inventor and businessman. However, he is in a tradition of rugged individualists – his name even echoes Thomas Jefferson and there is a sense that these books resonate with the idea that the best kind of government is that 'which governs least'. The name has another resonance in that it is also shared by Thomas Didymus, the sceptical disciple who needed proof of Jesus's resurrection. Thomas is even spoken of by his peers as a kind of Nietzschean Übermensch – after their traumatic but victorious night in the maze, Minho praises his new friend's 'willpower and strength' (*MR*, p. 159). He recognizes that he is 'different from everyone else in the glade' and discovers latent telepathic abilities (*MR*, p. 175). Thomas is both a nascent man of action and a problem-solver. His forbidden excursion into the Maze reveals a capacity to think under pressure (he saves Alby with an ingenious use of vines), a capacity for self-sacrifice (the act puts his own life at risk) and he outwits the Grievers, the first of the Glade's residents to defeat the relentless beasts. In folkloric terms, Thomas 'overcomes the monster' – or, at least, the avatar of a bigger, invisible enemy. However, he is also placed in conflict with a range of his peers and his struggle with Gally and Alby is part of a social experiment, a kind of controlled form of Social Darwinism designed to save the species.

The self-sacrificial risk that Katniss and Thomas undertake voluntarily is enforced on the majority of the participants in Panem's annual games. However, some tributes are a rather different kind of volunteer known as 'Careers', who have been raised, in wealthier or less oppressed districts, to compete and are indoctrinated to kill in the arena with no more compunction than Katniss might have in stalking a rabbit. Both would be done in the name of survival. Katniss's spontaneous decision is a rare act of self-sacrifice, an assertion of agency, but it might also be read as a form of conformity. The Capitol merely requires youthful scapegoats and Katniss, charismatic and defiant, is televisual – the fact that she bravely replaces her younger sister becomes a marketable part of the annual spectacle. However, the selfless deed is also the first step in precipitating the eventual end of the Games and the downfall of the Capitol by the trilogy's conclusion.

Alternative forms of looking, watchfulness and visual perception act as both crucial motif and plot device in the trilogy.[18] This is most clearly embodied in the annual screening of the games, venerated and feared by rich and poor, respectively, and what Katniss refers to as 'the prying eyes of Panem' (*HG*, p. 362). Moments of distress, personal danger and intimacy are continually screened in the nation's coercive visual economy via the Capitol's tyrannical gaze. Ocular imagery pervades Collins's sequence and there are more than one hundred references to eyes in the first novel alone. 'The Hunger Games' echoes the ideas of Guy Debord's enormously influential 1967 Situationist manifesto on the mass media. Debord famously saw television and advertising as a quietly manipulative force; his 'society of the spectacle' is one in which citizens are ruled by consumer dreams that are perpetuated to prevent revolution. 'The spectacle', argues Scott Bukatman, 'controls by atomizing the population and reducing their capacity to function as an aggregate force'.[19] Bukatman is writing about the new technologically driven subjectivities anticipated in late twentieth-century SF and philosophy, but his words might also apply to Collins's dystopian society. The annual Hunger Games are a spectacle that is designed to maintain the status quo; the wealthy are entertained, the poor are both humiliated and warned. There is no escape from the arena, either for the Tributes who, with one exception, will die during the games or for the citizens of the districts whose daily life is also an arena in which they are, in effect, subject to predatory laws. There are echoes of this surveillance culture in both *Divergent* and *The Maze Runner*, though neither explores television or entertainment as a mode of social control. In Roth's novel, the initiates who are competing for a place in their chosen faction are openly watched and judged. In the novel's denouement, however, they are also injected with tracking devices that make them subject to direct control by members of the Erudite faction who seek to usurp the current political leadership; the young members of Dauntless are rendered 'brain-dead, obedient, and trained to kill. Perfect soldiers' (D, p. 418). The leader of the Erudite faction, Jeannie, has a utopian dream that involves enslaving much of the population, rendering citizens 'pliable and easy to control' (D, p. 429). Indeed, the belief that 'free will' is under siege is central to the anxieties of these twenty-first-century YA sequences (D, p. 432). The world of The Maze Runner does not even sustain the illusion of free, civil society, though the Glade attempts to preserve order by sticking to a strict set of rules and roles. Significantly, however, the boys are aware that their behaviour is policed via a near omniscient technological eye: the so-called beetle blades are mobile robot cameras that relay images: it is 'how the Creators watch us', notes Alby, the community's effective leader (MR, p. 64).

In 'The Hunger Games', a number of other spectators are subtle rivals to the apparently all-seeing eye of the Capitol. Katniss is represented, from the very beginning, as a quiet observer of her environment: her aptitude as a hunter in the outlawed wilds of District 12 depends on visual acuity and the wit to hide her bow and arrows from 'unwanted eyes' (HG, p. 7). When she reaches the Capitol, Katniss's ability to conceal herself in nature is inverted as she becomes, against her wishes, a celebrity, subject to an intense media gaze and converted, by her quietly subversive stylist, into 'the girl who was on fire' (HG, p. 82). The metropolis is a place in which extravagant aesthetics dominate: a spendthrift economy that thrives on overindulgence and plastic surgery to prolong youth is prevalent. Katniss's austere simplicity is a vivid contrast to the artifice of the decadent city. Alice Curry argues that Katniss's 'consciousness of the oppressive social injustices on which the Capitol relies [...] is communicated through her critique of Capitol aestheticism'; her eye is as acute and unsparing as the controlling gaze of the elite.[20] Before Katniss enters the arena, during the bizarre series of parades, television interviews, training events and public appearances, she gradually learns ways of manipulating the manipulators, of using the gaze against itself. As Amy L. Montz observes, 'the novel understands the purposeful exhibition of the female form' and Katniss, together with Cinna, her stealthily subversive stylist, begins a process of shaping an identity that may help her

to survive.[21] This public image is subsequently feared and appropriated by both Panem's dictatorship and the underground rebel
movement, hidden in the ostensibly destroyed District 13. Katniss's
first-person narrative, across three novels, tracks her endeavour to
find an identity that is not one simply scripted by a bigger cultural
force: she hungers for justice but is always more concerned about
the human cost, particularly to those whom she encounters, than an
abstract political settlement.

The trope of a disadvantaged teenage protagonist succeed-
ing against the odds is a standard device in popular narrative,
but Collins's sequence is particularly self-aware in its exploration of social status: Katniss, reluctantly, gains fame and celebrity
but wishes only to use them to achieve the survival of those she
loves and, ultimately, a more just society. Can the novel itself, or
its extraordinarily successful film adaptations use their own status
for progressive aims? In her exploration of YA fiction, technology
and post-human subjectivity, Victoria Flanagan notes that surveillance in the sequence is 'a tool of class oppression' and, in line with
Michel Foucault's thinking, 'this produces a paranoid subjectivity
that is permanently conscious of being watched'. However, she also
argues that Katniss 'does not remain an interpellated subject of surveillance', but 'becomes adept at manipulating surveillance to her
own advantage'.[22] Technology, as Flanagan suggests, occupies an
ambiguous role in 'The Hunger Games': the mediated spectacle of
the games is used to oppress viewers (and the coerced participants)
but it can also be appropriated as a tactics of resistance. Flanagan
notes, in particular, the way in which Katniss becomes 'aware that
surveillance is no longer just a function of institutional power, but
an avenue for self-construction' and is therefore 'capable of fashion-
ing her own subjectivity' for the spectators of the games.[23] Similarly,
Montz argues that because the Games have been designed as a spectacle 'with a voyeuristic agenda, it becomes easy to place Katniss
and the other tributes into positions of passivity'. However, she
also suggests that even in the first novel, in which agency is apparently stripped from them in the deadly arena and in the spotlight
of the Capitol, both Katniss and Peeta Mallark, her fellow tribute
from District 12, achieve a 'modicum of control' by quiet acts of
resistance.[24]

The complicated relationship between Katniss and Peeta, offi-
cially her deadly rival since there can be only one winner, is crucial

to the narrative's political critique and to its representation of the oppressive nature of an intensively mediated society. Their relationship is initially brokered not via conversation but in a series of visual skirmishes. Collins echoes conventional romantic plots by locating the two both as adversaries and as belonging to different parts of the social hierarchy. 'The Hunger Games' has a self-reflexive awareness of the ways in which stories are appropriated and turned into commodities. For example, the Capitol takes a perverse delight in a narrative twist that is announced shortly before the Games. The romantic subplot of the novel – precipitated by Peeta's sudden, and indeed televised, declaration of love for Katniss – becomes the story that the decadent Capitol dwellers want to believe; it is also the thing that ultimately saves the pair. Katniss and Peeta become adept at manipulating this narrative as a survival strategy. Broad observes that the 'romance plot self-consciously calls attention to itself as a way of manipulating an audience's emotions to ensure its continued engagement'.[25] We might read this as Collins's critique of the ways in which YA fiction itself operates and is consumed. A readership may be divided between those who wish Katniss to find love with the gentle Peeta and others who favour his rival, the hunter Gale. Other readers might question the politics of including such a conventional love plot in a twenty-first-century narrative at all. Surely this independent narrator needs no masculine saviour or counterpart to complete her story? Katniss is represented as hostile to standard expectations of romance from the beginning of her own narrative: in chapter one she flatly tells Gale that she 'never' wants to 'have kids' and, in the arena, as the possibility of her own survival increases, she privately reflects that she will 'never marry' because of the 'risk of bringing a child into the world' (HG, pp. 11, 378). Katniss's view of the nuclear family is far from sentimental: she is protective of her younger sister, but treats her depressed and grieving mother with contempt. Post-apocalyptic Panem retains patriarchy as a default system of power. Yet Collins presents a world in which ingrained male privilege is less significant than class status. President Snow, the nation's long-standing dictator, uses his sovereign status against both men and women of the districts. The bodies and minds of the poor and powerless, male and female, are exploited, consumed and discarded as a way of ensuring compliance amongst the mass of subjugated citizens.

The trilogy is marked by violence, betrayal and a massive number of human casualties but the conflict is also conducted as a media war. Katniss's key responsibility, in the eyes of the rebel authorities, is to become a living symbol of the insurgency against the Capitol: the Mockingjay must appear to be a near transcendent embodiment of resistance rather than an ordinary flesh-and-blood fighter. In the final volume, the improbably named Plutarch Heavensbee, a former Gamemaker turned tactical leader of the rebellion, reminds his most telegenic fellow dissents that they must 'put on a good show' and praises Katniss's awareness of the medium that she also detests: 'she understands the power of that screen'.[26]

Love plots are frequently crucial in YA fiction, and both *Divergent* and *The Maze Runner* introduce elements of romantic awakening and frustrated desire: Tris is attracted to her mysterious, brooding mentor, Four (so named because he fears only four real-world phenomena, a rare level of courage), but he initially appears to treat her with unusual toughness; Thomas is aware that he and Teresa share a deep emotional link, but one that he cannot remember. Such plots are highly conventional but they also connect to bigger social debates. Critical readings of 'The Hunger Games', for example, often privilege the novels' construction of gender identity and performance.[27] Katniss's relationship with Peeta complicates the idea that the trilogy is a confidently feminist post-apocalyptic fable in which a woman is able to assert freedom purely on her own terms.[28] Katniss's most distinctive memory of her rival, their only 'real interaction', occurred years earlier: Peeta, raised in the merchant class, risked the punitive violence of his mother by silently leaving Katniss two loaves as she lurked, starving, in the lanes near his parents' bakery; 'the boy never even glanced' at his starving schoolmate even though she 'was watching him' (*HG*, p. 37). She credits the ambiguous and unacknowledged act of kindness as a turning point: it saved her family from starvation by reminding her of the potential of the woodland in which her late father once hunted and, more significantly, in pushing her towards a very American form of self-reliance. Her encounters with Peeta in subsequent years were brief and, again, based on furtive acts of seeing: she recalls that 'more than once, I have turned in the school hallway and caught his eyes trained on me, only to flit quickly away' (*HG*, p. 39). When, on the day of reaping, they both become tributes, the two do not speak but Peeta 'looks [Katniss] right in the eye' (*HG*, p. 39). Intimate visual contact becomes part of the shifting power dynamic in the narrative. Peeta's penchant for covertly watching Katniss might easily be read as a symptomatic masculine gaze. Yet the narrative complicates this bond: Katniss never capitulates to the status of a passively observed object; she returns and stares down the gaze. The two characters, in a number of respects, invert traditionally gendered romantic rapport: Katniss is primarily associated with predatory instincts; she is a leader and an energetic, athletic presence who continually asserts her own liberty in a world stripped of basic freedoms. Broad, however, argues that though 'stereotypical gender associations' are disturbed because Peeta is linked 'with the utopian gentleness and Katniss with dystopian violence', it does not follow that 'their gender roles are truly reversed or that the text offers more open examples of gender possibilities'.[29] The experiences of both protagonists during the spectacular violence of the Games result in lifelong traumatic memories, the consequences of which are explored in the sequels set in the immediate months and years after the first novel and, ultimately, in an epilogue, written from the perspective of Katniss when she is in her mid-thirties, years after the final Games and the revolutionary war against the Capitol.

The 'vast outdoor arena', packed with cameras that record the tributes' every move, the narrative crucible of *The Hunger Games*, in which twenty-four children and very young adults are confined, is in Kelley Wezner's terms a 'panoptic structure'.[30] The combatants cannot escape the gaze of the Capitol and even their bodies are not sacrosanct as tracking devices have been inserted beneath the skin to ensure that hiding or escape is not possible, even for the eventual victor. The malleable, postmodern amphitheatre 'could hold anything from a burning desert to a frozen wasteland' in which 'over a period of several weeks, the competitors must fight to the death' (*HG*, p. 22). Only when all but one of these captive gladiators has been slain is a victor named. In order to survive, a child must become a ruthless killer of his or her peers. They will then become lauded by the Capitol and part of a bizarre celebrity system that encourages bloodlust in the wealthy and fear among the powerless. The games deliberately blur the line between artifice and reality, a political strategy that perpetuates confusion and obedience to the state. In a reading of the trilogy via the work of Jean Baudrillard and Louis Althusser, Helen Day argues that the Capitol propagates the illusion that the arenas are 'places of violence in order to make [its] citizens believe that they are safe, to conceal the fact that violence and repression are everywhere'.[31] This theme is developed in the two sequels during the revolutionary war against the Capitol when the 'games' are displaced from the arena into the districts and the streets of the metropolis. The first novel also registers a strong sense of environmental disaster, one that has appalling consequences for both the voiceless land and disenfranchised young. As Curry observes, 'by turning environmental suffering into spectacle, the Gamemakers render the earth both threatened [...] and threat: the same position as that of the young tributes who must defend themselves by learning how to kill'; in Curry's terms, both children and the artificially enhanced environment are 'denatured'.[32] This violent 'denaturing' is a recurrent feature of post-apocalyptic fiction: for example, the scorched, ash-strewn America of McCarthy's *The Road* also frames the unnatural horror of human beings preying on each other as a source of food or, at the very least, of seeing every other individual as a threat or rival. In *Divergent* and *The Maze Runner* the young protagonists are also manipulated into fighting each other. Tris and her fellow initiates are required to complete terrifying and sometimes deadly trials that have been ordained by an adult hierarchy: the faction on which the novel focuses, 'Dauntless', is supposedly defined by courage, but it also tacitly allows cheating, bullying and manipulation. The teenagers are forced to undergo powerful, artificially induced dream states in which they encounter subconscious fears. The ostensible rationale is to determine an individual's aptitude for a particular faction. However, the trials also perpetuate the existing hierarchy and allow an increasing militarization of the city's youth. After a number of obstacles and an assault that almost results in her death, Tris, like Katniss, emerges as a singularly brave and smart individual. However, she is also compelled to commit acts of violence. In the novel's final section, Tris fights to escape from her peers who have been turned into machine-like soldiers by a serum that destroys their free will and makes them obedient to the orders of an elite. Tris's difference as central protagonist – her 'divergence' – renders her immune to this nightmarish, hallucinatory state but, in self-defence, she shoots and kills her friend, Will ('It was him or me. I chose me. But I feel dead too', *D*, p. 446). This traumatic moment of loss and guilt, the result of a manipulative, adult world, embodies the high stakes at play in contemporary YA fiction: romantic subplots are a significant element of their popular appeal, but the narratives often undermine the security of such relationships with acts of violence, perpetrated both against and by the adolescent protagonists.

A similarly defining moment in *The Hunger Games* is the death of Rue, a twelve-year-old girl from District 11. Although she is a rival combatant, Rue is represented from her introduction as a familial figure for Katniss, who first sees the child on television, during a 'recap of the reapings': the child is 'very like' Prim, Katniss's younger sister, 'in size and demeanour' and this proto-sisterly bond informs their relationship as allies throughout the vicious competition (*HG*, p. 55). Unlike Prim, no heroic siblings or friends offer to stand in Rue's place as 'tribute'. Rue, however, saves Katniss's life in the arena and is figured as a person of extraordinary integrity and blamelessness. Ultimately her young life is sacrificed to remind readers of the ruthless horrors of the competition. Katniss is hardly well disposed to her captors from the Capitol, but the traumatic event is fundamental in her resolve both to survive and, ultimately, to defeat those responsible for the death of a child. The self-sacrificial death of Chuck at the end of *The Maze Runner* serves a similar purpose of rousing its central protagonist. However, *The Hunger Games* also tacitly engages with racial politics. Rue, with her 'dark brown skin and eyes' is also one of the very few non-white characters in the sequence and, perhaps, in YA fiction more widely (*HG*, p. 55). Mary J. Couzelis, who makes a persuasive argument that 'contemporary young adult dystopian novels do little to question today's racial hierarchies', observes that Rue and her fellow District 11 tribute are the only characters whose 'skin tone' Katniss notes, 'thereby highlighting their difference from the others'.[33] Although the novel is never precise in identifying these characters as African American, Couzelis sets out a number of signifiers associated with a history of racial oppression that set out good reasons why Rue is read as black. District 11, she notes, is an agricultural region whose mode of exploitative work, including a regime of near starvation, beatings and enforced infant labour, is strongly reminiscent of slavery. Katniss's own background is one of near poverty and working-class struggle, but even so she is distressed by Rue's tales of life in the orchards and, in Couzelis words, 'a dichotomy is established that reaffirms white privilege'.[34] Rue's death, she argues, is a 'stereotypical trope' of modern narrative in which 'African American characters appear briefly to assist in the development of a white protagonist and then either disappear after or are sacrificed as part of the white character's transformation'.[35] In one sense, Rue is at least a big an influence on the momentum of the subsequent revolution as Katniss. The event is a turning point not only in the novel, but also in the entire trilogy since it consolidates an incipient sense of political outrage against the Capitol and ultimately galvanizes the oppressed population.

We might question the politics of a novel that itself uses vicarious sacrifice to emblematize all that is wrong with a regime based on preserving affluence via spectacular violence. Indeed, a number of critics are sceptical about readings of YA fiction, and 'The Hunger Games' in particular, that emphasize their politically progressive credentials. For such readers, the teenage revolutionaries of such novels might be more conservative than their fight for justice appears to suggest. The logic of this argument suggests that Katniss and Tris's parallel resistance to authoritarian states is motivated by a desire for personal independence rather than communal liberty. These adolescent dissidents are not, according to this reading, real revolutionaries but avatars of a reactionary politics of self, one invested in old American shibboleths of family, faith and security. Ewan Morrison, for example, argues that such novels 'propose a laissez-faire existence, with heroic individuals who are guided by the innate forces of human nature against evil social planners'.[36] In an article for *Salon*, Andrew O'Hehir describes Collins and Roth's sequences as 'propaganda for the ethos of individualism, the central ideology of consumer capitalism, which also undergirds both major political parties and almost all American public discourse.' This 'capitalist agit-prop' in the form of bestselling fiction, according to O'Hehir, performs a 'structural function [...] in the cultural economy'.[37] In vivid contrast, Karl Hand compares Katniss's gradual 'transformation' with the 'revolutionary consciousness' of Jesus, particularly as represented in the gospel of Luke.[38] Another critic notes that the first novel 'treats the political conflict as a secondary theme and focuses most intensely on the emerging moral consciousness of the protagonist'.[39] This interpretation, however, rather underplays the extent to which Katniss's 'emerging moral consciousness' is represented as a political phenomenon in *The Hunger Games*, even before she becomes the shared symbol of the rebellion against the injustices of the Capitol.

The politics of Katniss's evolution from self-reliant hunter to leading figure in the anti-Capitol insurgency, are certainly complicated and ambiguous. However, the bildungsroman, in this instance, is not one in which a youthful narrator, full of dissident energy, is eventually tamed by society and gradually learns to conform, though the end of the trilogy includes a turn towards conventional romantic resolution in her eventual life, many years later, with Peeta, as partner and mother of their children. 'The Hunger Games' sequence has been appropriated and maligned by both left and right. Katha Pollit, focusing on the film adaptations of Collins's novels, notes the range of rival political readings: 'You can see it as a savage satire of late capitalism [...] Tea Partiers can imagine an allegory of oppressive Washington, and traditionalists can revel in the ancient trope of the moral superiority of the countryside.'[40] Another critic notes that the films have become 'a canvas onto which disparate and even opposing ideologies are enthusiastically projected'.[41] The politics of commercially successful dystopias written for teenage or 'crossover' audiences are too ideologically complex to be understood as political manifestoes. However, it is also facile to simply dismiss 'The Hunger Games' as an insidiously individualist tract that covertly endorses personal fulfilment above collective struggle. Yonah Ringelstein's argument that Collins's trilogy 'advocates for a persistently critical perspective of all kinds of constructed worlds and all realities' is particularly persuasive.[42] However, the 'constructed world', as we know, occasionally exceeds its bounds and seeps into everyday (political) reality. In a strange twist, 'real world' politics have, on occasion, deliberately borrowed from the iconography of Collins's sequence. A three-fingered salute, initially performed as a sign of mournful respect in the first instalment of Katniss's narrative that ultimately becomes a mode of indicating dissent, was used in 2014 by protestors against the military coup in Thailand. Indeed, a group of five students was arrested for using the gesture in front of their prime minister.[43]

Twenty-first-century apocalyptic fiction, not exclusively novels written for young adults, frequently focuses on the figure of the child or the teenager. The flashback sequences that counterpoint the post-catastrophe future in Atwood's 'MaddAddam' trilogy (2003–13), for example, are primarily concerned with the adolescent experiences of Jimmy and Ren; the memories of their young lives, though far from idealized versions of secure childhood years, are a counterpoint to their present, post-catastrophe, 'experienced' selves. The sequence also concludes with the coming of age of Blackbeard, one of Crake's post-human children, who takes on the twin mantle of storyteller for his evolving community and becomes the novel's final narrator. McCarthy's *The Road* is divided between the voice of weary experience (the man) and open innocence (his son); the latter is faced with the responsibility of 'carrying the fire', a metaphor for their tentative (and questionable) preservation of hope and virtue, when the father dies and he continues their journey with another wandering family. The figure of the child fits the messianic logic that is a displaced legacy of Judeo-Christian apocalypse: s/he might be a herald of new possibilities, an alternative to the failed, decaying old order. Children and young adult characters in both fable and contemporary fiction are frequently burdened with a responsibility of overturning the world created by previous generations and, in particular, of putting right their parents' horrible mistakes. This idea not only is familiar to readers of dystopian fiction, but will also be recognizable to anybody who has been a parent or who remembers the moral outrage of their own childhood against adult injustice. Roth, Dashner and Collins's sequences splice genres, incorporating elements of conventional bildungsroman and SF tropes of disaster, dystopia and environmental ruin. YA fiction featuring rebellious protagonists might be profitable, but the status of these novels as popular commodities does not necessarily neuter their ability to confront the political crises of our era.

7

Conclusion: 'Survival is insufficient'

All things, convention dictates, must come to an end: empires, relationships, novels – everything reaches a conclusion, if only a very unsatisfactory one. The sole phenomenon that seems stubbornly resistant to closure is the continuing fascination with the end of the world. Are such narratives, at best, a bizarre style of escapism? In *After Virtue* (1981), the philosopher Alasdair McIntyre argues that ethical living is only thinkable with what he calls 'conceptions of a possible shared future':

> There is no present which is not informed by some image of some future and an image of the future which always presents itself in the form of a *telos* – or of a variety of ends or goals – towards which we are either moving or failing to move in the present. Unpredictability and teleology therefore coexist as part of our lives.[1]

Is it possible to imagine the future as anything more than a dispiritingly inevitable product of our wrecked present? Gerry Canavan, glossing Fredric Jameson's thoughts on the apparent inability of postmodern culture to imagine an end to capitalism, observes: 'The apocalypse is the only thing in our time that seems to have the capacity to shake the foundations of the system and "jumpstart" a history that now seems completely moribund.'[2] In Maggie Gee's *The Flood* (2004), Rhuksana tells her husband the story of the Snow Queen and concludes that because the fairy tale has 'everything' that children like ('courage, love, a happy ending') its author 'will never die'.

Her husband, however, qualifies this faith in the perseverance of narrative with a suggestion that the memory of the author will perish if 'all the readers' also pass away.[3] Perhaps the only apocalypse truly feared by novelists – and perhaps by any of us – is a readerless future, one in which the transmission of our shared stories of disaster and loss is wholly impossible. Apocalyptic fiction since 2000 is frequently ambivalent about its own status as a meaning-making medium. Cormac McCarthy's *The Road*, for example, represents the future of literature in a 'charred library where the blackened books lay in pools of water'.[4] As Peter Boxall comments, this is 'one version of the future of the novel'.[5]

The future of fiction is, however, not the only thing that keeps people awake at night. A number of contemporary thinkers view the apocalyptic tendencies of modern culture as fundamentally destructive. 'The myth of the End', claims John Gray, 'has caused untold suffering and is now as dangerous as it ever was'.[6] The bad news, from this perspective, is that apparently enlightened, democratic and liberated politics (what Gray calls 'secular religions') in seeking to bring an end to oppression have unintentionally made the world home to yet more violence. Apocalypse, in its destructive rather than revelatory sense, has not been discarded as a relic of a different, less enlightened era. Similarly, in a 'clerical rejoinder' to what he names the 'logic of the apocalypse', Michael Titlestad concludes that the proliferation of catastrophist ideas in contemporary fiction, film and political discourse says something rather shocking about our relationship with the end. 'The truth of late-modernity is that we love the apocalypse. We truly love it.'[7] This is a stark and somewhat depressing claim, but it is not the solitary preserve of academic debate; similar ideas are also explored in mainstream popular culture. For example, late in Brad Bird's SF adventure film, *Tomorrowland: A World Beyond* (2015), David Nix, leader of the titular utopia and chief antagonist of the film, gives an eloquent if embittered speech about the human proclivity for end-of-the-world stories. He is first puzzled and then disgusted by the realization that, far from frightened of future destruction, audiences seem to be thrilled by it. This aesthetic pleasure taken in easily marketed apocalyptic fictions is, he suggests, a sign that civilization has given up. Humanity, he claims, will not make the effort to believe in a better, more just society. It is a curious speech, particularly as it is delivered in a film that emerges from the Disneyland theme park.

Nix's utopianism is revealed as autocratic and extreme. However, in this piece of anti-apocalyptic rhetoric he sounds like a rational critic of a world that seems ready both to destroy itself and, meanwhile, to enjoy the spectacle. The fact that the looming catastrophe is averted, in true Hollywood style, with a blend of empathy and ingenuity, does not quite dispel the uncomfortable image of social apathy described by the idealistic, and ultimately vanquished, villain.

There are other, rather more hopeful ways of thinking about narratives of the end. In *Hope against Optimism* (2015) Terry Eagleton claims that Judeo-Christianity 'breaks the link' between hope and what he calls 'the doctrine of progress'. This is not to say that this particular religious world view dismisses the phenomenon of social and scientific improvement, but that such advancements are 'not to be confused with redemption'. The eschaton that Eagleton identifies as fundamental to New Testament teaching is 'not to be mistaken for the consummation of history as a whole [...] but as an event that breaks violently, unpredictably into the human narrative, upending its logic, defying its priorities, unmasking its wisdom as foolishness'.[8] Indeed, one alternative perspective on fictions of apocalypse might be found in philosophies of 'the event'. Slavoj Žižek describes the 'event' as 'something shocking, out of joint, that appears to happen all of a sudden and interrupts the usual flow of things; something that emerges seemingly out of nowhere, without discernable causes, an appearance without solid being as its foundation'.[9] This 'miraculous' sense of event is rather different, for example, from violent incidents or an environmental catastrophe. They are categories of phenomena that can be explained, their causes understood and their implications assessed. Žižek suggests that the disparate examples of believing in Christ, falling in love and political protests in Cairo might all have an eventual quality; standard ways of explaining these occurrences do not quite work. For the Marxist–Lacanian philosopher an 'event is [...] *the effect that seems to exceed its causes*'.[10]

Many of the catastrophes that cause the collapse of civilization in twenty-first-century fiction do not, I think, qualify as an event, in these terms. However, the narratives of survival, involving extraordinary acts of resistance, compassion and, on occasion, something that could be described as forgiveness, might be closer to Žižek's definition. The protagonists who come together in the denouement of Atwood's 'MaddAddam' trilogy, for example, have witnessed appalling brutality; some of them have behaved aggressively, perhaps in self-defence but in ways that implicitly endorse the abiding myth of redemptive violence. Yet the end of the novel emphasizes what Toby, the reluctant priest–storyteller to the 'Children of Crake', and Blackbeard, her apprentice who is learning the art of narrative, name 'a thing of hope'.[11] Neither the horrors of the dystopian, aggressively consumerist era narrated in flashback nor the pandemic orchestrated by Crake represent apocalypse in its primary sense. The tentative community, seeking to live peacefully, could, however, be read as non-violent revelation.

One characteristic of twenty-first-century apocalyptic fiction, particularly narratives set after the collapse of society, is a tacit antipathy for the corrupt present in which the novel is written. The ruined worlds that they evoke are, it is implied, frequently a product of our current propensities and trajectories: the legacy of the early twenty-first century to these near-future eras is often environmental degradation, consumer greed, the loss of human rights and the exploitation of future generations who will pay a high price for current folly or cruelty. We are, the subtext is clear, making a horrible mess of things and nostalgia for the present is relatively rare. The apocalyptic tradition is sometimes highly misanthropic; the earth, it suggests, would be in better condition if *Homo sapiens* were no longer around. However, not all iterations of apocalypse display such disdain for current human endeavours.

'One way to write about something', notes Emily St John Mandel, author of *Station Eleven* (2014), 'is to consider its absence, which is why I set much of the book in a post-apocalyptic landscape'.[12] The novel presents a very unusual perspective on the trauma of global catastrophe. *Station Eleven* is both a horrifying story of the fragility of civilization and, in her words, 'a love letter to the modern world, written in the form of a requiem'.[13] A pandemic, known as the Georgia Flu, 'explode[s] like a neutron bomb over the surface of the earth' and, within a few months, has killed the vast majority of the world's population.[14] Civilization, including government, infrastructure and motorized transport, it would seem, is over. 'What was lost in the collapse: almost everything, almost everyone, but there is still such beauty' (*SE*, p. 53). This is not the kind of sentence included in *The Road*. A defining difference between the post-catastrophe worlds of *Station Eleven* and McCarthy's novel is that the latter appears to show more faith in the sparks of ingenuity that create civilizations. At the end of the novel's opening section, the narrator, gifted a god-like perspective, gives 'an incomplete list' of all of those things that disappear at the end of this modern, techno-logical era as a litany of 'no more':

> No more diving into pools of chlorinated water lit green from below. No more ball games played out under floodlights. No more porchlights with moths fluttering on summer nights. No trains running under the surface of cities [...] No more cities. No more films, except rarely, except with a generator drowning out half the dialogue, points of glimmering light. No more flight. No more towns glimpsed from the sky through airplane win-dows [...] no more looking down from thirty thousand feet and imagining the lives lit up by those lights at that moment [...] No more countries, all borders unmanned (*SE*, p. 31).

This fragmented inventory of the era of finance capitalism or 'supermodernity' is a kind of nostalgic liturgy, an enumeration of the everyday that might make a reader homesick for the pre-sent. However, the narrative is more than a sentimental evocation of our world: it is an ambitious, and multi-genre, exploration of the human capacity to create and to pursue meaning via art, story and shared community. One of the reasons that the world dies so quickly in *Station Eleven* is because of its relentless mobility and the ordinary miracle of air travel: people travel across the globe in hours and the virus, horribly resistant to treatment, goes with them. These tropes of complacency followed by escalating panic and then years of struggle by a group of survivors are standard elements of apocalyptic fiction. Many of the characters are aware that the unhappy story in which they find themselves is uncannily familiar. As the pandemic unfolds, during the 'days before the end of televi-sion', one character observes that the crisis is 'like those disaster movies' and thinks about reality compared to 'the movie version of this' in which 'there's the apocalypse, and then afterward' (*SE*, p. 193). The novel acknowledges the appeal of apocalyptic clichés, but resists a formula of death, destruction and regret in favour of a rather stranger, more resourceful, narrative. This fable of the end is also unusually engaged with the value of human creativity: it folds a number of narrative forms into its structure, including elements

of drama, newspaper interviews and a dystopian story, the titular
Station Eleven, an obscure graphic novel created by a relatively
minor character, that is obsessively read and reread by two young
survivors in the years following the crisis.

The novel begins in a Toronto theatre on the night that the flu
epidemic starts to spread beyond limit. This opening playhouse
setting is a reminder that the narrative is a world of artifice, one
not only with a perceptible logic, but also in which a variety of
theatrical devices may alter perceptions of the line between reality and illusion. The play on stage, a distinguished tragedy, is also
proleptic of imminent loss and grief. An innovative interpretation
of Shakespeare's *King Lear* is being performed with a successful, if
careworn Hollywood actor, named Arthur Leander in the titular
role. He dies on stage, during Act 4, as three children, who perform
younger versions of Lear's daughters, eventually return 'as halluci-
nations in the mad scene' (*SE*, p. 4). The death of an actor playing
a dying sovereign foreshadows 'the end of everything' (*SE*, p. 274).
The flashback structure of the narrative that moves between episodes in Arthur's life as an actor and the two decades after the pandemic means that he remains a presence throughout the narrative.
In memory, he is a pseudo-survivor of the Georgia Flu. The linear
elements of the narrative follow the post-collapse lives of a number
of characters connected to Arthur, including his young son, Tyler;
Kirsten Raymonde, who played one of Lear's daughters; and Clark
Thompson, Arthur's best friend.

Tyler is an intense child, partially estranged from his father,
who, together with his mother, one of Arthur's three ex-wives,
survives the plague. They are stranded, with a number of other
terrified travellers, at an airport that gradually develops into
a makeshift community, with rules, responsibilities and work.
Tyler, encouraged by his mother's eccentric mixture of creeds,
believes that survivors have been 'saved' and the pair eventually
leave the airport with a group of religious wanderers (*SE*, p. 259).
He is also one of only two people to whom the actor gifts copies of *Station Eleven*. The graphic novel, painstakingly written,
drawn and self-published by one of Arthur's ex-wives, is a SF
fable about a space station that is a refuge for the exiled inhabitants of an invaded planet. Its themes of longing for a lost world
('the sweetness of life on earth') and the resilience of its physicist
central character, Dr Eleven, make it an arresting mise en abyme

that illuminates the framing story of survivors attempting to live in a world after catastrophe (*SE*, p. 42). It has the aura of a rare object: only ten copies of its two issues were printed. Kirsten, eight years old at the time of the catastrophe that killed her family, is the other recipient of Arthur's gift of the comic. She is haunted by its narrative and, by the time of adulthood, has memorized the two issues. Kirsten suffers from traumatic memory loss following the horrors of her first year on the road but, in another odd narrative repetition, she has become, in her adult life, a Shakespearean actor once again as a member of The Travelling Symphony. This group of musicians and performers has been touring, on foot, for twenty years 'travelling back and forth along the shores of Lakes Huron and Michigan, west as far as Traverse City, east and north over the 49th parallel to Kincardine'. Their theatrical repertoire has a very specific focus:

They'd performed more modern plays sometime in the first few years, but what was startling, what no one would have anticipated, was that audiences seemed to prefer Shakespeare to their other theatrical offerings. 'People want what was best about the world' (*SE*, p. 38).

The quixotic endeavours of the group are emblematic of a refusal to capitulate to despair or aggressive rejection of community. Significantly, the tragedy of *King Lear* performed in the opening chapter is replaced by *A Midsummer Night's Dream*, the title of the novel's second section. This movement from tragedy to supernatural comedy is indicative of the different ways in which Shakespeare's writing is used in the narrative. A maxim – 'Survival is insufficient' – is painted on the lead caravan of The Travelling Symphony and tattooed on the arm of one of its actresses; the phrase is borrowed not from Dante or Marx or the Bible or JFK, but from an episode of *Star Trek Voyager*. The novel defends the pleasures and imaginative possibilities of popular culture. A counterpoint to this celebration of narrative in its many forms is the threatening presence of a wandering messianic religious cult, led by a mysterious, charismatic and vicious preacher known only as the Prophet. The group dominate communities and they eventually come into violent conflict with The Travelling Symphony. The Prophet claims that everything including the suffering of his victims is 'all part of a greater plan' (SE, p. 290). He and his followers fulfil a similar role to the GR cult in Tom Perrotta's *The Leftovers*. In both cases, the pious believers are represented as victims of a persistent grief who need to believe in absolutes. This defence of certainty often leads to bloodshed. Both cults are believers in the secondary sense of apocalypse: a violent end that glories in death. St John Mandel places ersatz, messianic religion in symbolic competition with the consolations of art and shared storytelling.

In a narrative twist, that most apocalyptic of literary devices, it is revealed that the Prophet is a grown-up Tyler. After he is killed by one of his disciples, Kirsten discovers that the two have a very strange affinity. Inside his heavily annotated copy of the New Testament ('nearly illegible, a thicket of margin notes and exclamation points and underlining') is a fragment of another text: a page of the first issue of *Station Eleven*, the first that Kirsten had 'ever seen that hadn't come from her own copies of the book' (SE, p. 303). This scrap of paper is more than a textual connection: it is a reminder that the two share other things. The Prophet is, among other things, 'just another dead man on another road, answerless, the bearer of another unfathomable story about walking out of one world and into another' (SE, p. 304). She also recognizes that she and the Prophet are a similar age: 'he'd once been a boy adrift on the road, and perhaps he'd had the misfortune of remembering everything' (SE, p. 304).

In the novel's conclusion, The Travelling Symphony arrive at the airport in Severn City, itself a kind of avatar of Station Eleven, a dwelling place that is not quite a surrogate for the world that has been lost. Kirsten encounters Arthur's best friend, Clark, who has survived to become the curator of the airport community's makeshift Museum of Civilization. During a twenty-year period Clark gathers a collection of objects (laptops, iPhones, a turntable, a toaster) that become a secular shrine to the 'spectacular world' in which he once lived (SE, p. 254). This idiosyncratic archive is a link to 'the pre-pandemic world that he remembered so sharply' (SE, p. 232). The curator also acts as a guide to a potential new era when, from the air traffic control tower he hands Kirsten a telescope and in the distance she sees 'pinpricks of light arranged into a grid. There, plainly visible on the side of a hill some miles distant: a town, or a village, whose streets were lit up with electricity' (SE, p. 311). As the novel ends, The Travelling Symphony departs from the airport and its 'passing into unknown territory' is a sign of life continuing, in defiance of the odds (*SE*, p. 331). Kirsten leaves one of her two treasured issues of *Station Eleven* with Clark in the Museum of Civilization. The novel ends with three things: an act of reading; a departure, on foot; and the imagined possibility of other forms of mobility as Clark 'likes the thought of ships moving over the water, towards another world just out of sight' in 'this awakening world' (*SE*, p. 332).

The novel takes the risk of believing that an ethical, cooperative, version of society might be achievable. The nightmare of ruined worlds, it suggests, are vital to our collective imagination, but there are alternatives, if we do not capitulate to the idea that the future has already been written.

NOTES

Chapter 1

1 Douglas Coupland, *JPod* (London: Bloomsbury, 2006), pp. 329–30.

2 Jim Crace, *The Pesthouse* (London: Picador, 2013, Kindle edition), p. 6.

3 Margaret Atwood, *MaddAddam* (London: Bloomsbury, 2013), p. 351. All subsequent references will be given parenthetically.

4 Patrick Parrinder, 'The Ruined Futures of British Science Fiction', in *On Modern British Fiction*, ed. Zachary Leader (Oxford: Oxford University Press, 2002), pp. 209–33.

5 Veronica Hollinger, 'Stories about the Future: From Patterns of Expectation to Pattern Recognition', *Science Fiction Studies*, 33, no. 3 (Nov. 2006), 452–72 (p. 452).

6 Chad Harbach, 'The End', *n+1*, issue 6 (December 2007), https://nplusonemag.com/issue-6/reviews/the-end-the-end-the-end/ (accessed 9 March 2015).

7 Peter Boxall, *Twenty-First-Century Fiction* (Cambridge: Cambridge University Press, 2013, Kindle edition), p. 14.

8 David Mitchell, *The Bone Clocks* (London: Sceptre, 2014), pp. 533–4.

9 Bill McGuire, *A Guide to the End of the World: Everything You Never Wanted to Know* (London: Oxford: Oxford University Press), pp. 36–7.

10 Adam Trexler, *Anthropocene Fictions: The Novel in a Time of Climate Change* (Charlottesville: University of Virginia Press, 2015), p. 8.

11 George Monbiot, 'Civilization Ends with a Shutdown of Human Concern. Are We There Already?' 30 October 2007, *The Guardian* (http://www.theguardian.com/commentisfree/2007/oct/30/comment.books) (accessed 27 February 2016).

12 Emily St John Mandel, *Station Eleven* (London: Picador, 2015), p. 25.

13 Fiction after 9/11 has been explored in a number of studies. See, for example, Ann Keniston and Jeanne Follansbee Quinn, eds, *Literature*

after 9/11 (New York: Routledge, 2008); Arthur Bradley and Andrew Tate, *The New Atheist Novel: Fiction, Philosophy and Polemic after 9/11* (London: Bloomsbury, 2010); Richard Gray, *After the Fall: American Literature since 9/11* (Oxford: Wiley-Blackwell, 2011).

14 James Berger, *After the End: Representations of Post-Apocalypse* (Minneapolis: University of Minnesota Press, 1999), p. xiii.

15 Karl Hand, 'Come Now, Let Us Treason Together: Conversion and Revolutionary Consciousness in Luke 23: 35–38 and *The Hunger Games* Trilogy', *Literature and Theology*, 29, no. 3 (2015), 348–65 (p. 350).

16 Brian W. Aldiss, *Billion Year Spree: The History of Science Fiction* (London: Weidenfeld and Nicolson, 1973), pp. 293–4.

17 Nick Hornby, *How to Be Good* (London: Penguin, 2001), p. 243.

18 David Nicholls, *Us* (London: Hodder, 2014), p. 330. All subsequent references will be given parenthetically as *Us*, followed by page number.

19 Joshua Ferris, *To Rise Again at a Decent Hour* (London: Viking, 2014), pp. 9–10. All subsequent references will be given parenthetically as *TRA*, followed by page number.

20 Dave Eggers, *Your Fathers, Where Are They? And the Prophets, Do They Live Forever?* (London: Penguin, 2014), pp. 45–6.

21 Ibid., p. 36.

22 Joseph L. Mangina, *Revelation* (London: SCM Press, 2010), p. 37.

23 Michael Wheeler, *Ruskin's God* (Cambridge: Cambridge University Press, 1999), pp. 263–5.

24 Tom Wright, *Surprised by Hope* (London: Society for Promoting Christian Knowledge, 2007), p. 6.

25 Michael Northcott, *A Political Theology of Climate Change* (London: SPCK, 2014), pp. 26–7.

26 Judith Kovacs and Christopher Rowland, *Revelation* (Oxford: Blackwell, 2004), p. 7.

27 Will Self, introduction to The Revelation of St John the Divine, in *Revelations: Personal Responses to the Bible*, ed. Richard Holloway (Edinburgh: Canongate, 2005), pp. 375–83 (p. 381).

28 Kathleen Norris, introduction to The Revelation of St John the Divine, in *Revelations*, pp. 367–73 (p. 370).

29 James Annesley, 'Decadence and Disquiet: Recent American Fiction and the Coming "*Fin de Siècle*"', *Journal of American Studies*, 30, no. 3 (1996), 365–79 (p. 365). See also Annesley's *Blank Fictions* (London: Pluto, 1998), p. 108.

30 James Atlas, 'What Is Fukuyama Saying?', *The New York Times Magazine*, p. 38. Cited in Annesley, 'Decadence and Disquiet', p. 365.

31 Frank Kermode, *The Sense of an Ending: Studies in the Theory of Fiction* (Oxford: Oxford University Press, 1967), p. 6.

32 Paul S. Fiddes, *The Promised End: Eschatology in Theology and Literature* (Oxford: Blackwell, 2000), p. 6.

33 Ibid.

34 Greg Garrard, *Ecocriticism* (Abingdon: Routledge, 2004), p. 89.

35 Thomas Carlyle, *The Works of Thomas Carlyle*, 30 vols. (London: Chapman & Hall, 1899), Vol. 27, p. 59.

36 John Wolffe, *God and Greater Britain: Religion and National life in Britain and Ireland 1843–1945* (London: Routledge, 1994), p. 159.

37 Garrard briefly traces Lawrence's impact on ecologists such as Del Ivan Janik and Rolf Gardiner, the founder of the Soil Association, pp. 89–90. He also emphasizes the ways in which *The Rainbow* (1915) both echoes biblical narrative – especially the 'poetry of the Authorized Version' – and foregrounds a critique of 'Christian Anthropomorphism', p. 92.

38 See Maria Kalnins discussion of Lawrence's spirituality in D. H. Lawrence, *Apocalypse and the Writings on Revelation*, ed. Mara Kalnins (Cambridge: Cambridge University Press, 1980), p. 17. For a wider discussion of Lawrence's relationship with the Bible, see T. R Wright, *D. H. Lawrence and the Bible* (Cambridge: Cambridge University Press, 2000).

39 Lawrence, *Apocalypse and the Writings on Revelation*, pp. 61–2.

40 Ibid., pp. 66, 143.

41 Ibid., p. 144.

42 Ibid., p. 66.

43 John Gray, *Black Mass: Apocalyptic Religion and the Death of Utopia* (London: Penguin, 2008), p. 261.

44 Lee Quinby, *Anti-Apocalypse: Exercises in Genealogical Criticism* (Minneapolis: University of Minnesota Press, 1994), p. xii.

45 Matthew Avery Sutton, *American Apocalypse: A History of Modern Evangelicalism* (Cambridge, MA: Harvard University Press, 2014), p. 3.

46 Ibid., p. 6.

47 Ibid.

48 Ibid., p. 7.

49 Cormac McCarthy, *The Road* (London: Picador, 2007), p. 120. All subsequent references will be given parenthetically as *TR*, followed by page number.

50 Hannah Stark, ' "All These Things He Saw and Did Not See": Witnessing the End of the World in Cormac McCarthy's *The Road*', *Critical Survey*, 25, no. 2 (2013), 71–84; Stefan Skrimshire, ' "There Is no God and We Are His Prophets": Deconstructing Redemption in Cormac McCarthy's *The Road*', *Journal for Cultural Research*, 15, no. 1 (2011), 1–14. McCarthy's novel has inspired a range of rival theological interpretations. See, for example, Thomas A. Carlson, 'With the World at Heart: Reading Cormac McCarthy's *The Road* with Augustine and Heidegger', *Religion & Literature*, 39, no. 3 (2007), 47–71; Shelly L. Rambo, 'Beyond Redemption?: Reading Cormac McCarthy's *The Road* after the End of the World', *Studies in the Literary Imagination*, 41, no. 2 (2008), 99–120; D. Marcel DeCoste, ' "A Thing That Even Death Cannot Undo": The Operation of the Theological Virtues in Cormac McCarthy's *The Road*', *Religion and Literature*, 44, no. 2 (2012), 67–91; Allen Josephs, 'The Quest for God in *The Road*', in *The Cambridge Companion to Cormac McCarthy*, ed. Steven Frye (Cambridge: Cambridge University Press, 2013), pp. 133–45.

51 'For yourselves know perfectly that the day of the Lord so cometh as a thief in the night', King James Version, 1 Thessalonians 5. 2.

Chapter 2

1 Jamie Wilson, 'The Whole Damn City Is under Water', *The Guardian*, 30 August 2005 (http://www.theguardian.com/world/2005/aug/30/hurricanekatrina.usa; accessed 6 October 2015).

2 Justin McCurry and Tracy McVeigh, *The Guardian*, 12 March 2011 (http://www.theguardian.com/world/2011/mar/12/japan-counts-death-toll-destruction); Tim Walker, *The Independent*, 18 April 2013 (http://www.independent.co.uk/news/world/americas/texas-explosion-biblical-scene-of-destruction-on-waco-s-doorstep-8577619.html; accessed 6 October 2015).

3 J. G. Ballard, *Kingdom Come* (London: Fourth Estate, 2014), p. 7. All subsequent references will be given parenthetically as *KC*, followed by page number.

4 Marc Augé, *Non-Places: Introduction to an Anthropology of Supermodernity*, trans. John Howe (London: Verso, 1995).

5 For a detailed, comparative reading of Ballard's representation of consumerism and the apocalypse, see, for example, Alexis Paknadel, 'Anywhere But Here: The Competing (and Complementary) Postmodern Nostalgias of J. G. Ballard and Douglas Coupland', Unpublished doctoral thesis, Lancaster University, 2011.

6 Ballard, *Kingdom Come*, pp. 276, 280.

7 J. G. Ballard, *The Drowned World* (London: Harper Perennial, 2008), p. 175. For a valuable reading of the novel, see Andrzej Gasiorek, *JG Ballard* (Manchester: Manchester University Press, 2005), pp. 31–9.

8 H. G. Wells, a forefather of contemporary apocalypticism, contributed to this tradition with *All Aboard for Ararat* (Secker & Warburg, 1940). For a valuable overview of postmodern rewritings of the flood, with particular emphasis on Winterson, see Terry R. Wright, *The Genesis of Fiction: Modern Novelists as Biblical Interpreters* (Aldershot: Ashgate, 2007), pp. 69–84.

9 For a detailed reading of Self's novel alongside Sam Taylor's *The Island at the End of the World*, see Diletta De Cristofaro, 'Beyond the Sense of an Ending: Post-Apocalyptic Critical Temporalities', Unpublished PhD thesis, University of Nottingham, July 2015, pp. 139–89.

10 Maggie Gee, *The Flood* (London: Saqi, 2005), pp. 146, 200. All subsequent references will be given parenthetically as *F*, followed by page number.

11 Maggi Dawn, *The Writing on the Wall: High Art, Popular Culture and the Bible* (London: Hodder, 2005), p. 35.

12 Jürgen Moltmann, *In the End – The Beginning*, trans. Margaret Kohl (London: SCM, 2004).

13 Norman Cohn, *Noah's Flood: The Genesis Story in Western Thought* (New Haven: Yale University Press, 1996), xi. Cohn cites, inter alia, James Frazer, *Folklore in the Old Testament* (London: Macmillan, 1918) and Alan Dundes, ed., *The Flood Myth* (Berkeley: University of California Press, 1988).

14 Walter Brueggemann, *Genesis* (Louisville: John Knox Press, 2010, Kindle edition), Location 1727.

15 Ibid., Location 1808.

16 Julian Barnes, *A History of the World in 10 ½ Chapters* (London: Random House, 2009), p. 29 (iBooks edition). All subsequent references will be given parenthetically as *AHOTW*, followed by page number.

17 David Maine, *The Flood* (Edinburgh: Canongate, 2004), p. 83. All subsequent references will be given parenthetically as *TF*, followed by page number.

18 Josh Lacey, 'What Noe Did Next', *The Guardian*, 9 October 2004 (http://www.theguardian.com/books/2004/oct/09/featuresreviews.guardianreview17; accessed 11 November 2015).

19 Kasia Boddy, 'Rich People and Foxes Desert the City' [review of Maggie Gee, *The Flood*], *The Daily Telegraph*, 24 February ᵃᵃᵃ

(http://www.telegraph.co.uk/culture/books/3612667/Rich-people-and-foxes-desert-the-city.html; accessed 10 November 2015).

20 Sarah Dillon, 'Imagining Apocalypse: Maggie Gee's *The Flood*', *Contemporary Literature*, 48, no. 3 (2007), 374–97 (p. 376). For a wider perspective on Gee's writing, including the apocalyptic strand, see also Mine Özyurt Kiliç, *Maggie Gee: Writing the Condition-of-England Novel* (London: Bloomsbury, 2013); Sarah Dillon and Caroline Edwards, eds, *Maggie Gee: Critical Essays* (Canterbury: Gylphi, 2015).

21 Dillon, 'Imagining Apocalypse', p. 377.

22 Ibid., p. 381. Dillon cites M. H. Abrams, 'Apocalypse: Theme and Variations', *The Apocalypse in English Renaissance Thought and Literature*, ed. C. S. Patrides and Joseph Wittreich (Manchester: Manchester University Press, 1984), pp. 342–68 (p. 343).

23 Dillon, 'Imagining Apocalypse', p. 377.

24 Adam Trexler, *Anthropocene Fictions: The Novel in a Time of Climate Change* (Charlottesville: University of Virginia Press, 2015), p. 115.

25 David Lodge, *Paradise News* (London: Penguin, 1992), p. 352.

Chapter 3

1 Tom Perrotta, *The Leftovers* (London: Fourth Estate, 2012), pp. 10, 12. All subsequent references will be given parenthetically as *TL*, followed by page number.

2 Ron Charles also cites these words about grief in his perceptive review of *The Leftovers*; *The Washington Post*, 30 August 2011 (https://www.washingtonpost.com/entertainment/books/ron-charles-reviews-the-leftovers-by-tom-perrotta/2011/08/22/gIQA22rWqJ_story.html; accessed 9 October 2011).

3 21 May was the precise date that Camping predicted for the apocalyptic event.

4 Michael Northcott, *An Angel Directs the Storm: Apocalyptic Religion and American Empire* (London: SCM, 2007), p. 59.

5 Matthew Avery Sutton, *American Apocalypse: A History of Modern Evangelicalism* (Cambridge, MA: Harvard University Press, 2014), p. 3.

6 Ibid., p. 372. He cites Pew Research Center, 'Jesus Christ's Return to Earth', 14 July 2010 (www.pewresearch.org/daily-number/jesus-christs-return-to-earth/); Philip Goff, Arthur E. Farnsley II and Peter J. Thuesen, *The Bible in American Life*, A National Study by the Center for the Study of Religion and American Culture, Indiana

University–Purdue University, Indianapolis, 6 March 2014, p. 22 (http://www.raac.iupui.edu/files/2713/9413/8354/Bible_in_American_Life_Report_March_6_2014.pdf).

7 For a reading of the complexity of gender politics in relation to 'the literary practice of belief' in the *Left Behind* novels, see Amy Hungerford, *Postmodern Belief* (Princeton: Princeton University Press, 2010), pp. 121–31.

8 For an overview of LaHaye's career, cultural influence and affiliations with particular reference to *Left Behind*, see Avery Sutton, *American Apocalypse* (2014), pp. 363–6.

9 Jennie Chapman, *Plotting Apocalypse: Reading, Agency and Identity in the Left Behind Series* (Jackson: University Press of Mississippi, 2013), pp. 8–10.

10 Ibid., p. 4.

11 Amy Johnson Frykholm, *Rapture Culture: Left Behind in Evangelical America* (Oxford: Oxford University Press, 2004), p. 4.

12 Thanks to Ben Whitehouse who described *Player One* as a 'collage novel' in a pub chat in December 2009.

13 Douglas Coupland, *Player One* (London: Heinemann, 2009), p. 240.

14 Douglas Coupland, *Generation A* (London: Windmill, 2010), pp. 296–7.

15 http://coupland.com/tag/museum-of-the-rapture/ (accessed 8 October 2015).

16 Barbara Sibbald, 'Coupland's *Museum of the Rapture* Needs Contributions', *Canadian Medical Association Journal*, 19 December 2011, http://www.cmaj.ca/content/184/1/80 (accessed 8 October 2015).

17 Peter O'Leary, *The Leftovers* (review of television series), *Religious Studies Review*, 41, no. 1 (2015), 19.

18 Tom Perrotta, '*The Leftovers* Won't Be Like Lost – It'll Have an Ending', *Wired*, 27 June 2014 (http://www.wired.com/2014/06/the-leftovers-tom-perrotta/; accessed 20 November 2015).

19 Pew Research Center, 'America's Changing Religious Landscape', 12 May 2015, (http://www.pewforum.org/2015/05/12/americas-changing-religious-landscape/; accessed 26 November 2015).

20 The survey indicates that 70.6 per cent of Americans describe themselves as Christians, a significant fall from the 78.4 per cent established in the 2007 survey. This decline of Christianity is countered by a 1.2 per cent increase in other faiths and a 6.7 per cent rise of those who are 'unaffiliated'. (http://www.pewforum.org/2015/05/12/americas-changing-religious-landscape/; accessed 26 November 2015).

21 Slavoj Žižek, *Event: Philosophy in Transit* (London: Penguin, 2014), p. 2.

22 Steven Poole, 'Life after the Rapture' (review of *The Leftovers*), *The Guardian*, 30 March 2012 (http://www.theguardian.com/books/2012/mar/30/leftovers-tom-perrotta-review; accessed 9 October 2015).

23 For a wider discussion of literary responses to September 11, see, for example, Ann Keniston and Jeanne Follansbee Quinn, eds, *Literature after 9/11* (New York: Routledge, 2008); Arthur Bradley and Andrew Tate, *The New Atheist Novel: Fiction, Philosophy and Polemic after 9/11* (London: Continuum, 2010); Richard Gray, *After the Fall: American Literature since 9/11* (Oxford: Wiley-Blackwell, 2011).

24 Stephen King, 'The Eerie Aftermath of a Mass Exit' (Review of *The Leftovers*), *The New York Times*, 25 August 2011 (http://www.nytimes.com/2011/08/28/books/review/the-leftovers-by-tom-perrotta-book-review.html?_r=0; accessed 9 October 2015).

25 Robert McGill, 'The Sublime Simulacrum: Vancouver in Douglas Coupland's Geography of Apocalypse', *Essays on Canadian Writing*, 70 (2000), 252–76 (p. 270).

26 Mark Knight, *An Introduction to Religion and Literature* (London: Continuum, 2009), pp. 127–8.

Chapter 4

1 Margaret Atwood, *MaddAddam* (London: Bloomsbury, 2013), p. xiv. All subsequent references will be given parenthetically as *MA*, followed by page number.

2 Katherine V. Snyder, '"Time to Go": The Post-apocalyptic and the Post-traumatic in Margaret Atwood's *Oryx and Crake*', *Studies in the Novel*, 43, no. 4 (Winter 2011), 470–89 (p. 470).

3 Margaret Atwood, *Oryx and Crake* (London: Virago, 2009), p. 397. All subsequent references will be given parenthetically as *OC*, followed by page number.

4 Margaret Atwood, *The Year of the Flood* (London: Virago, 2010), p. 3. All subsequent references will be given parenthetically as *YF*, followed by page number.

5 Cormac McCarthy, *The Road* (London: Picador, 2007), p. 31.

6 For a reading of *Oryx and Crake* in relation to 'Last Man' fiction, see Barbara Korte, 'Fundamentalism and the End: A Reading of Margaret Atwood's Oryx and Crake in the Context of Last Man Fiction', in *Literary Encounters of Fundamentalism: A Case Book*, ed. Klaus

Stierstofer and Annette Kern-Stähler (Heidelberg: Universitätsverla g, 2008), pp. 151–63; see also Gerry Canavan, 'Hope, But Not for Us: Ecological Science Fiction and the End of the World in Margaret Atwood's *Oryx and Crake* and *The Year of the Flood*', *Lit: Literature Interpretation Theory*, 23, no. 2 (2012), 138–59 (p. 140).

7   Karen F. Stein, 'Problematic Paradice in *Oryx and Crake*', in *Margaret Atwood: The Robber Bride, The Blind Assassin, Oryx and Crake*, ed. J. Brooks Bouson (London: Continuum, 2010), pp. 141–55 (pp. 143, 147).

8   Ibid., p. 143.

9   James Berger, *After the End: Representations of Post-Apocalypse* (Minneapolis: University of Minnesota Press, 1999), pp. 5–6.

10   Maggie Gee, *The Flood* (London: Saqi, 2005), p. 215.

11   Calina Ciobanu, 'Rewriting the Human at the End of the Anthropocene in Margaret Atwood's *MaddAddam* Trilogy', *The Minnesota Review*, 83 (2014), 153–62 (p. 154).

12   I conducted this interview via Skype in the Summer of 2010. Andrew Tate, 'Natural Lore', Interview with Margaret Atwood, *Third Way*, 33, no. 7 (September 2010), 26–31.

13   Shannon Hengen, 'Moral Environmental Debt in *Payback* and *Oryx and Crake*', in Bouson, *Margaret Atwood* (2010), pp. 129–40 (p. 129).

14   Ibid., p. 130.

15   Peter Scott, *A Political Theology of Nature* (Cambridge: Cambridge University Press, 2003), p. 8. Scott is quoting Lynn White, 'The Historical Roots of our Ecologic Crisis', *Science* 155 (1967), 1203–7.

16   Pete Moore, 'Gaia Warning' [Interview with James Lovelock], *Third Way*, 28, no. 5 (June 2005), pp. 18–22 (p. 20). Cited in Richard Bauckham, *Bible and Ecology: Rediscovering the Community of Creation* (London: Darton, 2010), p. 2.

17   Bauckham, *Bible and Ecology* (2010), p. 28.

18   Michael Northcott, *A Moral Climate: The Ethics of Global Warming* (London: Darton, 2007), p. 7.

19   'Religious Groups' Views of Global Warming', Pew Research Center, Religion and Public Life, 16 April 2009 (http://www.pewforum.org/2009/04/16/religious-groups-views-on-global-warming/; accessed 18 November 2015). For further analysis of the survey, see Leo Hickman, 'Just What Is It with Evangelical Christians and Climate Change?', *The Guardian*, 17 April 2009 (http://www.theguardian.com/environment/blog/2009/apr/17/climate-change-religion; accessed 18 November 2015).

20 The essay, 'Burning Bushes: Why Heaven and Hell Went to Planet X', was originally delivered as part of the Richard Ellman Lectures in Modern Literature that Atwood delivered at Emory University, Atlanta, 24–26 October 2010.

21 Margaret Atwood, *In Other Words: SF and the Human Imagination* (London: Virago, 2011), p. 40. All subsequent references will be given as *IOW*, followed by page number.

22 Andrew Hoogheem, 'Secular Apocalypses: Darwinian Criticism and Atwoodian Floods', *Mosaic*, 45, no. 2 (2012), 55–71 (p. 57).

23 J. Brooks Bouson, ' "It's Game Over Forever": Atwood's Satiric Vision of a Bioengineered Posthuman Future in *Oryx and Crake*', *Journal of Commonwealth Literature*, 39, no. 3 (2004), 139–56 (p. 141).

24 Coral Ann Howells, *Margaret Atwood*, 2nd ed. (Houndmills: Palgrave, 2005), p. 171.

25 Ibid., p. 182.

26 Bouson, 'It's Game Over Forever' (2004), pp. 140–1.

27 Howells, *Margaret Atwood*, p. 182.

28 John Milton, *Paradise Lost*, Book 12, line 646.

29 'Of the Creation, and of the Naming of the Animals, Spoken by Adam One', *YF*, pp. 13–15.

30 Howells, in one of the first critical responses to the novel, also explores Crake's warning about art and Jimmy's subsequent subversion of the injunction; Howells, *Margaret Atwood*, p. 182.

31 Ralph Pordzik, 'The Posthuman Future of Man: Anthropocentrism and the Other of Technology in Anglo-American Science Fiction', *Utopian Studies*, 23, no. 1 (2012), 142–61 (p. 154).

32 Ibid., p. 154.

33 Ibid., p. 156.

34 Andrew Sean Greer, 'Final Showdown' (review of Margaret Atwood's *MaddAddam*), *The New York Times*, 6 September 2013 (http://www.nytimes.com/2013/09/08/books/review/maddaddam-by-margaret-atwood.html?pagewanted=all&_r=1; accessed 21 February 2016).

35 Ibid.

36 Ciobanu, 'Rewriting the Human' (2014), p. 161.

37 Mark Bosco, 'The Apocalyptic Imagination in *Oryx and Crake*', in Bouson, *Margaret Atwood* (2010), pp. 156–71 (p. 157).

38 Ibid., p. 156.

39 Tate, 'Natural Lore' (2010), p. 29.

Chapter 5

1 Frédéric Gros, *A Philosophy of Walking*, trans. John Howe (London: Verso, 2015), p. 1.

2 Ibid., pp. 4–5.

3 Cormac McCarthy, *The Road* (London: Picador, 2007), p. 186. All subsequent references will be given parenthetically as *TR*, followed by page number.

4 Joseph A. Amato, *On Foot: A History of Walking* (New York: New York University Press, 2004), pp. 151, 264.

5 Thoreau originally delivered 'Walking' as a pair of lectures in 1851. The essay was posthumously published in 1862. Henry D. Thoreau, *Walden, Civil Disobedience and Other Writings*, ed. William Rossi, 3rd ed. (New York: Norton, 2008), pp. 5, 262. All subsequent references will appear parenthetically as *W*, followed by page number.

6 Quoted in Amato, *On Foot* (2004), p. 127. Amato cites *Walking Magazine, The Quotable Walker* (New York: R. D.Walking, 2000), p. 100.

7 Rebecca Solnit, *Wanderlust: A History of Walking* (London: Granta, 2014, Kindle edition), n. p.

8 Ibid., p. 7.

9 Ibid., p. 8.

10 Douglas Coupland, *Miss Wyoming* (London: Flamingo, 2000), pp. 51–2. All subsequent references will be given parenthetically as *MW*, followed by page number.

11 For a more detailed exploration of Coupland's drifters, walkers and seekers, see Andrew Tate, *Douglas Coupland* (Manchester: Manchester University Press, 2007), p. 107 ff.

12 Joshua Ferris, *The Unnamed* (London: Penguin, 2010), p. 196. All subsequent references will be given parenthetically as *U*, followed by page number.

13 Tim Adams, 'The *Unnamed* by Joshua Ferris' (review), *The Guardian*, 21 February 2010 (http://www.theguardian.com/books/2010/feb/21/the-unnamed-joshua-ferris; accessed 9 December 2015).

14 Michael Titlestad, 'The Logic of the Apocalypse: A Clerical Rejoinder', *Safundi: The Journal of South African and American Studies*, 14, no. 1 (2013), 93–110 (p. 95).

15 Diletta De Cristofaro, 'Beyond the Sense of an Ending: Post-Apocalyptic Critical Temporalities', Unpublished PhD thesis, University of Nottingham, July 2015, p. 55.

16 Ibid., p. 56.

17 Peter Boxall, *Twenty-First-Century Fiction* (Cambridge: Cambridge University Press, 2013, Kindle edition), p. 220.

18 Ashley Kunsa, '"Maps of the World in Its Becoming": Post-Apocalyptic Naming in Cormac McCarthy's *The Road*', *Journal of Modern Literature*, 33, no. 1 (2009), 57–74 (p. 62).

19 Amy Hungerford, *Postmodern Belief: American Literature and Religion since 1960* (Princeton: Princeton University Press, 2010), p. 134.

20 Shelly L. Rambo, 'Beyond Redemption?: Reading Cormac McCarthy's *The Road* after the End of the World', *Studies in the Literary Imagination*, 41, no. 2 (2008), 99–120 (p. 100).

21 For readings of the representation of region in McCarthy's fiction see, for example, Lydia R. Cooper, 'McCarthy, Tennessee, and the Southern Gothic', in *The Cambridge Companion to Cormac McCarthy*, ed. Steven Frye (Cambridge: Cambridge University Press, 2013), pp. 41–53; Brian Evenson, 'History and the Problem of Evil in McCarthy's Western Novels', in Frye, *The Cambridge Companion to Cormac McCarthy* (2013), pp. 67–78.

22 Rambo, 'Beyond Redemption?' (2008), p. 102.

23 Ibid., p. 100.

24 Lydia Cooper, 'Cormac McCarthy's *The Road* as Apocalyptic Grail Narrative', *Studies in the Novel*, 43, no. 2 (2011), 218–36. A more detailed exploration of the novel's biblical echoes is included in the introduction to this book.

25 Ibid., p. 220.

26 Jim Crace, *The Pesthouse* (London: Picador, 2013, Kindle edition), p. 6. All subsequent references will be given parenthetically as *TP*, followed by page number.

27 Philip Tew, *Jim Crace* (Manchester: Manchester University Press, 2006), pp. 194–5.

28 Caroline Edwards, 'Microtopias: The Post-apocalyptic Communities of Jim Crace's *The Pesthouse*', *Textual Practice*, 23, no. 5 (2009), 763–86 (p. 769).

29 Ibid., p. 779.

30 Gros, *A Philosophy of Walking* (2015), p. 6.

Chapter 6

1 Nick Hornby, *Otherwise Pandemonium* (London: Penguin, 2005), pp. 16, 24. All subsequent references will be given parenthetically as *OP*, followed by page number.

2 Kimberley Reynolds, *Radical Children's Literature: Future Visions and Aesthetic Transformations in Juvenile Fiction* (Houndmills: Palgrave, 2007), p. 154.

3 Miranda A. Green-Barteet, '"I'm Beginning to Know Who I Am": The Rebellious Subjectivities of Katniss Everdeen and Tris Prior', in *Female Rebellion in Young Adult Dystopian Fiction*, ed. Sara K. Day, Miranda A. Green-Barteet and Amy L. Montz (Aldershot: Ashgate, 2014), pp. 33–50 (p. 33).

4 Balaka Basu, Katherine R. Broad and Carrie Hintz, 'Introduction', in *Contemporary Dystopian Fiction for Young Adults: Brave New Teenagers*, ed. Balaka Basu, Katherine R. Broad and Carrie Hintz (Abingdon: Routledge, 2013), pp. 1–15 (p. 7).

5 See, for example, Roberta Seelinger Trites, *Disturbing the Universe: Power and Repression in Adolescent Literature* (Iowa City: Iowa University Press, 2000); Claudia Mills, ed., *Ethics and Children's Literature* (Farnham: Ashgate, 2014); George A. Dunn and Nicholas Michaud, eds, *The Hunger Games and Philosophy: A Critique of Pure Treason* (Hoboken: Wiley, 2012).

6 Brian Jansen, 'Zygmunt Bauman, Postmodern Ethics, and Utopia as Process in Suzanne Collins' *The Hunger Games*: "It's the First Gift That's Always the Hardest to Payback"', *Jeunesse: Young People, Texts, Cultures*, 7, no. 1 (2015), 18–41 (p. 21).

7 James Dashner, *The Maze Runner* (Frome: Chicken House, 2013), p. 201. All subsequent references will be given parenthetically as *MR*, followed by page number.

8 Suzanne Collins, *The Hunger Games* (London: Scholastic, 2011), p. 21. All subsequent references will be given parenthetically as *HG*, followed by page number.

9 Suzanne Collins, *Mockingjay* (New York: Scholastic, 2010), p. 82.

10 Indeed, Basu describes *Divergent* as 'what happens when Harry Potter meets *The Hunger Games* [...] an adventure-*cum*-romance set in a dystopian society based around the wizarding world's Sorting Hat': 'What Faction Are You In? The Pleasure of Being Sorted in Veronica Roth's *Divergent*', in Basu, Broad and Hintz (2013), pp. 19–33 (p. 22).

11 Veronica Roth, *Divergent* (London: HarperCollins, 2013), p. 22. All subsequent references will be given parenthetically as *D*, followed by page number.

12 Basu, Broad and Hintz, *Contemporary Dystopian Fiction for Young Adults* (2013), p. 20.

13 Susan Louise Stewart, 'Dystopian Sacrifice, Scapegoats, and Neal Shusterman's *Unwind*', in Basu, Broad and Hintz (2013), pp. 159–73 (p. 162).

14 Karl Hand, 'Come Now, Let Us Treason Together: Conversion and Revolutionary Consciousness in Luke 23: 35–38 and *The Hunger Games* Trilogy', *Literature and Theology*, 29, no. 3 (2015), 348–65 (pp. 350, 352).

15 Veronica Hollinger, 'Stories about the Future: From Patterns of Expectation to Pattern Recognition', *Science Fiction Studies*, 33, no. 3 (Nov. 2006), 452–72 (p. 452).

16 Jansen, 'Zygmunt Bauman, Postmodern Ethics, and Utopia' (2015), p. 30.

17 Green-Barteet, 'I'm Beginning to Know Who I Am' (2014), p. 34.

18 I highly recommend a quartet of essays grouped under the section heading 'Resistance, Surveillance and Simulacra', in *Of Bread, Blood and the Hunger Games: Critical Essays on the Suzanne Collins Trilogy*, ed. Mary F. Pharr, Leisa A. Clark, Donald E. Palumbo and C. W. Sullivan III (Jefferson: McFarland, 2012): see Amy L. Montz, 'Costuming the Resistance: The Female Spectacle of Rebellion', pp. 139–47; Kelley Wezner, '"Perhaps I Am Watching You Now": Panem's Panopticons', pp. 148–57; Shannon R. Mortimore-Smith, 'Fueling the Spectacle: Audience as "Gamemaker"', pp. 158–66; Helen Day, 'Simulacra, Sacrifice and Survival in *The Hunger Games*, *Battle Royale*, and *The Running Man*', pp. 167–77.

19 Scott Bukatman, *Terminal Identity: The Virtual Subject in Post-Modern Science Fiction* (Durham: Duke University Press, 1993), p. 36.

20 Alice Curry, *Environmental Crisis in Young Adult Fiction: A Poetics of Earth* (Houndmills: Palgrave, 2013), p. 47.

21 Montz, 'Costuming the Resistance' (2012), p. 139. See also Curry on the exploitation of Katniss, both in and out of the arena, 56ff.

22 Victoria Flanagan, *Technology and Identity in Young Adult Fiction: The Posthuman Subject* (Basingstoke: Palgrave, 2014), pp. 137–8.

23 Ibid., pp. 132, 143.

24 Montz, 'Costuming the Resistance' (2012), p. 140.

25 Katherine R. Broad, '"The Dandelion in the Spring": Utopia as Romance in Suzanne Collins's *The Hunger Games* Trilogy', in Basu, Broad and Hintz, (2013), pp. 117–30 (p. 119).

26 Collins, *Mockingjay*, p. 255.

27 See, for example, Kathryn Strong Hansen, 'The Metamorphosis of Katniss Everdeen: *The Hunger Games*, Myth and Femininity', *Children's Literature Association Quarterly*, 40, no. 2 (2015), 161–78 (p. 161); Ellyn Lem and Holly Hassel, '"Killer" Katniss and "Lover Boy" Peeta: Suzanne Collins's Defiance of Gender-Genred Reading', in Pharr et al. (2012), pp. 118–27; Jennifer Mitchell, 'Of Queer Necessity: Panem's Hunger Games as Gender Games', in Pharr et al. (2012), pp. 128–38; Katha Pollitt, '*The Hunger Games*' Feral Feminism', *The Nation*, 3 April 2012 (http://www.thenation.com/article/hunger-games-feral-feminism/; accessed 6 November 2015).

28 For readings of gender politics and the romantic plots of the sequence, see, for example, Broad, 'The Dandelion in the Spring', in Basu, Broad and Hintz, (2013), pp. 117–30 (p. 118).

29 Ibid., p. 126.

30 Wezner, 'Perhaps I Am Watching You Now' (2012), p. 149.

31 Day, 'Simulacra, Sacrifice and Survival' (2012), p. 176.

32 Curry, *Environmental Crisis in Young Adult Fiction* (2013), p. 105.

33 Mary J. Couzelis, 'The Future Is Pale: Race in Contemporary Young Adult Dystopian Novels', in Basu, Broad and Hintz (2013), pp. 131–44 (pp. 132, 138).

34 Ibid., p. 139.

35 Ibid., p. 140.

36 Ewan Morrison, 'YA Fiction Teaches Children to Submit to the Free Market, Not Fight Authority', *The Guardian*, 1 September 2014 (http://www.theguardian.com/books/2014/sep/01/ya-dystopias-children-free-market-hunger-games-the-giver-divergent; accessed 25 February 2015).

37 Andrew O'Hehir, '"Divergent" and "Hunger Games" as Capitalist Agitprop', *Salon*, 22 March 2014 (http://www.salon.com/2014/03/22/divergent_and_hunger_games_as_capitalist_agitprop/; accessed 25 February 2015).

38 Hand, 'Come Now, Let Us Treason Together' (2015), p. 349.

39 Martha Rainbolt, 'Katniss Everdeen's Emerging Moral Consciousness in *The Hunger Games*', in *Ethics and Children's Literature*, ed. Claudia Mills (Farnham: Ashgate, 2014), pp. 223–32 (p. 223).

40 Pollitt, 'The Hunger Games' Feral Feminism' (2012).

41 Steven Zeitchik, 'What The Hunger Games Really Means', Los Angeles Times, 24 March 2012 (http://articles.latimes.com/2012/mar/24/entertainment/la-et-hunger-politics-20120324; accessed 6 November 2015).

42 Yonah Ringlestein, 'Real or Not Real: The Hunger Games as Transmediated Religion', Journal of Religion and Popular Culture, 25, no. 3 (2013), 372–87 (p. 384).

43 'Five Thai Students Held for "Hunger Games" Salute at PM', 19 November 2014, BBC news (http://www.bbc.co.uk/news/world-asia-30110280; accessed 4 January 2016).

Chapter 7

1 Alasdair McIntyre, After Virtue (London: Bloomsbury, 2013), p. 250.

2 Gerry Canavan, 'Hope, But Not for Us: Ecological Science Fiction and the End of the World in Margaret Atwood's Oryx and Crake and The Year of the Flood', Lit: Literature Interpretation Theory, 23, no. 2 (2012), 138–59 (p. 139). Canavan cites, in particular, three texts by Jameson that debate this perspective: The Seeds of Time (New York: Columbia University Press, 1994); 'Future City', New Left Review 21 (May–June 2003): n. p. (http://newleftreview.org/?view=2449); and Archaeologies of the Future: The Desire Called Utopia and Other Science Fictions (New York: Verso, 2007).

3 Maggie Gee, The Flood (London: Saqi, 2005), p. 133.

4 Cormac McCarthy, The Road (London: Picador, 2007), p. 199.

5 Peter Boxall, Twenty-First-Century Fiction (Cambridge: Cambridge University Press, 2013, Kindle edition), p. 226.

6 John Gray, Black Mass: Apocalyptic Religion and the Death of Utopia (London: Penguin, 2008), p. 297.

7 Michael Titlestad, 'The Logic of the Apocalypse: A Clerical Rejoinder', Safundi: The Journal of South African and American Studies, 14, no. 1 (2013), 93–110 (p. 104).

8 Terry Eagleton, Hope without Optimism (New Haven: Yale University Press, 2015), p. 27.

9 Slavoj Žižek, Event: Philosophy in Transit (London: Penguin, 2014), p. 2.

10 Ibid., p. 3.

11 Margaret Atwood, *MaddAddam* (London: Bloomsbury, 2013), p. 390.

12 Charlie Jane Anders, 'Why Are Many of Today's Hottest Authors Writing Post-Apocalyptic Books?', *IO9: We Come from the Future*, 21 October 2014 (http://io9.com/how-did-post-apocalyptic-stories-become-the-hottest-boo-1649022270; accessed 11 March 2015).

13 Ibid.

14 Emily St John Mandel, *Station Eleven* (London: Picador, 2015), p. 36. All subsequent references will be given as *SE*, followed by page number.

PRIMARY
BIBLIOGRAPHY

Atwood, Margaret, *Oryx and Crake* (London: Virago, 2009).

Atwood, Margaret, *The Year of the Flood* (London: Virago, 2010).

Atwood, Margaret, *MaddAddam* (London: Bloomsbury, 2013).

Atwood, Margaret, *The Heart Goes Last* (London: Bloomsbury, 2015).

Ballard, J. G., *The Drowned World* (London: Harper Perennial, 2008).

Ballard, J. G., *Kingdom Come* (London: Fourth Estate, 2014), Kindle edition.

Barnes, Julian, *A History of the World in 10 ½ Chapters* (London: Random House, 2009), iBooks edition.

Collins, Suzanne, *Catching Fire* (New York: Scholastic, 2009).

Collins, Suzanne, *The Hunger Games* (London: Scholastic, 2009).

Collins, Suzanne, *Mockingbird* (New York: Scholastic, 2010).

Coupland, Douglas, *JPod* (London: Bloomsbury, 2006).

Coupland, Douglas, *Generation A* (London: William Heinemann, 2009).

Coupland, Douglas, *Player One* (London: William Heinemann, 2010).

Crace, Jim, *The Pesthouse* (London: Picador, 2007), Kindle edition.

Dashner, James, *The Death Cure* (Frome: Chicken House, 2013).

Dashner, James, *The Kill Order* (Frome: Chicken House, 2013).

Dashner, James, *The Maze Runner* (Frome: Chicken House, 2013).

Dashner, James, *The Scorch Trials* (Frome: Chicken House, 2013).

Eggers, Dave, *Your Fathers, Where Are They? And the Prophets, Do They Live Forever?* (London: Penguin, 2014).

Ferris, Joshua, *The Unnamed* (London: Penguin, 2010), Kindle edition.

Ferris, Joshua, *To Rise Again at a Decent Hour* (London: Penguin, 2014), Kindle edition.

Gee, Maggie, *The Flood* (London: Saqi, 2005).

Grant, Michael, *Gone* (London: Harper Collins, 2008), Kindle edition.

Hornby, Nick, *How to Be Good* (London: Penguin, 2001).

King, Stephen, *Under the Dome* (London: Hodder, 2009), Kindle edition.

Lodge, David, *Paradise News* (London: Penguin, 1992).

McCarthy, Cormac, *The Road* (London: Pan, 2007).

McEwan, Ian, *Solar* (London: Vintage, 2011).

Maine, David, *The Flood* (Edinburgh: Canongate, 2005).

Mitchell, David, *Ghostwritten* (London: Sceptre, 1999).

Mitchell, David, *Cloud Atlas* (London: Sceptre, 2004).

Mitchell, David, *The Bone Clocks* (London: Sceptre, 2014).

Nicholls, David, *Us* (London: Hodder, 2014).

Perrotta, Tom, *The Leftovers* (London: Fourth Estate, 2012), iBooks edition.

Robinson, Kim Stanley, *Forty Signs of Rain* (London: HarperCollins, 2004).

Robinson, Kim Stanley, *Fifty Degrees Below* (London: HarperCollins, 2013), Kindle edition.

Robinson, Kim Stanley, *Sixty Days and Counting* (London: HarperCollins, 2013), Kindle edition.

Roth, Veronica, *Divergent* (London: HarperCollins, 2013).

Self, Will, *The Book of Dave* (London: Viking, 2007), Kindle edition.

ANNOTATED SECONDARY BIBLIOGRAPHY

The long tradition of thinking about the end of the world is a concern for many different academic disciplines. Theology and religious history provide vital contexts, but apocalyptic discourse also haunts continental philosophy, sociology and, in recent years, scholarship on cinema and the visual arts. Although this book engages with the specifics of one aspect of popular culture in a particular moment – the novel in the early twenty-first century – it is indebted to the rich variety of sources that seek to understand alternative projections of the future.

The field is enormous and still expanding. This bibliography could not hope to be exhaustive, but it is, I hope, useful for readers who are interested in engaging with apocalyptic discourse in its different iterations. I have divided the material into a variety of subheadings, including sections on theology and the broader tradition of end-of-the-world narratives that inform contemporary writing as well as material on eco-criticism and mobility.

The apparently increasing fascination with catastrophe and future-fear that shaped many late-twentieth-century popular narratives has been matched by the interest of literary and cultural critics. Art and scholarship seem equally beguiled by the possibility of our collective downfall and there are no signs of a change in this mood. The section on contemporary fiction, film and culture indicates the breadth of a distinctive and often contentious area of debate. Two texts have generated so much critical attention that they have been granted their own subsection: Margaret Atwood's 'MaddAddam' trilogy (2003–13) and Cormac McCarthy's *The Road* have inspired more critical discussion than many successful writers receive for their entire oeuvre. The novels are relatively rare in matching critical praise, commercial success and sustained academic interest.

Scholarship on children's literature and YA fiction forms a significant part of literary debate regarding the representation of the family of genres related to catastrophe, dystopia and post-collapse societies. To date, Collins's series has received more academic (and popular) attention than either the 'Divergent' or 'Maze Runner' sequences. The increasing interest in 'crossover' fiction that is not only ostensibly written for teenagers, but also bought by older readers suggests that many of these narratives are likely to be explored side by side with novels by, for example, Atwood and McCarthy. However, the current critical convention tends to see YA fiction as a separate, emerging canon. The focus of recent monographs and articles on twenty-first-century YA apocalyptic or dystopian fiction is often on the politics of representation and a range of urgent social concerns including post-humanism, technologies of surveillance and environmentalism.

The apocalyptic tradition

Aldiss, Brian W., *Billion Year Spree: The History of Science Fiction* (London: Weidenfeld and Nicolson, 1973).

Bukatman, Scott, *Terminal Identity: The Virtual Subject in Post-Modern Science Fiction* (Durham: Duke University Press, 1993).

Darsey, James, *The Prophetic Tradition and Radical Rhetoric in America* (New York: New York University Press, 1997).

Fitch, Raymond E., *The Poison Sky: Myth and Apocalypse in Ruskin* (London: Ohio University Press, 1982).

Goldsmith, Steven, *Unbuilding Jerusalem: Apocalypse and Romantic Representation* (Ithaca, NY: Cornell University Press, 1993).

Hanley, Keith, 'The Discourse of Natural Beauty', in Wheeler (1995), pp. 10–37.

Harrison, J. F. C., *The Second Coming: Popular Millenarianism, 1780–1850* (London: Routledge, 1979).

Huntington, John, 'The Science Fiction of H. G. Wells', in Parrinder (1979), pp. 34–50.

Knight, Mark, *An Introduction to Religion and Literature* (London: Continuum, 2009).

Lawrence, D. H., *Apocalypse and the Writings on Revelation*, edited by Mara Kalnins (Cambridge: Cambridge University Press, 1980).

Mills, Kevin, *Approaching Apocalypse: Unveiling Revelation in Victorian Writing* (Lewisburg: Bucknell University Press, 2007).

Parrinder, Patrick, ed., *Science Fiction: A Critical Guide* (Longman: London, 1979).

Parrinder, Patrick, 'The Ruined Futures of British Science Fiction', in Leader (2002), pp. 209–33.

Roberts, Jonathan, 'Wordsworth's Apocalypse', *Literature and Theology*, 20, no. 4 (2006), 361–78.

Rogers, Jane, 'Jane Rogers's Top 10 Cosy Catastrophes', *The Guardian*, 5 July 2012 (http://www.theguardian.com/books/2012/jul/05/jane-rogers-top-10-cosy-catastrophes).

Wheeler, Michael, ed., *Ruskin and Environment: The Storm-Cloud of the Nineteenth-Century* (Manchester: Manchester University Press, 1995).

Wheeler, Michael, ed., 'Environment and Apocalypse', in Wheeler (1995), pp. 165–86.

Wheeler, Michael, *Ruskin's God* (Cambridge: Cambridge University Press, 1999).

Wright, T. R., *D. H. Lawrence and the Bible* (Cambridge: Cambridge University Press, 2000).

Biblical apocalypse and theological contexts

Burdett, Michael S., *Eschatology and the Technological Future* (Abingdon: Routledge, 2015).

Cohn, Norman, *Noah's Flood: The Genesis Story in Western Thought* (New Haven: Yale University Press, 1996).

Dawn, Maggi, *The Writing on the Wall: High Art, Popular Culture and the Bible* (London: Hodder, 2005).

Ellul, Jacques, *Apocalypse: The Book of Revelation* (New York: Seabury Press, 1977).

Holloway, Richard, ed., *Revelations: Personal Responses to the Bible* (Edinburgh: Canongate, 2005).

Jasper, David, *The Sacred Desert: Religion, Literature, Art, and Culture* (Oxford: Blackwell, 2004).

Keller, Catherine, *Apocalypse Now and Then: A Feminist Guide to the End of the World* (Boston: Beacon, 1996).

Keller, Catherine, *God and Power: Counter-Apocalyptic Journeys* (Minneapolis: Fortress, 2005).

Kovacs, J. L., Christopher Rowland and Rebekah Callow, *Revelation: The Apocalypse of Jesus Christ* (Oxford: Blackwell, 2004).

Kyle, Richard, *Awaiting the Millennium: A History of End-Time Thinking* (Leicester: IVP, 1998).

McDannell, Colleen and Bernhard Lang, eds, *Heaven: A History* (New Haven: Yale University Press, 1988).

McGrath, Alister E., *A Brief History of Heaven* (Oxford: Blackwell, 2003).

Mangina, Joseph L., *Revelation* (London: SCM Press, 2010).

Messer, Neil, ed., *Theological Issues in Bioethics: An Introduction with Readings* (London: Darton, 2002).

Moltmann, Jürgen, *In the End – The Beginning*, translated by Margaret Kohl (London: SCM, 2004).

Moyise, Steven, ed., *Studies in the Book of Revelation* (Edinburgh: T&T Clark, 2001).

Newport, Kenneth G. C., *Apocalypse and Millennium: Studies in Biblical Eisegesis* (Cambridge: Cambridge University Press, 2000).

Northcott, Michael S., *An Angel Directs the Storm: Apocalyptic Religion and American Empire* (London: SCM, 2007).

Plate, Brent S., *The Apocalyptic Imagination: Aesthetics and Ethics at the End of the World* (Glasgow: Trinity St Mungo Press, 1999).

Pleins, J. David, *When the Great Abyss Opened: Classic and Contemporary Readings of Noah's Flood* (Oxford: Oxford University Press, 2003).

Resseguie, James L., *The Revelation of John: A Narrative Commentary* (Grand Rapids: Baker Academic, 2009).

Sandeen, Ernest R., *The Roots of Fundamentalism; British and American Millenarianism, 1800–1930* (Chicago: University of Chicago Press, 1970).

Sutton, Matthew Avery, *American Apocalypse: A History of Modern Evangelicalism* (Cambridge, MA: Harvard University Press, 2014).

Thompson, Leonard L., *The Book of Revelation: Apocalypse and Empire* (New York: Oxford University Press, 1990).

Wright, Tom, *Surprised by Hope* (London: Society for Promoting Christian Knowledge, 2007).

Contemporary fiction, film and culture

Anders, Charlie Jane, 'Why Are Many of Today's Hottest Authors Writing Post-Apocalyptic Books?', *IO9: We Come from the Future*, 21 October 2014 (http://io9.com/how-did-post-apocalyptic-stories-become-the-hottest-boo-1649022270).

Annesley, James, 'Decadence and Disquiet: Recent American Fiction and the Coming "*Fin de Siècle*"', *Journal of American Studies*, 30, no. 3 (1996), 365–79.

Annesley, James, *Blank Fictions* (London: Pluto, 1998).

Barber, Nicholas, 'The End is Nigh. Again', *The Guardian*, 28 April 2014, pp. 16–17.

Boxall, Peter, *Twenty-First-Century Fiction: A Critical Introduction* (Cambridge: Cambridge University Press, 2013).

Bradley, Arthur and Andrew Tate, *The New Atheist Novel: Fiction, Philosophy and Polemic after 9/11* (London: Bloomsbury, 2010).

Chapman, Jennie, *Plotting Apocalypse: Reading, Agency and Identity in the Left Behind Series* (Jackson: University Press of Mississippi, 2013).

Childs, Peter and James Green, *Aesthetics and Ethics in Twenty-First Century British Novels: Zadie Smith, Nadeem Aslam, Hari Kunzru and David Mitchell* (London: Bloomsbury, 2013).

Curtis, Claire P., *Postapocalyptic Fiction and the Social Contract* (Plymouth: Lexington, 2010).

De Cristofaro, Diletta, 'Beyond the Sense of an Ending: Post-Apocalyptic Critical Temporalities', Unpublished PhD thesis, University of Nottingham, July 2015.

Diaz, Junot, 'Apocalypse: What Disasters Reveal', *The Boston Review*, 36, no. 3 (1 May 2011) (http://bostonreview.net/junot-diaz-apocalypse-haiti-earthquake).

Dillon, Sarah, 'Imagining Apocalypse: Maggie Gee's *The Flood*', *Contemporary Literature*, 48, no. 3 (2007), 374–97.

Dillon, Sarah and Caroline Edwards, eds, *Maggie Gee: Critical Essays* (Canterbury: Gylphi, 2015).

Dixon, Wheeler Winston, *Visions of the Apocalypse: Spectacles of Destruction in American Cinema* (Columbia: Columbia University Press, 2003).

Edwards, Caroline, 'Microtopias: The Post-apocalyptic Communities of Jim Crace's *The Pesthouse*', *Textual Practice*, 23, no. 5 (2009), 763–86.

Falconer, Rachel, *Hell in Contemporary Fiction: Western Descent Narratives Since 1945* (Edinburgh: Edinburgh University Press, 2007).

Fiddes, Paul S., *The Promised End: Eschatology in Theology and Literature* (Oxford: Blackwell, 2000).

Gasiorek, Andrzej, *JG Ballard* (Manchester: Manchester University Press, 2005).

Goldman, Marlene, *Rewriting Apocalypse in Canadian Fiction* (Montreal: McGill-Queen's Press, 2005).

Gray, Richard, *After the Fall: American Literature since 9/11* (Oxford: Wiley-Blackwell, 2011).

Harbach, Chad, 'The End', *n+1*, issue 6 (December 2007) (https://nplusonemag.com/issue-6/reviews/the-end-the-end-the-end/).

Hungerford, Amy, *Postmodern Belief: American Literature and Religion since 1960* (Princeton: Princeton University Press, 2010).

Johnson Frykholm, Amy, *Rapture Culture: Left Behind in Evangelical America* (Oxford: Oxford University Press, 2004).

Keniston, Ann and Jeanne Follansbee Quinn, eds, *Literature after 9/11* (New York: Routledge, 2008).

Kiliç, Mine Özyurt, *Maggie Gee: Writing the Condition-of-England Novel* (London: Bloomsbury, 2013).

Leader, Zachary, ed., *On Modern British Fiction* (Oxford: Oxford University Press, 2002).

McClure, John A., *Partial Faiths: Postsecular Fiction in the Age of Pynchon and Morrison* (Athens: University of Georgia Press, 2007).

Paik, Peter Y., *From Utopia to Apocalypse: Science Fiction and the Politics of Catastrophe* (Minneapolis: University of Minnesota Press, 2010).

Paknadel, Alexis, 'Anywhere But Here: The Competing (and Complementary) Postmodern Nostalgias of J. G. Ballard and Douglas Coupland', Unpublished doctoral thesis, Lancaster University, 2011.

Parrinder, Patrick, 'The Ruined Futures of British Science Fiction', in Leader (2002), pp. 209–33.

Partridge, Christopher H., ed., *Anthems of Apocalypse: Popular Music and Apocalyptic Thought* (Sheffield: Sheffield Phoenix Press, 2012).

Tate, Andrew, *Contemporary Fiction and Christianity* (London: Continuum, 2008).

Tew, Philip, *Jim Crace* (Manchester: Manchester University Press, 2006).

Thompson, Kirsten Moana, *Apocalyptic Dread: American Film at the Turn of the Millennium* (Albany: State University of New York Press, 2007).

Versluys, Kristiaan, *Out of the Blue: September 11 and the Novel* (New York: Columbia University Press, 2009).

Watkins, Susan, 'Future Shock: Rewriting the Apocalypse in Contemporary Women's Fiction', *Lit: Literature Interpretation Theory*, 23, no. 2 (2012), 119–37.

Margaret Atwood

Atwood, Margaret, '*The Handmaid's Tale and Oryx and Crake* "In Context"', *PMLA*, 119, no. 3, Special Topic: Science Fiction and Literary Studies: The Next Millennium (May 2004), 513–17.

Atwood, Margaret, *In Other Worlds: SF and the Human Imagination* (London: Virago, 2011).

Bergthaller, Hannes, 'Housebreaking the Human Animal: Humanism and the Problem of Sustainability in Margaret Atwood's *Oryx and Crake* and *The Year of the Flood*', *English Studies*, 91, no. 7 (2010), 728–43.

Bouson, J. Brooks, *Brutal Choreographies: Oppositional Strategies and Oppositional Design in the Novels of Margaret Atwood* (Amherst: University of Massachusetts Press, 1993).

Bouson, J. Brooks, '"It's Game Over Forever": Atwood's Satiric Vision of a Bioengineered Posthuman Future in *Oryx and Crake*', *Journal of Commonwealth Literature*, 39, no. 3 (2004), 139–56.

Bouson, J. Brooks, ed., *Margaret Atwood: The Robber Bride, The Blind Assassin, Oryx and Crake* (London: Continuum, 2010).

Bouson, J. Brooks, '"We're Using Up the Earth. It's Almost Gone": A Return to the Post-Apocalyptic Future in Margaret Atwood's *The Year of the Flood*', *The Journal of Commonwealth Literature*, 46, no. 1 (2011), 9–26.

Canavan, Gerry, 'Hope, But Not for Us: Ecological Science Fiction and the End of the World in Margaret Atwood's *Oryx and Crake* and *The Year of the Flood*', *Lit: Literature Interpretation Theory*, 23, no. 2 (2012), 138–59.

Ciobanu, Calina, 'Rewriting the Human at the End of the Anthropocene in Margaret Atwood's *MaddAddam* Trilogy', *The Minnesota Review*, 83 (2014), 153–62.

Glover, Jayne, 'Human/Nature: Ecological Philosophy in Margaret Atwood's *Oryx and Crake*', *English Studies in Africa*, 52, no. 2 (2009), 50–62.

Greer, Andrew Sean, 'Final Showdown' [Review of Margaret Atwood's *MaddAddam*], *The New York Times*, 6 September 2013 (http://www.nytimes.com/2013/09/08/books/review/maddaddam-by-margaret-atwood.html?pagewanted=all&_r=1).

Hollinger, Veronica, 'Stories about the Future: From Patterns of Expectation to Pattern Recognition', *Science Fiction Studies*, 33, no. 3 (2006), 452–72.

Hoogheem, Andrew, 'Secular Apocalypses: Darwinian Criticism and Atwoodian Floods', *Mosaic*, 45, no. 2 (2012), 55–71.

Howells, Coral Ann, *Margaret Atwood*, 2nd ed. (Houndmills: Palgrave, 2005).

Howells, Coral Ann, 'Margaret Atwood's Dystopian Visions: *The Handmaid's Tale* and *Oryx and Crake*', in *The Cambridge Companion to Margaret Atwood*, edited by Coral Ann Howells (Cambridge: Cambridge University Press, 2006), pp. 161–75.

Hume, Kathryn, 'Diffused Satire in Contemporary American Fiction', *Modern Philology*, 105, no. 2 (November 2007), 300–25.

Ingersoll, Earl G., 'Survival in Margaret Atwood's Novel *Oryx and Crake*', *Extrapolation*, 45, no. 2 (2004), 162–75.

Korte, Barbara, 'Fundamentalism and the End: A Reading of Margaret Atwood's Oryx and Crake in the Context of Last Man Fiction', in *Literary Encounters of Fundamentalism: A Case Book*, edited by Klaus Stierstofer and Annette Kern-Stähler (Heidelberg: Universitätsverlag, 2008), pp. 151–63.

Martin, Tim, 'Review of *MaddAddam*', *The Daily Telegraph*, 25 August 2013 (http://www.telegraph.co.uk/culture/books/fictionreviews/

10259661/MaddAddam-by-Margaret-Atwood-review.html; accessed 19 October 2015).

Pordzik, Ralph, 'The Posthuman Future of Man: Anthropocentrism and the Other of Technology in Anglo-American Science Fiction', *Utopian Studies*, 23, no. 1 (2012), 142–61.

Snyder, Katherine V., '"Time to Go": The Post-apocalyptic and the Post-traumatic in Margaret Atwood's *Oryx and Crake*', *Studies in the Novel*, 43, no. 4 (2011), 470–89.

Stein, Karen F., 'Problematic Paradice in *Oryx and Crake*', in Bouson (2010), pp. 141–55.

Tate, Andrew, 'Natural Lore' (Interview with Margaret Atwood), *Third Way*, 33, no. 7 (2010), 26–31.

Cormac McCarthy

Cant, John, *Cormac McCarthy and the Myth of American Exceptionalism* (New York: Routledge, 2008).

Carlson, Thomas A., 'With the World at Heart: Reading Cormac McCarthy's *The Road* with Augustine and Heidegger', *Religion and Literature*, 39, no. 3 (2007), 47–71.

Cooper, Lydia, 'Cormac McCarthy's *The Road* as Apocalyptic Grail Narrative', *Studies in the Novel*, 43, no. 2 (2011), 218–36.

DeCoste, D. Marcel, '"A Thing That Even Death Cannot Undo": The Operation of The Theological Virtues in Cormac McCarthy's *The Road*', *Religion and Literature*, 44, no. 2 (2012), 67–91.

Frye, Steven, ed., *The Cambridge Companion to Cormac McCarthy* (Cambridge: Cambridge University Press, 2013).

Gruber Godfrey, Laura, '"The World He'd Lost": Geography and "Green" Memory in Cormac McCarthy's *The Road*', *Critique*, 52, no. 2 (2011), 163–75.

Gwinner, Donovan, '"Everything Uncoupled from Its Shoring": Quandries of Epistemology and Ethics in *The Road*', in Spurgeon (2011), pp. 137–56.

Josephs, Allen, 'The Quest for God in *The Road*', in Frye (2013), pp. 133–45.

Knox, Paul D. '"Okay Means Okay": Ideology and Survival in Cormac McCarthy's *The Road*', *The Explicator*, 70, no. 2 (2012), 96–99.

Kollin, Susan, '"Barren, Silent, Godless": Ecodisaster and the Post-Abundant Landscape in *The Road*', in Spurgeon (2011), pp. 157–71.

Kunsa, Ashley, '"Maps of the World in Its Becoming": Post-Apocalyptic Naming in Cormac McCarthy's *The Road*', *Journal of Modern Literature*, 33, no. 1 (2009), 57–74.

Lagayette, Pierre, 'The Border Trilogy, *The Road* and the Cold War', in Frye (2013), 79–91.

Morgenstern, Naomi, 'Postapocalyptic Responsibility: Patriarchy at the End of the World in Cormac McCarthy's *The Road*', *Differences*, 25, no. 2 (2014), 33–61.

Mullins, Matthew, 'Hunger and the Apocalypse of Modernity in Cormac McCarthy's The Road', *Symplokē*, 19, nos. 1–2 (2011), 75–93.

Murphet, Julian, and Mark Steven, eds, *Styles of Extinction: Cormac McCarthy's The Road* (London: Continuum, 2012).

Phillips, Dana, ' "He Ought Not Have Done It": McCarthy and Apocalypse', in Spurgeon (2011), 172–88.

Rambo, Shelly L., 'Beyond Redemption?: Reading Cormac McCarthy's *The Road* after the End of the World', *Studies in the Literary Imagination*, 41, no. 2 (2008), 99–120.

Skrimshire, Stefan, ' "There Is No God and We Are His Prophets": Deconstructing Redemption in Cormac McCarthy's *The Road*', *Journal for Cultural Research*, 15, no. 1 (2011), 1–14.

Snyder, Phillip A., 'Hospitality in Cormac McCarthy's *The Road*', *Cormac McCarthy Journal*, 6 (2008), 69–86.

Spurgeon, Sara L., ed., *Cormac McCarthy: All the Pretty Horses, No Country for Old Men* (London: Continuum, 2011).

Stark, Hannah, ' "All These Things He Saw and Did Not See": Witnessing the End of the World in Cormac McCarthy's *The Road*', *Critical Survey*, 25, no. 2 (2013), 71–84.

Titlestad, Michael, 'The Logic of the Apocalypse: A Clerical Rejoinder', *Safundi: The Journal of South African and American Studies*, 14, no. 1 (2013), 93–110.

Young adult fiction

Basu, Balaka, 'What Faction Are You In? The Pleasure of Being Sorted in Veronica Roth's *Divergent*', in Basu, Broad and Hintz (2013), pp. 19–33.

Basu, Balaka, Katherine R. Broad and Carrie Hintz, eds, *Contemporary Dystopian Fiction for Young Adults: Brave New Teenagers* (Abingdon: Routledge, 2013).

Bradford, Clare, Kerry Mallan, John Stephens and Robyn McCallum, *New World Orders in Contemporary Children's Literature: Utopian Transformations* (Houndmills: Palgrave, 2008).

Broad, Katherine R., ' "The Dandelion in the Spring": Utopia as Romance in Suzanne Collins's *The Hunger Games* Trilogy', in Basu, Broad and Hintz (2013), pp. 117–30.

Couzelis, Mary J., 'The Future Is Pale: Race in Contemporary Young Adult Dystopian Novels', in Basu, Broad and Hintz (2013), pp. 131–44.

Curry, Alice, *Environmental Crisis in Young Adult Fiction: A Poetics of Earth* (Houndmills: Palgrave, 2013).

Day, Helen, 'Simulacra, Sacrifice and Survival in *The Hunger Games*, *Battle Royale*, and *The Running Man*', in Pharr et al. (2012), pp. 167–77.

Day, Sara K., Miranda A. Green-Barteet and Amy L. Montz, eds, *Female Rebellion in Young Adult Dystopian Fiction* (Aldershot: Ashgate, 2014).

Dunn, George A., and Nicholas Michaud, eds, *The Hunger Games and Philosophy: A Critique of Pure Treason* (Hoboken: Wiley, 2012).

Flanagan, Victoria, *Technology and Identity in Young Adult Fiction: The Posthuman Subject* (Basingstoke: Palgrave, 2014).

Green-Barteet, Miranda A., '"I'm Beginning to Know Who I Am": The Rebellious Subjectivities of Katniss Everdeen and Tris Prior', in Day, Green-Barteet and Montz (2014), pp. 33–50.

Hand, Karl, 'Come Now, Let Us Treason Together: Conversion and Revolutionary Consciousness in Luke 23: 35–38 and *The Hunger Games* Trilogy', *Literature and Theology*, 29, no. 3 (2015), 348–65.

Hintz, Carrie, and Elaine Ostry, eds, *Utopian and Dystopian Writing for Children and Young Adults* (London: Routledge, 2003).

Jansen, Brian, 'Zygmunt Bauman, Postmodern Ethics, and Utopia as Process in Suzanne Collins' *The Hunger Games*: "It's the First Gift That's Always the Hardest to Payback"', *Jeunesse: Young People, Texts, Cultures*, 7, no. 1 (2015), 18–41.

McCallum, Robyn, *Ideologies of Identity in Adolescent Fiction: The Dialogic Construction of Subjectivity* (New York: Garland, 1999).

Mills, Claudia, ed., *Ethics and Children's Literature* (Farnham: Ashgate, 2014).

Montz, Amy L., 'Costuming the Resistance: The Female Spectacle of Rebellion', in Pharr et al. (2012), pp. 139–47.

Morrison, Ewan, 'YA Dystopias Teach Children to Submit to the Free Market, Not Fight Authority', *The Guardian*, 1 September 2014 (http://www.theguardian.com/books/2014/sep/01/ya-dystopias-children-free-market-hunger-games-the-giver-divergent; accessed 19 October 2015).

Mortimore-Smith, Shannon R., 'Fueling the Spectacle: Audience as "Gamemaker"', in Pharr et al. (2012), pp. 158–66.

O'Hehir, Andrew, '*Divergent* and *The Hunger Games* as Capitalist Agitprop', *Salon.com*, 22 March 2014, (http://www.salon.com/2014/03/22/divergent_and_hunger_games_as_capitalist_agitprop/; accessed 19 October 2015).

Pharr, Mary F., Leisa A. Clark, Donald E. Palumbo, and C. W. Sullivan III, eds, *Of Bread, Blood and the Hunger Games: Critical Essays on the Suzanne Collins Trilogy* (Jefferson: McFarland, 2012).

Pollitt, Katha, 'The *Hunger Games'* Feral Feminism', *The Nation*, 3 April 2012 (http://www.thenation.com/article/hunger-games-feral-feminism/; accessed 6 November 2015.

Rainbolt, Martha, 'Katniss Everdeen's Emerging Moral Consciousness in *The Hunger Games*', in Mills (2014), pp. 223–32.

Reynolds, Kimberley, *Radical Children's Literature: Future Visions and Aesthetic Transformations in Juvenile Fiction* (Houndmills: Palgrave, 2007).

Ringlestein, Yonah, 'Real or Not Real: *The Hunger Games* as Transmediated Religion', *Journal of Religion and Popular Culture*, 25, no. 3 (2013), 372–87.

Seelinger Trites, Roberta, *Disturbing the Universe: Power and Repression in Adolescent Literature* (Iowa City: Iowa University Press, 2000).

Stewart, Susan Louise, 'Dystopian Sacrifice, Scapegoats, and Neal Shusterman's *Unwind*', in Basu, Broad and Hintz (2013), pp. 159–73.

Strong Hansen, Kathryn, 'The Metamorphosis of Katniss Everdeen: *The Hunger Games*, Myth and Femininity', *Children's Literature Association Quarterly*, 40, no. 2 (2015), 161–78.

Wezner, Kelley, ' "Perhaps I Am Watching You Now": Panem's Panopticons', in Pharr et al. (2012), pp. 148–57.

Wilkinson, Alissa, 'Why *The Hunger Games* Is about Racism', *Christianity Today*, 24 November 2014 (http://www.christianitytoday.com/ct/2014/november-web-only/why-hunger-games-is-about-racism.html; accessed 4 January 2016).

Philosophies of the future, catastrophe and other kinds of end

Agamben, Giorgio, *The Time That Remains: A Commentary on the Letter to the Romans*, translated by Patricia Dailey (Stanford: Stanford University Press, 2005).

Augé, Marc, *The Future*, translated by John Howe (London: Verso, 2014).

Bull, Malcolm, ed., *Apocalypse Theory and the Ends of the World* (Oxford: Blackwell, 1995).

Butler, Judith, *Precarious Life: The Power of Mourning and Violence* (London: Verso, 2004).

Calder Williams, Evan, *Combined and Uneven Apocalypse* (Winchester: Zero Books, 2010).

Crosthwaite, Paul, ed., *Criticism, Crisis and Contemporary Narrative: Textual Horizons in an Age of Global Risk* (Abingdon: Routledge, 2011).

Dellamora, Richard, *Postmodern Apocalypse: Theory and Cultural Practice at the End* (Philadelphia: University of Pennsylvania Press, 1995).

Derrida, Jacques, *Spectres of Marx: The State of the Debt, the Work of Mourning, and the New International*, translated by Peggy Kamuf (New York and London: Routledge, 1994).

Eagleton, Terry, *Hope without Optimism* (New Haven: Yale University Press, 2015).

Ermath, Elizabeth Deeds, *Sequel to History: Postmodernism and the Crisis of Representational Time* (New Jersey: Princeton University Press, 1992).

Fukuyama, Francis, *Our Posthuman Future: Consequences of the Biotechnology Revolution* (New York: Farrar, Straus and Giroux, 2002).

Gold, Joshua Robert, 'Jacob Taubes: "Apocalypse from Below"', *Telos*, 134 (Spring 2006), 140–56.

Hall, John R., *Apocalypse: From Antiquity to the Empire of Modernity* (Cambridge: Polity Press, 2009).

Jameson, Fredric, *Archeologies of the Future: The Desire Called Utopianism and Other Science Fictions* (London: Verso, 2005).

Kermode, Frank, *The Sense of an Ending: Studies in the Theory of Fiction* (Oxford: Oxford University Press, 1967).

Quinby, Lee, *Anti-Apocalypse: Exercises in Genealogical Criticism* (Minneapolis: University of Minnesota Press, 1994).

Quinby, Lee, *Millennial Seduction: A Skeptic Confronts Apocalyptic Culture* (Ithaca: Cornell University Press, 1999).

Wallace, Molly, 'Will the Apocalypse Have Been Now? Literary Criticism in an Age of Global Risk', in Crosthwaite (2011), pp. 15–30.

Žižek, Slavoj, *Living in the End Times* (London: Verso, 2011).

Žižek, Slavoj, *Event: Philosophy in Transit* (London: Penguin, 2014).

Eco-criticism, climate change, the anthropocene

Canavan, Gerry, and Kim Stanley Robinson, eds, *Green Planets: Ecology and Science Fiction* (Middletown, CT: Wesleyan University Press, 2014).

Clarke, Jim, 'Reading Climate Change in J. G. Ballard', *Critical Survey*, 25, no. 2 (2013), 7–21.

Garrard, Greg, *Ecocriticism* (London: Routledge, 2004).

McGuire, Bill, *A Guide to the End of the World: Everything You Never Wanted to Know* (London, Oxford: Oxford University Press).

Moore, Pete, 'Gaia Warning' [interview with James Lovelock], *Third Way*, 28, no. 5 (June 2005), 18–22.

Morton, Timothy, *The Ecological Thought* (Cambridge, MA: Harvard University Press, 2010).

Morton, Timothy, *Hyperobjects: Philosophy and Ecology after the End of the World* (Minneapolis: University of Minnesota Press, 2013).

Northcott, Michael S., *A Moral Climate: The Ethics of Global Warming* (London: Darton, 2007).

Northcott, Michael S., *A Political Theology of Climate Change* (London: SPCK, 2014).

Rigby, Kate, 'Confronting Catastrophe: Ecocriticism in a Warming World', in Westling (2014), pp. 212–25.

Scott, Peter, *A Political Theology of Nature* (Cambridge: Cambridge University Press, 2003).

Skrimshire, Stefan, ed., *Future Ethics: Climate Change and Apocalyptic Imagination* (London: Continuum, 2010).

Trexler, Adam, *Anthropocene Fictions: The Novel in a Time of Climate Change* (Charlottesville: University of Virginia Press, 2015).

Westling, Louise, ed., *The Cambridge Companion to Literature and the Environment* (Cambridge: Cambridge University Press, 2014).

Space, mobility, walking

Amato, Joseph A., *On Foot: A History of Walking* (New York: New York University Press, 2004).

Augé, Marc, *Non-Places: Introduction to an Anthropology of Supermodernity*, translated by John Howe (London: Verso, 1995).

Gros, Frédéric, *A Philosophy of Walking*, translated by by John Howe (London: Verso, 2015).

Richardson, Tina, ed., *Walking Inside Out: Contemporary British Psychogeography* (London: Rowman and Littlefield), 2015.

Solnit, Rebecca, *Wanderlust: A History of Walking* (London: Granta, 2014), Kindle edition.

Thoreau, Henry D., *Walden, Civil Disobedience and Other Writings*, edited by William Rossi, 3rd ed. (New York: Norton, 2008).

INDEX